The Wolf and
the Watchman

The Wolf and the Watchman

A FATHER, A SON, AND THE CIA

Scott C. Johnson

W. W. NORTON & COMPANY
New York • London

"Later" by Yevgeny Yevtushenko (p. 145) reproduced by kind permission of Penguin Books. Poetry on pp. 1, 73, and 237 from "The Stranger" by Rudyard Kipling.

Author's Note: To write this book I spoke to many people, including family members, friends, and current and former CIA officers, over a period of years. I also drew on my own experiences, memories, notes, and video recordings to complete the picture. Whenever possible, I researched historical documents to verify the stories I had heard.

I have changed the names of some individuals to protect their privacy, and in some cases I have also modified identifying details to help preserve their anonymity. Others appear under their real names. There are no composite characters or composite situations in this book; all of the events are real.

To my father

Contents

What was silent in the father speaks in the son,
and often I found in the son the unveiled secret of the father.
—**Friedrich Nietzsche**

Prologue

"Don't write anything about your father, for God's sake!" Cy was saying. "You can't do that, can you?"

Cy was a friend in Mexico. He had spent most of his life on the other side of the law, smuggling drugs and running planes. He was in the country to escape the police. He lived on the coast somewhere, far enough not to be found, to feel safe for another day on the run.

I sometimes stayed in a house nearby. At night, I sat around with Cy and listened to his stories about his past lives. There was one in particular that stands out for me now, several years later.

One day, a long time before we met, one of his long-lost daughters had managed to track him down. She just walked up the driveway and into Cy's house, wanting to talk. He invited her up to the living room and sat her down on the couch. "You've got fifteen minutes," he told her. "Fifteen minutes and you can ask me anything you want, and I swear to God I won't lie to you."

Cy's daughter had asked him why he left her and her mother so many years before. He swayed in the memory of it as he talked, as if the recollection was as difficult as the decision itself. His eyes glassed over, and a sad smile swept across his face.

I wondered what I would have asked my father if I'd had only fifteen minutes. Have you ever killed anyone? What's the saddest thing that's ever happened to you? Do you know that I love you?

"He doesn't have to tell me anything, does he?" I said to Cy one night, as he rolled a joint. He dropped his hands into his lap, not letting go of the joint, and stared at me with a look of surprise for asking. His mouth formed a small *o*. A rill of sea-colored light shone off the lenses of his reading glasses. He shook his head.

"Hell, no! He doesn't." He almost shouted it, irritated at my impertinence. "It's his own goddamn business."

Everyone who came around to Cy's house knew that my father had worked for the CIA. I had told him once, and word must have spread. Many of them had been involved in something illegal over the years. Most of them accepted my father's job as a matter of course, part of the natural order of the universe. It was an entirely nonjudgmental position. They joked about it with me, and Cy encouraged them. "I swear the other day he introduced himself with a fake name," he said to his ragtag crew once. "He introduced himself as Scott Jorgenson."

The men would wink at me when I came in. "What are you writing over there?" they would ask. "What's your last name, anyway?"

I would smile. To this group of outlaws, my writing inspired more suspicion than anything about my dad's job. It was as if the recording of events, the endless reworking and rewiring and self-prognostications, were the source of the real problem. They, like him, preferred the darker corners.

"Where you going next, anyway?" one would usually ask, and I would say one place or another. If it was a war, which it usually was in those years, they would all nod. "And what are you gonna do over there, huh?" another would ask, and they'd laugh.

"Don't worry," said Cy. "I won't tell your old man."

Just a bunch of harmless old criminals sitting around in Mexico, getting stoned and joking about the journalist-spy who lived next door. If anyone understood my father, they did. They were living just outside the law, on the sidelines—in a parallel universe of secrecy, of codes and conduct in which deceit and betrayal were sources of consistency and of fear.

"They're not all bad, you know," Cy mused, referring to the lawmen he had clashed with for many years. "I've spent my whole life in criminal enterprise, but people are just people, any way you cut it. I swear to God, that's the truth." It was the voice of moderation and restraint from the other side of the law, from the dark recesses of a man who had done bad things, pleading for the understanding and forgiveness of those who didn't sympathize.

I gave him a curious look.

"I'm lying; I'm dyin'," he said insistently, and took a shot of the back-alley tequila he had gotten from a friend. The crow's lines at his eyes were deep and weary, worn from use; the creases tanned into life, the humility scratched as if into bone.

"Here," he said. "Have another shot of this. Best damn tequila you ever had. I swear to God, it'll make you cry."

Part I

The Stranger within my gate,
He may be true or kind,
But he does not talk my talk—
I cannot feel his mind.
I see the face and the eyes and mouth
But not the soul behind.
    —"The Stranger," Rudyard Kipling

CHAPTER 1

New Delhi, 1973

When I was a child in India, a snake-charmer came to our house now and again. When he rang the bell, my mother gathered me in her arms and ushered him into the garden, where linen shirts and shalwar kameez swung in the breeze.

He set his wicker basket on the ground and brought out a wooden flute. Playing it, he swayed back and forth, circling the end of his flute down into the basket and up again, in hypnotic circular eights, until a black cobra appeared. Its head rose slowly, and it flicked and lashed its tongue. I was scared, half-believing the snake was under the man's control and half-sure it would lash out and strike me. He whistled to it as my mother held me tight, whispering in my ear that everything was okay; the snake was in a trance.

Eventually, the charmer made the cobra disappear back into the wicker, into darkness, and the world returned to its normal bright glow. The charmer blessed us, bowed his head, and left.

Other times it was a music-man, with a ratty wooden harmonium and a tangled beard. He sang and played songs. He had sad and wise eyes, and his music reflected the world back at me. Once, my mother invited him into the house and drew his portrait.

These two men were among my earliest memories. They

3

came to me with what they knew, and I imagine each of us left with a little bit more of the other.

My parents had arrived in India during the rains. Refugees from the war in Bangladesh were pouring into Calcutta with tales of violence. In an already overpopulated city, the deluge of humanity only added to the aura of a war-torn wasteland. The airport that early morning was thick with heat and sickness. My mother's memory of it makes it seem like walking into a nightmare: she remembers inert bodies, some naked, some wrapped in a gauzy white cloth as if they had been mummified, sprawled in doorways and along walls. A swarm of huge insects, half-scorpion and half-spider, leeched along the floors and sallow, yellow-eyed men skulked down alleys. They stayed for a few hours in a dingy hotel before their next flight, and my mother clung to my father throughout, unsure of what kind of pact she had entered—but sure that the man on her arm was strong enough to carry her through it.

They landed in Madras the next morning. A consulate man met them at the airport and took them to their hotel, where my mother collapsed in exhaustion. The long voyage, a new marriage, and the prospects of a new life—all of it became crushingly real.

In Madras, my father inherited a house with its own name: "The Flame," because of the fuchsia bougainvillea blazing on the arched latticework around the door. The Flame was home to five Tamil-speaking servants. The previous occupant was a consulate man too, and he and his wife, Alice, had been there the day my parents had arrived to look things over. It was hot and muggy, and Alice greeted them from under the shade of the verandah, careful not to step too far into the sun. She looked haggard. She had a distended belly, and my mother thought she might be dying. They sat on a pillowed teak couch as Alice gave her a tutorial, woman to woman, on her new country. Alice was sick of India, she said, with all the parasites and bugs, the rodents and unidentifiable dark shadows that scuttled back and forth along the floors—and if the bugs didn't get you, the snakes and scorpions surely would. "My nails are going, my skin's going," she said bitterly, and raised a scaly arm to prove it. The threats went unnumbered. She sipped a bitter gin fizz and ran a few bony fingers through a mat of dry hair, and gazed at my horrified mother with eyes full of pity and defeat.

But my mother thought it was beautiful. Outside the windows of her new home, which a good cleaning soon purged of the psychological rot left by Alice, bunches of bananas hung from trees. When the wind was still at midday, the eggshell-blue and linoleum-pink on the leaves froze in the heat, and to my mother the garden looked like a still life framed by the windows. The rooms were airy and spacious and dark, and she slipped along the terrazzo floors and breathed in the scent of her new life, making it her own. She was twenty-five, fresh out of college, and her servants would become her closest friends.

The days began to acquire a rhythm. My father often rose early and went to the Madras Club to play tennis. My mother began to explore India. She learned some Tamil because she wanted to know more about the country, and because it seemed easier and more fun than grappling with the ins and outs of the wives' club; the isolation from Indian society; and the catty, gossiping lunches. She wanted to help people. She volunteered for a YWCA project in a drought-devastated town beset by famine, and she met children mutilated or crippled by the beggar gangs. She bought an Olivetti typewriter and started to write. Then she hired a young Indian man to guide her on longer excursions; she talked to people about fishing and hygiene and witchcraft, and she tried writing about it. One day, on a whim, she went to Afghanistan by herself. She flew to Kabul and drove out into the nearby countryside, where she spent an afternoon with villagers who slaughtered and bled a goat and roasted the meat in an open pit. With her Olivetti, she wrote letters home about her adventures.

My father nurtured her and supported her. They were dutifully social, giving and attending parties. They went to the Madras Club to swim or play tennis or dine on white linen, served by gracious turbaned waiters in white Nehru jackets near a reflective pool in which white swans floated. The benevolent nostalgia, the atmosphere of decayed luxury—all your needs could be met, and yet sometimes he wondered why she wasn't more content to be a wife, like the other wives.

But despite the ease, theirs was also a world of intrigue and secrets, in which wit and flashy derring-do were rewarded. In such circles, people began to call my father Silver Tongue, and so my mother did, too, smiling and teasing him about his ease with people and his facility with words, all the while feeling intimidated by those things herself. My father also presented well: his black hair was always combed, he wore pressed safari shirts, and he did yoga and tennis in the morning to keep fit.

After some time had passed, my father began to ease my mother into the more serious work at hand. Sometimes, before or after dinner parties, when they were all dressed up, they made excursions into the city. These trips were missions: they were searching for dark alleyways or quiet back streets that could provide good cover for the face-to-face meetings with Indian agents that my father would need to arrange at a later date. In time, and in other countries, the grunt work he was logging there in Madras would evolve into more sophisticated operations: dead drops or pick-ups or, sometimes, just drives to look for signs or plant a decoy or confuse someone that might be following them. In years to come, he would learn how to deliver some eagerly anticipated cargo of money, or instructions in invisible ink, or a small canister of film. He would leave a bill-laden newspaper or a rumpled sack innocuously down underneath a bench, or behind a tree, or in a particular rubbish bin.

On other quiet evenings in Madras, he looked for places to park, safe enough for her to linger innocently, looking into the mirror from her purse, while he casually strolled away to survey the terrain. He hesitated, or tied his shoe. He returned to the car, to her nervous giggling and her beauty. He smiled, and kissed her. There was something luscious about the intrigue for her, strolling through these dirty, washed-out streets, thinking how strange it was to find herself there. She liked the tinge of the illicit. She found it fun, at least at first—her handsome husband skillfully navigating them through the endless valves of rickshaw alleyways opening and closing around them. She sat in the passenger seat and, in her compact or the vanity mirror under the visor, watched to make sure they weren't being followed. But often they were, so it was her very presence that helped to give him cover—made him seem more benign, his comings and goings less fraught with significance.

The moment I was born in 1973, my father took hold of me and only rarely let go, and never for very long. He was possessive. He sat outside and held me during hot nights, and I sank easily into his chest.

When I was one, we moved to New Delhi. Once again we lived in roomy diplomatic quarters, and we had servants and a garden. In the yard was a shade-giving pepper tree, and its dark branches hung loosely over us. I remember bursts of red and white from the flowerbeds, and the smells of pepper and smoke and sandalwood. Some days the Indian air would be yellow, thick with pollution or dust; on others it would fill with alabaster clouds or seem heavy with the anticipation of rain.

I remember my father standing in the yard during the hot summer, gazing up curiously at a tree full of black crows. He wore a beige khaki suit with pockets on the breasts and hips. He had a wide and angular face, with brown eyes and a full mouth. The crows screamed at him, a deafening caw. Their wings were dry. The world smelled of lemon and dust. Behind them the sky shone white, a color that erased distances. My father carried a sling-shot and took aim at the birds. He wanted to calm their ruckus. Every now and again he fired, a rock slung through the air, and the tumult of many hundreds of wings stirred, fluttered, and then hammered to flee, their cries lingering as they hauled out over the rooftops.

It was an idyllic existence in many ways. We went on trips all the time. When I was four my parents took me up to Kashmir, where we rode ponies high into the Himalayas. I christened the white stallion my father rode Grassy Whitey because of the pro-digious amount of greenery he consumed while walking. And I called the mare my mother and I rode, a sluggish brown beast that seemed intent on marking our path with a steady stream of droppings, Brownie Poo-Peep. I can still see those mountains, lit-tle trickling streams, tall pines, and hear the clippety-clop of horse feet underneath us.

When I was young, and I asked for "backpack, Daddy," my father carried me in a little sack on his back. Later, when I could walk, my mother held my hand. There is a picture of the three of us in a nineteenth-century English riding trolley—I'm sitting between them like a spoiled prince and they are smiling grandly, looking past the photographer to something on the horizon.

On a picnic once, I stepped barefoot into a steaming pile of bull dung. It squeezed through my toes and I felt a rush of fear. I squalled and didn't move. My father picked me up, cleaned my foot, and laughed the pain away in my ear.

Sometimes at night, when I was sitting in my father's lap in the vinyl lawn chair outside, he would pull out our big, illus-trated copy of Rudyard Kipling's *The Jungle Book* and read from it. I loved to hear about Mowgli, the boy abandoned by his parents and raised by wolves. Under the stars my father cooed to me those angry words from "Mowgli's Song Against People": *I will let loose against you the fleet-footed vines—I will call in the Jungle to stamp out your lines! The roofs shall fade before it, the*

*house beams shall fall; and the Karela, the bitter Karela, shall cover
it all!*

The language of Kipling's poems was the bulwark of my
young imagination. I felt protected by those words, and by Baloo,
the great jungle bear, as alive to me as the geckos on my ceiling
and the crows in the pepper tree outside. There was the cobra
Kaa, whose hissing I could hear in my father's rendition, but
also in the mornings or at night, when the hallways of our house
became the sleek surfaces for slippered feet. *Rikki-tikki-tikki-
tikki-tikki-tikki-tikki-tikki-tikki*, my father would croon, when
he whispered to me about the exploits of Rikki-Tikki-Tavi, the
cobra-eating mongoose. And before I went to sleep I stared at
the mobile of Shere Khan, the tiger, which my mother had hung
above my bed for me.

But it was Mowgli, raised by Mother Wolf and Father Wolf,
who captivated me most. I loved his freedom. I lived in his country, and I had seen some of his friends and enemies firsthand—
the snake, the mongoose. I heard his words so often they became
familiar. *Ye shall not hear my strikers; ye shall hear them and guess.
By night, before the moon-rise, I will send for my cess. And the wolf
shall be your herdsman by a landmark removed; for the Karela, the
bitter Karela, shall seed where ye loved!*

Unbeknown to me, as in the jungle, there were threats to
my existence. I was a young Mowgli, reliant on the protection
of those who knew the world I lived in. One evening, my parents had gone out to dinner, leaving me at home with my *ayah*,
Mary, who took care of me. Our house was a sprawling neoco-
lonial mansion, and at night it was quiet. In the dim light the
doorbell rang, and Mary went to answer it, carrying me in her
arms. A dapper-looking man stood there, having parked his car
in the driveway. He was dressed in fine Indian-tailored linen and
a handsome Stetson, which he took off when Mary arrived. He
told her he was there at the request of "the sahib"—the master
of the house, my father. My father had asked him to fetch me

and bring me back to the dinner party. He gave no reason as to why, no explanation or note. But he was an elegant man, dark and articulate, and Mary wasn't sure what to think.

She looked at the man carefully and told him to wait. She shut the door behind her, stood on the marble tiles of the foyer, and began to think. Why hadn't the sahib rung? Or sent a note? She considered calling him at the restaurant, but then thought better of it. He wouldn't want to be disturbed. If he had wanted the child so urgently, perhaps he wouldn't want to be questioned.

She looked down and saw our cocker spaniel, Toby, at her feet. Turning, she headed for the door again, bringing the dog with her. The man was still standing there. She looked down at Toby, who was normally docile and friendly. He began to growl and bare his teeth; his tail went rigid. Following her instincts, Mary told the elegant man to leave and never return.

When my parents returned from the party later that night, Mary nervously told them about the man who had tried to take me away.

"My God!" my mother said.

My father comforted her, and told Mary she had done the right thing. But they realized there was no accounting for danger. It was diffuse, ever-present. The right kind of children were valuable commodities in this world, provided that you could find and steal one. And everyone, even the strongest men, had their points of weakness. My mother and father would have to be more vigilant.

That night, in bed, my father told me again the story of Rikki-Tikki-Tavi, who protects the house from the cobras lurking in the yard, and of Mowgli, the brave wolf-boy who was raised in the jungle, and of Shere Khan the tiger and Baloo the bear. He whispered me to sleep with his deep, reassuring voice and promised that he would always protect me.

Soon after, it was our last dim dawn in India, and I was following him out the door, a suitcase in his hand. I was wearing a miniature version of the blue-and-white striped Indian suit he often wore. The marble floors of our huge house were especially cold, the walls white and empty without our pictures and paintings. He winked at me from under sleek black hair. *Keep quiet*, everything about that morning seemed to say. *Leave only when the world is fast asleep.*

CHAPTER 2
Belgrade, 1981

A few years later, I was seven and living in Belgrade. My father had been assigned to the embassy there. Our small stone cottage was in a quiet diplomatic enclave on the south side of the city, perched on the banks above a bend in the Danube River where yellow forsythia and chestnut trees jostled for space. From the branches of the cherry trees came the shouting of the neighborhood kids until dark, and sometimes well beyond.

My father and I walked our dog, a golden retriever called Duke, in the evenings. We did so slowly; my father liked to amble. Hands in pockets, he'd whistle through his teeth, Brahms or one of the old show tunes he'd sung as a member of the college glee club. He usually wore a brown beret and a puffy blue parka, under which his big frame disappeared entirely. Sometimes, he smoked a pipe.

He often stopped by one of the park's giant trees, behemoths that had been there for half a century or more, and reached down to examine the ground at its base. He was looking for good chestnuts, he said. As I played, or watched the dog, he'd root around on his knees, running his hands through the beet-colored leaves. Sensing a hunt, Duke would come racing up, disturb the scene, and cause my father to topple over, laughing, against the tree. He'd emerge holding a chestnut out for me.

"We used to roast these when I was a kid," he'd say. "There's nothing like the smell of a roasted chestnut." He'd look around, relishing the afternoon.

Then he'd smile and off we'd go, Duke trailing behind or ahead, or spinning through the bushes. Life was an adventure, and he was my guide.

In Belgrade, I lived with my father, Janet, and Amy. He and my mother had divorced the year before, when I was six, and I had left her behind in Virginia—or she had left me (these things all depend on perspective). My father had married Janet promptly after the divorce, a circumstance that came to mean more to me in later years. Janet's daughter, Amy, was five years older than me. The four of us were a new family, and Belgrade was our first collective home.

Children are malleable, and I no less than most, so the novelty of the situation inspired more curiosity than terror. The fact that we were behind the Iron Curtain, or at least right on its edge, had a special significance for me. I imagined a wall that stretched from the ground to the sky, a veil of rust-colored chain-link through which the rest of the world was visible, but not reachable. My mother, I knew, was on the other side of the curtain. Little did she know how pleasant it actually was in the iron gardens of Belgrade.

At that age, I didn't really know why I was always moving, only that it was an irreducible component of life with my father. When I asked him about it, he said he worked for the Foreign Service, and that was enough for me. I understood that this involved embassies and functions and parties, which was why we entertained on a regular basis, throwing cocktail parties and dinners to which large numbers of people from many different countries came. I thought it to be a rather dignified, urbane kind of job, something I might like to do one day.

One night, I snuck from my bedroom and peeked around

a corner to watch one of these parties. My dad spoke Serbo-Croatian fluently, and the local ladies trilled in his presence. His eyes twinkled as he talked to them, and one eyebrow would often arch up mischievously. The other men, I thought, seemed harsh next to his charm.

After the party, my father went out with Duke alone. He did this sometimes: they'd go on long walks, much longer than the ones I ever took. I was impatient, like most boys, and if Duke veered off in one direction I'd yank him back as hard as I could until he morosely succumbed, or until I decided it was time to go home. Duke listened to and obeyed my father; he hardly had to be leashed at all.

Off they went into the woods, as I sat at the window next to the front door and watched their bodies disappearing into the darkness. I followed the last moving fragments as they deepened out of the lamplight that smeared the cobblestones. Then I went to my room to wait. I played with my Lego set and read Hardy Boys mysteries to pass the time. They were gone for so long that I became worried; the house seemed empty without him. When they eventually returned, and I heard the rhythmic jangling of Duke's collar and his excited trot toward my room, my father came in. It was late, and he was surprised to find me awake and at my desk, but he smiled.

"What are you working on, Scotty?" he asked.

I made something up. He came over to investigate and I shoved some previously used paper his way as proof of my labors. But he loved me, and didn't doubt me, or I him, and that's the way it was. He was a magical man to me, and there was little about him that I didn't study for clues as to how the world worked.

"How was your walk?" I asked.

"Great," he beamed. He'd always say something like that. And because so few encounters in life were ever less than exceptional for my father, he would recount some detail that stood out: a brightly colored leaf, a woman with one leg, some thought he'd had about a prospective trip, or some suddenly and deeply felt emotion, such as his great love for me.

"But how do you see in the dark?" I asked, after he'd told me about what he'd seen. I was scared of the dark, and of the woods—sometimes even in the brightness of day. I cowered at the idea of setting off alone into that particular darkness with only a dog at your side—a dog you could no longer see but only hear, as a faint jingling of metal in the void, or a panting of breath and pitter-pattering over dry leaves and broken branches. And what if Duke suddenly became vicious, rabid—werewolf-like—and attacked you on those long walks?

But he just smiled. "You get used to it. Your eyes grow accustomed to the dark," he said. "It's okay out there."

I wanted him to hug me and he did, tucking me into bed and singing to me. In the morning when he came to wake me, he sat by my side, rubbed his hands on my chest, and sang to the melody of Reveille, "You gotta get up, you gotta get up, you gotta get up in the morning. You gotta get up, you gotta get up, you gotta get up today."

Being seven, my universe was small. I rarely ventured too far from our little three-bedroom cottage. During the morning, I went to an international school close by, and came home again. In the afternoons, I would be out in the cherry trees with my friends playing War or Dragons or a game in which you had to get from one place to another without touching the ground, or else you'd die. I had a secret fort in the backyard, and there I waged wars and staged battles and toppled mountains or towers, or whichever other edifices could be torn asunder, and built them back up again. I played soldiers or fort at friends' houses, or they played Lego at mine. My best friend, Zander, lived next door, and we strung up a telephone line made of string and passed secret messages to each other at night. My first semi-crush, an American girl named Kate, whose father worked with mine, lived right up the hill. Her braces and curly black hair were the closest I came to adoration for many years.

Thus the days went by in Belgrade, for two years. I didn't know much about what was happening around me—the simmering ethnic tensions, the slow exodus from the Soviet Bloc, and what that would mean for the generation of Yugoslavs with whom, in second grade, I was now learning to add and subtract.

But those many walks through the woods, sometimes alone, sometimes together, define my experience of Belgrade. Even today, I can see the outline of my father and me walking away through that forest, his arm about my shoulder, his head swiveling this way and that, eyes scanning. I can hear his deep voice ushering me along, and the long, mournfully repeating whistle he used to call Duke. "Come on, Scotty," he'd say, "we better get home for dinner." With him, the darkness of those woods was kept at bay just as the heft of the Earth kept the sun from obliterating us for twelve hours of each twenty-four. Then the light would begin to raze, to fray that ragged edge.

If I had looked around a bit closer, say at the base of one of those trees my father and I had been playing under, I might have noticed something different. The ground might have been loosely packed down. Whereas before we had arrived there had been nothing out of the ordinary, now I might notice a single gray branch placed loosely, almost haphazardly, against the base of the trunk. If I looked closely enough, I might see that in the dark hollow just above the roots a brown paper package had been left and was covered with a slight smattering of debris.

But if a person wasn't looking carefully—if, in fact, you didn't know exactly what you were looking for—you wouldn't notice a thing.

CHAPTER 3
Islamabad, 1983

The country, the circumstances, or the distance from the life we had previously lived—none of that mattered once our family arrived somewhere else; whatever disruption it caused soon vanished in reinvention. For days after we landed in Pakistan, none of us could sleep for jetlag. The sudden anomie didn't help, or being alone in the heat of third-world summer. But when the nights came and the insomnia hit, my dad transformed adversity into adventure. He bundled Janet and me into our little car and crept into Islamabad's night. Almost immediately we were lost, and we spent the rest of the night trying to find our way back home. I saw darkened streets, with sallow lights and hanging lamppost wires, and figures lingering in the shadows. I loved it that a place you called home could also be incomprehensible.

Eventually we settled into a house, a big white cake of a thing at the end of a long road lined with smaller houses. The embassy employed a guard from Sindh, and the house came adorned with a thick lawn and a rose garden—and for me, a giant bedroom with its own bathroom. As in New Delhi, geckos played on the ceilings. From my window I could see the neighborhood rooftops, a park filled with palms and hedges and, in the distance, a small mosque, whose muezzin woke me each morning with his call to prayer.

Soon after we arrived, Duke disappeared. At first my father thought he had simply gotten lost, as he had so often before, and that diligent searching would eventually lead us to him. But a week passed without a sign of our golden retriever. My father grew worried and morose. He put up signs in our neighborhood, but to no effect. He expanded the circumference so that soon the whole city was bristling with the fluttering posters bearing Duke's baleful, trusting face, and our telephone number.

Days passed. Now and again my dad would get a report of a Duke sighting, and he'd immediately jump in the car to investigate. The trips took him far from home, out to the edges of the city and beyond, to dusty villages that lay on its periphery. Duke was distractible and flighty; he could have wandered into somebody else's home and, finding it comfortable and sufficiently luxurious, decided to decamp and stay a while. But our thoughts tended toward the morbid. What if he was dead, chopped up for meat? What if he was wandering, alone, hungry, howling for my dad?

As more time passed, I became accustomed to Duke's absence. Eventually my thoughts returned to my own preoccupations. I started fourth grade at the International School of Islamabad. I biked around the city, and trawled through the green jungles that abutted my house in G-6/3 (the name given to our patch of Islamabad's angular grid) on my ten-speed Schwinn. I custom-ordered cassette tapes at the Jinnah Market with the songs of Michael Jackson or the Beatles. At home I ran up the winding staircase to my room, where I played Lego, or sang along with Michael or John, or constructed a pretend science laboratory on a built-in vanity counter, or lounged around on my bed listening to the muezzin sing his mournful prayer.

One of my close friends was an Indonesian boy named Peter. His father and mine were friendly. When my dad and I visited Peter's family, he and I would race upstairs to his room and watch

James Bond movies over and over again. We watched *The Man with the Golden Gun* and *Goldfinger* and *The Spy Who Loved Me*, and we fantasized for hours about being James Bond, the coolest man in the world.

My father and I spent lazy weekends at the embassy pool. He introduced me one day to John, a U.S. Marine who did guard duty at the embassy during the week and worked as a lifeguard on the weekends. At my father's urging, John and I became friends. I remember his beige uniform—the crisp tightness of it—and the pistol he carried on his waist. John would pick me up and swing me around on his shoulders before throwing me into the pool. I liked watching him salute my father and me from behind the bulletproof glass of the embassy gate.

One day at the pool, my father told me that John and the other marines were there to protect us. I asked why, and he told me that not too long before we had arrived in Pakistan, an angry mob had attacked the embassy. They had tried to shoot people, and had set fire to the embassy. People retreated to the embassy roof. One was killed by a sniper's bullet. The marines had drained the pool, and people took shelter inside it. But that was all over now, he said. He dangled his feet in the water and challenged me to an under-water race, from one end to the other. I watched him go, thinking of a crowd of people sitting scared where my legs now floated. As we swam I studied his long, powerful kicks; his hair washing backward and forward; and the push of his body, surging ahead of me so easily as I struggled to keep up.

On the weekends sometimes we drove north along the Grand Trunk Road to the North-West Frontier Province, and the border town of Peshawar, which in those years was filled with Afghans—refugees from their Soviet-occupied land. We often stopped at a hotel from the British era called Deans, and there we would have breakfast or lunch, freshly squeezed juice, and warm tea. There is a picture of the two of us in front of Deans on one of those occasions. My father is clean-shaven. He's wearing a red sweater, smiling, and holding me loosely in his right arm. I am getting bigger by then, still blond, my grin toothy, my hair neatly parted because in those years, like him, I always parted my hair and made sure to get the line as straight as possible.

We drove north from Peshawar, further toward the border with Afghanistan, which I knew was a lawless land of bandits and warriors. I knew there was a war against the Russians there, and that some of these men had come from the fighting. They were all around me, men in long, dusty shalwar kameezes and hectic beards. Most of them were part of the mujahideen resistance army, my father explained.

I have a vague memory of watching a large group of men I took to be Afghans stream down a dusty hillside one day. There was some commotion near the top of the hill—a fight or an argument, I couldn't be sure. I desperately wanted to know what lay on the other side of that hill: what men, what anger, what was driving them to us. I could see the concern on my father's face. But even he was hesitant to take us much further up the hill.

Sometimes we'd see light-skinned people, blue-eyed blonds or redheads on the road down, or heading east from, Islamabad. They were traveling toward a town called Murree, a name that some claimed was a bastardization of Mary—a linguistic hold-over from two thousand years before, when Jesus had apparently visited India, during the missing years of his life. But I was always more curious about those ragged men we had seen along the border, the ones with guns, on a mission I didn't understand. I pictured them on their hillsides with their weapons, staring at the arcing sun, shaking off the dust, marauding down the hills toward the border—toward us, and safety.

My home life was not completely idyllic. I was terrified of Amy. She was six feet tall, big-boned and mean. I rarely spoke to her unless spoken to, which wasn't often. She wore her bangs so they covered her eyes, and I remember a face full of hair more vividly than any particular expression. Amy was a teenager in Islamabad, concerned mostly with her Syrian boyfriend Basel and how to sneak in copious amounts of the marijuana that grew outside our house.

Janet and I were on better terms, but she was concerned about, and patient with, her daughter, and for that slight I did not forgive her. I called her "Mom" because my father thought doing so would somehow fix what was wrong. Even from my boy's vantage point, I sometimes questioned Janet's enthusiasm for the life she had inherited by marrying my father. She was a painter, and the things she had given up in Manhattan—the Chelsea apartment, the galleries, the café society—were painfully absent in Islamabad. I didn't know why she had left her fun life. But then, maybe it wasn't so fun: her firstborn, Timmy, had drowned only a few years before, after falling into a river, which led to a divorce and perhaps this remarriage and her current situation. I looked a lot like Timmy, I suppose—a reminder for her of what she had once had, but lost. That seemed to have broken her.

Janet was a terribly proficient and competent mother. She cooked and cared and fretted as only a loving mother could. When I got sick with West Nile fever that year, Janet spent weeks nursing me back to health. Her ministrations were proof for my father that he had made the correct choice in marrying her. Here was a woman who could fill the void that my mother's absence had created; a woman willing to follow him around the world and help care for the son that he would never have been able to look after on his own. His love for her, and his vision for our family, though, was wrapped up in the idea that she and I somehow fulfilled and complemented a need for the other. I could become the son that she had lost; she would become the replacement for a mother who was now several thousand miles away in darkness. It was a subtle, clever machination. He insisted upon it on a regular basis. "Mom sure took care of you, didn't she?" he'd say. "You know, she really cares about you."

Looking back, that was the first false note my father ever struck with me. He really wanted to believe it, for both our sakes, but I didn't. In addition to her ministrations, Janet showed early on that she was capable of great rages, emotional outbursts that left me angry and confused. Even in my child's mind I knew that my father was trapped between what he wanted and what he had. What he had wanted for all of us—the seamless creation of a new family—wasn't as easy as he'd hoped. Still, both of them tried to make our lives as expatriates as normal as possible. We ate dinner every night around a table. We entertained, just as we had in Yugoslavia, and went on family vacations: to Goa, India, one year; to a mountain retreat another. My father and I staged elaborate swimming races at the embassy pool. Sometimes in the evenings or on weekends we'd take off into the Margala Hills outside of town and walk up trails dotted with crystalline pools made azure by mineral deposits, take off our clothes, and jump in the water.

What I knew of my father was simple: he loved me. But I knew, too, that there was something unusual in all of this moving and remarrying and constant change—and there was very little I could do about it.

And then, one day, in the midst of all this, my father found Duke. He had wandered off innocently and slipped into another family's routine. Word had somehow filtered through to him about a golden dog lost in a village. But, somehow, that's not what I thought had happened. I came up with a much wilder story—a more sinister imagining that coincided with what I might have been starting to suspect about my father. As I saw it, kidnappers had stolen Duke and taken him to a small village on the outskirts of Islamabad, where they were holding him for ransom. Clearly, I thought, the kidnappers didn't want to run the risk of damaging a potentially lucrative source of revenue.

Then I came to this further erroneous conclusion: Duke wasn't even the target. I was.

CHAPTER 4
Williamsburg, Virginia, 1984

As we traveled to Williamsburg, my father sang, crooned, to me in the backseat of our car a song he and I had always sung together:

Oh, we ain't got a barrel of money
Maybe we're ragged and funny
But we'll travel along, singin' a song
Side by side.
. . .
Through all kinds of weather
What if the sky should fall?
Just as long as we're together
It doesn't matter at all.

It was hot and humid that autumn of 1984. The world coasted by alongside the humming regularity of the interstate's yellow lines. The song finished, my father and Janet snarled at each other quietly in the front seat. This at least was familiar, amid everything else that wasn't. Once again, I had no idea where we were headed—only that wherever we landed was going to be my new home.

I had spent the summer with my mother in Northern Virginia, learning new American music on the radio by listening to her singing. The arrangement between them was that I lived with my father during the school year and spent the summer months with her. Initially they had agreed to joint custody, but it hadn't worked out that way, and I knew she was sad about this. I also knew my father would do just about anything to keep me by his side.

My mother liked Lionel Richie's "Stuck on You," and she sang it to me in her car, which she called her blue jay. If she didn't know the words to a song, she hummed along to the melody anyway, and that summer was filled with the music of her gentle voice. She was remarried by then, and had a job as a technical editor. I told her about Pakistan: the sailing black birds called kites that rode hot-air currents, the games of soccer and cricket with the boys who had lived on my street, the cone-shaped paper cups of water at school, and the days our teachers let us go home because it was too hot.

My clothes had been out of style and gawky when I returned, and she took me shopping at Tysons Corner for striped tube socks and shorts with white trim and new Puma tennis shoes. She also indulged my endless hunger for Dannon yogurt. She stood next to me and watched me stir, prolonging the ordinary and the routine, something not infused with the extraordinariness of my visit. It was too short, too weighted with the anticipation of departure.

I was happy to be with my mother, but sad to be in America, which seemed like such a bland place. I hated these in-between times because they made me long for a decisive moment when I finally decided to be with one or the other of my parents. I hated them because they forced my hand.

My father came to pick me up from her townhouse at the end of summer. I hadn't seen him since Pakistan. He stood in the doorway talking in his deep voice, grinning and flirting. She put a hand on my shoulder and leaned against the wall of the house. I could have been mistaken, but I thought I caught her blush, perhaps momentarily swept back into the graces of his warmth. Or maybe it was something else entirely. When my mother waved goodbye, she bent her fingers at her first set of knuckles, an action that looked to me like she was imitating the wings of a small bird.

In the car, on the way south, my father raised the volume on the classical radio station. Janet absently twirled a finger through her auburn curls. I watched as rest stops and Winnebagos and signs for gas stations and Motel 6s and Denny's slid by. I had no idea where we were going; my father wanted to surprise me. He told me I would love our new home. It was a great place for a kid my age, he informed me.

After a couple of hours, we pulled off the highway and almost immediately began to pass tall poles with flashing orange lights and hatchings, like railroad crossings, that read "Warning" and "Government Property." I thought we had made a wrong turn.

But my father looked ahead, to where an American flag hung loosely from a pole beside a modest guardhouse. Two metal bars blocked the road. The guard came out and, after giving us the once-over, snapped sharply to attention as the security bar rose and our car moved through. People didn't normally gesture so officially to my father.

He turned to me with an oversized grin. "Welcome home, Scotty." He was the most excited person in the car.

"What is this place?" I asked.

He said it was called Camp Peary. That didn't answer much for me. He added that it was a base—like a military base, only different. More importantly, it was our new home, and I would find lots to enjoy here.

A road wound through forest laced with hanging moss. The sun sank through branches to rectangular fields where groups of deer grazed. I exclaimed when I saw them, and so did my father. Now, I was genuinely excited. Black iron lampposts were planted evenly every twenty yards Modern, one-story ranch houses with

covered carports, fake-wood siding, and winding gravel walk-
ways lined the perimeters of the fields.

A military jeep pulled up across from us. The soldiers inside
wore white armbands stitched with the letters *M* and *P*—for military police, my father explained. They waved, and we waved
back.

My father stopped at an intersection of three massive fields.
Across the smallest of the three was an old two-story farmhouse.
He turned around to face me. He was still grinning, full of excitement that we were together again in a new place with a new home,
about to start on some new adventure. The house had a huge front
yard and a circular driveway. Beside it was a little white garage, and
beyond that, through a copse of marshy trees and undergrowth, a
creek. The lush expanse of the land—its sheltered position behind
those gates, as if it were a magical kingdom—was enchanting.
I was transfixed, lost suddenly in a wilderness of America, surrounded by forests and rivers, happy to be so firmly planted again
within the magical realm that my father was able to create.

"Mom already fixed up your room," he said, breaking the
spell. "Go take a look." I silently cursed him for the word "mom,"
so soon on the heels of my visit to my mother. To hide my anger,
I tore across that field toward the house. On the porch there was
a floral-cushioned swinging chair, and potted palms and ferns
crawled up the screen door. Inside, I recognized my father's teak
tables. The foreignness of everything was what made it familiar. There was a red sandalwood box with gold clasps that held
cloth napkins, low table lamps from India, rugs from Iran and
Afghanistan, a dark wooden sculpture of the Hindu pantheon
that had hung in all our houses, and a delicate likeness of a plow
made from shesham wood. A rocking chair that had belonged to
my grandmother rested in one corner.

I raced upstairs to my room. The ceiling slanted over a bed in
the corner. Near my bed was a hatch, a passageway to an attic. I
opened it and peered down a long, unlit alcove, already planning

for its secret uses. A little red sailor's lamp with an anchor on the base sat on my bedside table. Most of my belongings had arrived by sea freight: a brown stuffed bear and a pink rabbit that used to belong to my father, toy soldiers of the American Revolution, boxes of my great-grandfather's WWII medals, an atlas and a globe, and rows of books—Zane Grey novels, my father's old books about cowboys and Indians, Hardy Boys mysteries, a token Nancy Drew. The small bronze horse my father had given me in Yugoslavia stood by my bed. I picked it up and polished it gently. Only then did it truly feel like home.

That evening, I sat with my father in his study. He had grown a beard over the summer, and he was smoking a pipe. He wanted to know if I liked Camp Peary. Yes, I told him, I loved it. It was true. The land was big and green and smelled of cut hay and clay and dried river salt. The elements left me feeling more prone to possibility.

We ate well that night, warm and open to the comfortable feel of a new country. Summer gnats swarmed outside the screen door. But inside, we were protected with candles and clean linen and the clink of glasses—and my father's deep voice extolling the activities and possibilities of our new home.

After dinner, it began to rain; long summer sheets descended through the trees. My father tucked me in. I lay with my head at the foot of the bed watching the giant maple thrash outside my window. Crickets chirped loudly, just audible through the din. The air smelled electric, of grass and pitch and wet road. But there were no geckos on the walls, no muezzin calling the faithful to prayer.

The next morning my father asked if I had made my bed. I shook my head. "This isn't Pakistan," he said. "We don't have servants here."

For those first few weeks, I missed my former country. I missed the smell of pepper trees, leaves being burned in the morning, and the pungent, rotting scent given off by flower petals being crushed under tires. I missed eating caramel in the kitchen while our cook, William, talked and cut carrots and measured spices. I had asked if we could bring William to America, and my father had said no.

Letters postmarked Pakistan and bearing the international red, white, and blue flag markers arrived for me. My friend Sohail wanted to tell me that my friends missed me. America was strange, I wrote back.

One Saturday I went swimming with my dad at the Camp Peary pool. The bottom was deep, and a dull green light leached upward. Unlike the outdoor pool in Islamabad, which was filled with children's boisterous voices, this one was quiet and empty, seconded away in the back room of a gymnasium and surrounded by concrete and a few opaque windows. We were the only ones there that day, and the sounds of our splashing echoed.

The following weekend, we played catch in our vast front yard. "Gotta keep your tongue in the right place," he said, indicating his own and punching his mitt with a balled fist. We drove around parts of the vast, unexplored base in his green Dodge pickup, and he let me sit on his lap and steer. That night, he tucked me in, sat on my bed, and made sure everything was okay.

Then, "You gotta get up, you gotta get up, you gotta get up in the morning," he sang in the morning before my first day of school. "You gotta get up, you gotta get up, you gotta get up today." I hesitated, and he leaned in close and ran his fingers along my chest. "You need a gowering," he threatened. "Gowering" was his word for tickling me with his beard. He rumbled his voice in anticipation of the impending attack. I squealed in delight. He moved in and I screamed until I was thrashing to get out of bed, panting and sweating and wide-awake.

One evening, two boys rode over to our street. Jeff was curly-haired and bright. Reid was an elfin boy with feathery blond hair that fell down to his sharp cheekbones. Reid and I had lived together in India as infants. They were the first boys I met at

Camp Peary, and when I saw how in command they seemed I realized how lost I had been feeling. They invited me to accompany them on their bike ride, and I happily acquiesced. My dad waved goodbye from the driveway.

That night, Reid told an improbable story about India that involved bottle rockets and firecrackers. I remembered nothing like that in my time there. "Remember?" he asked hopefully, and because I wanted to make friends I said yes.

Jeff and Reid were soon coming over most days after school, and if there had been a time when we weren't best friends, none of us could remember it. They took me all over. We biked down long dirt roads to the edge of the base, where chain-link fences rose up in long, vertical walls that cut through the forest. We played fantasy games like Dungeons & Dragons and Gamma World, creating alter egos and measuring our powers of charisma and intelligence. We walked to glassy lakes deep in the woods where the only noises were the resonant thumps of leaping bass. We went along the York River, past a sewage turbine and the small algae- and stone-filled tributaries, to an overlook, where we played with a giant M60 machine gun—the same kind used in *Rambo: First Blood*, Jeff informed me. The gun was mounted on an abandoned Huey helicopter.

Sometimes we would just set off in one direction in the morning and walk or ride our bikes until we couldn't anymore. We wound up lost in forests or wading through impossible streams. I lived for these excursions, so completely and perfectly did they manage to elicit equal amounts of fear and excitement. I longed for the daylight to last, for as long as it did I could prolong the absolute freedom those woods conferred.

But there were limits to our world. Camp Peary was not endless wilderness; it was under twenty square miles, and marked on maps as a Defense Department property. Long fences bisected the trees, stretching off in both directions. We went exploring because, sometimes, Camp Peary felt oddly empty. As the months wore on, I began to wonder why I was living there, and my father didn't make any effort to clarify this for me.

The bus that picked me up for school every morning had a prescribed route through the camp—the driver wasn't allowed to deviate at all. Kids from outside the base weren't allowed to get off the bus in Camp Peary without written permission. Every day we passed through those gates at the entrance and entered an outer world, one with restaurants and shopping malls, with litter and chaos, devoid of animals—the ordinary world. But no one was allowed to see my landscapes. It was reserved for the Camp Peary People. We were the Camp Peary Kids.

There was a movie theater in the camp that for many weeks played only one movie: *Red Dawn*. Jeff, Reid, and I went. I got shivers when I saw the opening scenes: a group of boys about our age sitting bored in a classroom until suddenly, out of the window, one of them sees a white parachute with a man attached drifting slowly to earth. A second chute follows, then a third, and soon the whole sky is filled with hordes of invading paratroopers. It was the story of a Soviet military invasion of the United States—the dawn of World War III as seen through the eyes of a group of kids from a small western town. I watched with unhinged fascination. I saw Jeff and Reid and myself as the boys who flee to the mountains to wage a guerrilla war against the occupying army. It was righteous. The kids loot the local hardware store of all its rifles and shotguns and ammunition, and its stocks of hunting reserves, camouflage jackets, shovels and axes, and spools of rope. They fill the pickup with cans of soup, macaroni, boxes of anything they can find. Their small resistance group, called the Wolverines, survives a harsh winter.

Toward the end of the film, the Russians are moving up a long, clear-cut field, just below the tree line, hunting for the rebels, and the ground suddenly rises up. A square patch of straw pops neatly up off the tundra, like a secret door. Then another. The advancing Russians are mowed down en masse. I whooped in silence.

This was reassuring and familiar to me. Our games were all about stocking up with weapons; our trips into the woods were calculated acts of resistance. And the Russians *were* near; you could feel them.

Scattered all about Camp Peary were restricted areas. Sometimes Jeff and Reid and I rode past them on our bikes, or stopped at the forbidding gates that warned us away: "This is a Restricted Area. No Access Allowed." Behind the gates long roads, so different from the mud tracks that crisscrossed the rest of the land, disappeared in straight lines into the oblivion of the forests, walled in on either side by pines and bramble.

Sometimes, helicopters thundered over Camp Peary. Black shadows flew along the ground. Looking up, I saw the underbelly, the straight tail, and the metal legs elongated. They flew toward the woods. They would wake me up in the mornings, or at night. Usually they came just as dusk was falling, in twos and threes, splayed out broadly against the sky. They scared and thrilled me, and they beckoned: I wanted to be part of the secret endeavor.

At other times, at dusk or in the afternoons, planes overhead dumped bodies through side cargo doors, and they would bloom into the delicate white blossoms of parachutes, wafting in spirals toward the pines. When I asked, my father said the military did training here, but that was all he would reveal.

What were the helicopters flying out there for? Who was doing military training? Those woods seemed to hold as many questions as answers. Sometimes, alone, I'd walk into the forest and weave among the trees, picking off branches like an Indian scout, leaving the track, looking for some clue to what was hiding in there.

But very often, those dusks were just still, with only the high-pitched thrumming and sawing of the cicadas. If I was still enough, the vast area where I lived and roamed felt like a large and complicated heart whose valves needed this position of repose to function properly.

In the mornings my father would bike calmly to work on his

twelve-speed Trek, taking the river route along the York. He had told me he was a teacher. What was he teaching? I asked. But the answer was not forthcoming.

One day Jeff told me I should follow him up the hill by the river, near the sewage turbines. He showed me where to go, stopping underneath a building with dark windows and pointing up. I saw the back of someone's head. Our fathers supposedly taught in these oddly nondescript buildings, in cloistered woods, away from public scrutiny. My father had told me he worked for the Foreign Service, as my grandfather had. I thought my father and his students must have been "diplomats." But this place wasn't "foreign." I wondered why we were stuck on a base in the middle of a wilderness of tidewater and marshes. And around this campus, the young men were stolid and serious, too old to be students. I was how old a student was.

Not long after this, my father left for a few days. He did this sometimes. "Gotta see a man about a horse," he chuckled. He had shaved his beard, but kept a mustache. He looked much thinner, almost like a different man.

"What kind of man?" I asked.

"Oh, the one about a horse," he replied with a wink, which meant there was nothing more to say. If I got ever mad at this secrecy, he would arch his stern eyebrows at me until I couldn't keep my frown any longer, and I'd start to laugh. "Don't smile," he'd say. "You can't smile if you're angry."

I thought, then and now, that this was his cleverest move. It was like trying not to think about a pink elephant when someone says not to—impossible.

But I had my own concerns, too. I was always behind in school because of the constant changes, the tardiness, and the many differences between the various school systems of my childhood. I didn't do well in classes and hated the work. I believed that learning was about convincing, and I was impossible to convince.

At school I argued with my teachers all the time. Ms. Williams, my teacher, told me I would make a good lawyer, so she staged mock trials and picked me to conduct public examinations and cross-examinations on whichever subject I chose.

Other teachers weren't so accommodating. One of them drew me aside and said that I, along with a feeble-looking kid with glasses and a silent Asian girl who barely spoke English, would be in a separate reading group called Special K. Special K turned out to be the remedial group.

My father kept telling me I was smart, but I knew otherwise. In the evenings, if he came home from work early, or on weekends, he sat me at the dining-room table and lectured me with unending patience on fractions and semicolons. He counted numbers on his hands, twisting them into unlikely shapes and folding his thick fingers into themselves. He tried to tutor me on the decimal system, but I couldn't or wouldn't understand. Sometimes Janet took over, patiently wading through grammar or science with me. I threw temper tantrums over homework. But my father persisted in his belief about my intelligence. "I love you more than the sky," he said, "'cause the sky never ends."

That first year at Camp Peary was marked by fun and frivolity, particularly with my father, but also the sense that something was unraveling. My father and I starred in a play together at a local base theater that year, a melodrama called *Dirty Work at the Crossroads*. He played a corn-fed farmer with a southern accent; I played a young maiden named Little Nell, and I had to wear a dress. People, in this case an audience of base employees, screamed with applause for my father, who put on a stellar performance with a baritone voice and a corn pipe, and they clapped courteously when I sang a solo in a very high-pitched falsetto.

When we were in Pakistan, my father had bought a Willys World War II jeep and had it shipped to Camp Peary. It took a year to get there, but finally it arrived one week. On nice days he parked it in our driveway for display, and when it rained, in the garage. He took family portraits of us in front of it to include with Christmas cards. When he left the jeep outside one night with the top down, it rained and the camouflage canvas shrank so that it became impossible to cover.

On weekends he asked us to dress up in nice clothes and took us for rides around the base. He always wore a long brown trench coat with a turned-up collar and a scarf on these occasions. He smoked his pipe and wore an English cap. Families came to their doors to watch us go by, and later commented on our tours. "We saw you and your father," they'd say. "Quite a car you have there."

He looked like a dandy. Spiffy, he'd say. When an in-law who played the bagpipes came to visit us one winter, my father drove us around in the Willys with the bagpipes blowing across the snowy fields. People shook their heads. Janet laughed in embarrassment. I sat in the back, alternately proud and embarrassed.

But at home it was often tense. Our house was small, the walls thin. At night I hung at the top of the creaky wooden stairs and strained to listen to the conversation coming from behind his closed doors. I would hear sighs and drawers being shut in various rooms, and now again a laugh, the general effect like some complicated breathing machine.

One day, Reid, Jeff, and I trekked into the woods on a mission to go as deep into the wilderness as we could—farther than we had ever ventured before. It was a Saturday, so we had the whole day. We had been riding our bikes for about an hour when Jeff suddenly stopped. In the distance we heard gunshots. Jeff dumped his bike and motioned for us to do the same. We stashed them in a grove and continued on foot. The sound of the firing grew louder. Eventually we came to a small berm and crawled up to its summit. We peeked our heads over and froze. There, in the distance, about a dozen men were shooting weapons into the woods. They looked determined and calm, like my father when he was concentrating. Behind the men were a smaller number of supervisors, wearing caps and carrying clipboards. One strolled with his hands behind his back, plastic earmuffs on his head, murmuring orders.

My first instinct was to run away, as quickly as possible. We weren't supposed to see this. I was afraid of what the men would do to us if they caught us spying on them: torture us with bamboo stalks like they had done to Rambo, or prod us with cold gun barrels like they did with James Bond? Worse, what if my father found out? Jeff's face was pale, and Reid was somber.

"What are they shooting for?" I asked.

"They're soldiers," said Jeff, with authority.

"How come they don't wear uniforms?" Reid asked.

"They don't need to wear them here."

We had shards of understanding—that was all.

Soon after this, the three of us took off early one weekend morning toward the southern edge of camp, following the river at first and then veering up into thicker parts of forest. Eventually the road we were following petered out, and we dropped our bikes and began walking. We passed one ridge, then another, and forded a trickle of stream that led to the river several hundred yards below. The woods were untamed, tangled with thistles, grass, and poison oak. We picked ticks off our bodies and thorns out of our socks. We were far from home. I had a grand feeling of independence. We played games while we hiked, imagining ourselves in a magical forest. Jeff talked about dragons and elves, and the treasures that awaited us at the end of our trip. My walking stick became a golden staff that could shoot lightning bolts. Reid threw stones like balls of fire.

Then, from a distance, one of us saw the glint of something metallic and shouted to the others. We raced toward this thing, which was shining like the hilt of a sword.

When we came to the clearing, we stopped running. There were two metal silos, whose sides shimmered in the light and shade as if underwater. A chain-link fence encased a house-sized square around them. Each silo was marked with white insignia and serial numbers. They were huge, at least fifty feet tall, and round as oil barrels, capped off by cylindrically shaped warheads with numbers painted on their sides. Nuclear missiles, I decided, based on my extensive viewing of war movies.

I had never seen a missile before, and yet here were two of them, so close I could reach out and lay my hands on the metal. They were tall and eerie—sleek instruments of death. I was afraid we would trigger unseen alarms or tripwires or pressurized antitank mines, as we had seen in movies. Jeff warned us there might be grenades scattered on the ground. I felt as if we were being watched, and peered into the shadows. All I could see were birch leaves clattering to the ground; a wind had come up and was blowing them around, thankfully erasing our tracks. Nearby there was a low, earth-colored concrete bunker with flat, sloping sides that led directly into the ground—and probably deep into it, I thought. I knew there were more missiles, hidden in underground silos, ready to blast off at any moment.

Guarding the bunker was a small M4 Patton tank, its small wheels wrapped in thin treads, and its round turret with a short gun barrel. We climbed up on the tank, too, and sat there marveling that such a fine weapon would be abandoned here in these woods.

After a while, I sat down on the bunker and leaned back so that I was looking up at the roof of tree branches, the sky peeking through. I figured the inside of the bunker was connected to an underground maze of tunnels that stretched deep into the earth, to an alternate city buzzing with activity—with computers and switches and men in white lab coats able to operate the buttons that would fire these missiles off at a moment's notice. I knew that presidents had red telephones for circumstances such as these, and I was sure that one of those lines must lead directly here.

But all was so quiet. I peeked inside the entrance and it was dank, covered with leaves and wet earth.

The bunker had a horizontal opening less than two feet high

on one side. It was dark inside, and we didn't know how far down it went. Reid and I held on to Jeff and lowered him in. He crawled around, poking at walls, but didn't find other tunnels. His voice echoed up to us.

From inside the fence the forest looked different, more like camouflage. The branches swayed and threw sunlight across their tops. I knew we were well hidden. I just didn't know why, or from what.

We pulled Jeff out looking a little afraid. "Where are we?" he asked, out of breath, suddenly disturbed by what we had stumbled upon.

We looked for other signs of missile activity, but could see none. I wondered how the missiles launched, how they looked when airborne, and what it would be like to see a missile coming toward you—a giant bird of death.

Jeff had wandered to the edge of the fence. "Come look at this," he shouted. He motioned for us to stop behind him. He was staring at the ground. There, nestled among the leaves, was a small oval-shaped metal object. Reid was transfixed.

"What is it?" I asked, feeling a wave of panic.

"It's a dud," said Jeff.

"A dud what?"

Reid explained that it was a grenade that couldn't explode. Jeff picked it up. There was no pin, he said, showing me the hole, explaining that all the explosive material had been emptied out. The grenade was small and round, and cut into squares. When it exploded, Jeff said, the squares broke up into little pieces and cut into your body. That was called shrapnel.

"That's what kills you," he said, "the shrapnel."

Reid held it and pretended to throw. So did Jeff. When it was my turn, I cradled it in my hand. I felt how it could roll off my fingers so easily. I wanted to throw it. I wanted to see it roll. I checked inside to make sure the explosive had all been emptied. It smelled of burnished metal.

We carried it around, tossing it back and forth as we played around the tank and the bunker. The afternoon began to fade; the air began to cool. We wondered who else knew about this place. Our fathers? Surely.

Eventually, some hours after we had discovered them, we realized the missiles were fakes. Jeff went up close and saw the seams. They were just lots and lots of oil barrels that had been stacked together and painted. If the missiles weren't real, what were they doing here? Someone had put them here on purpose. Was this a deliberate ploy to mislead the Soviets into thinking that they knew where America's military arsenal was stored? It seemed plausible.

We kept the mysterious discovery secret from our fathers. But we began to look for more clues as to what was going on in our bucolic riverside community. We discussed the possibilities over milkshakes at a place called The Café that overlooked the York River. It looked like something from a movie set. The waiter wore a little white hat—whether a sailor's or a chef's, it wasn't clear. On the wall above our usual table, a sign read "Loose Lips Sink Ships." The men around us always talked quietly, as if they were trying to figure out a puzzle. They drank coffee. But it felt like a simulacrum of friends talking over coffee, not the real thing.

The more the three of us explored, the more I realized that we didn't need to leave Camp Peary. The base had enough mystery of its own.

One day I went to a restricted area on my own. It was near the general store, on the way to the camp's main gate. I pulled my bike up to the perimeter and stashed it in the bushes. I walked to the edge of the gate, stepped under, took a few steps, and then went right in, around a small bend in the path. A little further on was a huge pile of tires and trash. I stood looking for a while, trying to figure out what was so forbidden about a pile of trash, when I heard a voice. It was Toot, the main guard at the front gate. He was the base policeman, and a deer hunter and former marine—not a man to be messed with. He stared at me.

"I got lost," I volunteered.

"No, you didn't. You snuck in here."

"I didn't."

Toot moved past me and walked to the other side of the pile, blocking my way. "Not allowed in here," he said.

"I know."

"So?"

"I don't know."

He nodded for me to leave. "I don't want to catch you in here again, or anywhere else that's off-limits."

I left, but the encounter hadn't thrilled me like my others. It just made me uneasy. I was suddenly aware that my trespasses were more than just a passing annoyance for the adults, and that perhaps the dangers on the base needed to be kept quiet for our own protection.

As the seasons changed and we became less enthralled by the mysteries of Camp Peary, the three of us began to see its downsides. The boys and I often dreamed of running away. Jeff told us he had done it once—just started walking down a road, prepared to leave and never return. I imagined doing it, too, but then I saw myself stopping for fear of the unknown, for fear of encountering or causing trouble and losing the things that were familiar to me. But the fantasy of escaping grew within us, and it was reinforced by our proximity to adults who acted strangely and were constantly dodging our questions. We knew there were lies in the air. We shared our frustrations with each other, and complained about being sequestered on a base where visits from outsiders required military authorization—where the whole outside world was, in fact, something people in the camp generally regarded with suspicion, or even derision.

When we did leave the base, it was often to visit the nearby colonial town of Williamsburg, which was a farcical illusion if there ever was one—an entire village devoted to keeping alive the customs and cares of eighteenth-century American colonists. The town was filled with blacksmiths and coppersmiths, horse-drawn carriages, and soldiers with tricornered hats prancing around talking in Old English. There were also hundreds of thousands of tourists who visited each year, turning it into even more of a circus than it already was. Between colonial Williamsburg and Camp Peary, it wasn't hard to choose which was the more pleasant reality; but the notion of reality itself was what began to seem fuzzy.

It wasn't just the stifling secrets of Camp Peary. At home, at night, my father and Janet continued to hiss at each other. I would try to listen in, but could never hear much. During the day, they were rarely together. Janet was in the kitchen much of the time, or outside in the garden picking lilies and hibiscus to arrange in vases or for garden parties. Her gardening seemed like dentistry to me—it was the science of rearranging roots in the flesh of the ground, pulling protruding random life into some more appropriate shape and poking it into bowls, where spikes held it in place. Tulips and lilies were caught in our front yard, along the sidewalk that led to the front porch. Sometimes I thought about booting their heads off with a swift kick—sending the seeds flying into space and leaving the petals there, gasping on the ground like red lips.

There was a long hill on the banks of the York that I had never managed to descend fully on my skateboard. It was too steep for me, and my skills were lacking. One day my dad suggested we go together. We got to the top of the hill and stood looking down at the steep incline. I glanced over at him nervously. He put his hand on my shoulder. "Bend your knees," he said. "Keep yourself low."

So I did. And then I started to roll. At first it was okay; I was coasting down nicely. But then the board began to wobble from side to side, and I began to lose control. Then suddenly I was off, looming out forward horizontally, until I landed on my face on the footpath. Blood began to pour from my nose and forehead. My father was there in an instant, cradling my head in his arms and wiping the blood away. When we got home, he took me into the kitchen and asked Janet to prepare a wet cloth.

"Don't treat him like a baby," she said, looking back at me from the kitchen sink.

"Just get the damn cloth," he snarled back at her. "Can't you see he's hurt?"

I sat there quietly and whimpered. I couldn't suppress the smile of vengeance. Whenever Janet and my father fought, I always chose his side.

A few months later, I did get the chance to leave Camp Peary. I went to California to spend the summer of 1985 with my mother and her second husband, a cruel air-force colonel who ran his house like a barracks. He stacked canned goods alphabetically in the cupboards and combed his hair neatly, even on weekend mornings, a habit that seemed charming with my dad but hateful somehow with this man. My mother was unhappy with him. He was a deeply unfeeling man, cold and controlling. He had no sense of smell, which I equated with having no emotion at all. He had two sons from a previous marriage, and both of them cowered in fear every time he appeared. I desperately wanted my mother to leave him. I could see she wanted to as well, but I think the threat of another domestic failure haunted her. I passed by their bedroom door on several occasions and heard hushed voices, and it soon became clear that they were having urgent discussions about the poor state of their relationship.

Toward the end of summer, as much as I wanted to stay in the warm glow of my mother, I was happy to get away from the colonel. But when I arrived back at Camp Peary, I discovered that Jeff and Reid had left for good while I was gone; I was friendless.

Amy was also going. She was only with us at Camp Peary for a year. I hardly ever saw her, anyway—she was either in her room or with her friends. At the beginning of our second year in Camp Peary, she left to finish high school in California and live with her father for a while. And though I hadn't seen much of her, her absence from the house made it all the quieter.

By then, I had stopped receiving letters from Pakistan. At my age, a year can seem an eternity, and half of that is a lifetime.

But just before I began seventh grade, a boy named Paul arrived at Camp Peary from Thailand. His brother rode a motor-cycle, and owned an AK-47 that he had somehow shipped from Thailand and hid in the woods, he said, and one day he would show it to me. We became friends. Soon the woods became a ref-uge for us, an escape from the cloistered atmosphere of the rest of the base.

One day Paul taught me how to smoke. We sat on a log, and he slapped the pack against his wrist, pulling out a cigarette and slipping it in his mouth. He struck a match and touched the flame to it. The smoke lingered in his mouth kind of sexily, and then disappeared. He handed one to me and I mimicked him, striking the match and inhaling. I began to cough violently. But I loved it—not only the smell of fresh smoke, but also the illicit nature of it.

We returned to the same spot, just out of sight of the trees, every day. After school Paul would put his fingers to his lips. "I need a drag," he'd whisper, and we'd head off. We had stashed the cigarettes in a tin can under a log. We smoked until we were dizzy. Afterward, we chewed gum to hide our breath, stashed our butts carefully in the canister, and rubbed our clothes with pine needles to erase the scent.

My father sensed my lies and smelled the smoke on me. One day he hid himself and pinpointed the spot where we emerged from the woods. He found the canister, the butts, and the matches. When we went back the next day, our stash had mysteriously dis-appeared without a trace. I went home, without a clue that my father was behind it.

When he came home from work that day, all he said was, "I found your stash." He had been tracking me while walking Duke in the fields, he said. In fact, I had seen him walking the dog from what I thought was the safety of the woods. I didn't imagine he was shadowing me. How benign his behavior had looked from a distance, how unaware he had appeared. That was the trick, then: lull your targets into safety and then ambush them. His discovery of my cigarettes was galling, but enlightening.

I lost my phone privileges, wasn't allowed into the woods, and was given more chores. By the time my restrictions were eventually lifted it was almost winter, and I took to the woods with my friends again.

When the snows fell, we had full-blown battles in the forests. We had gotten hold of pump-action BB guns that could hold up to 100 BBs at a time. We trekked into a patch of woods near a small creek and built an underground fort near one of the boulders that were scattered along the slopes. The shelter, like the one in *Red Dawn*, was a few yards deep and wide enough for two of us. We wove together branches and leaves and vines that we packed with dirt and flopped over the top for camouflage. When there, we sprayed the air and trees with gunfire, faces red and puffed with anger. Branches cracked and fell to the ground around us. There was laughter and panting, the rustle of leaves, the *clickity-click* of BBs being loaded. We screamed and killed each other again and again. I had never had so much fun.

But my father thought I might have even more fun if I followed in his footsteps and joined the Boy Scouts. So one night Paul and I accompanied him to a small cabin where the Camp Peary scouts held their weekly meetings. The front-gate guard, Toot, was the scoutmaster. The scouts were a sorry bunch, half a dozen or so boys in ragged uniforms, all sons of the base's employees. Many of them were stoned much of the time. Few had any merit badges, and most were unenthusiastic about earning them. However, my father encouraged us to make the best of it.

Sometimes Toot took us camping. Even he, our fearless leader, recognized the apathy of his scouts, and he concentrated instead on his signature achievement—making a killer venison stew, which he wouldn't stop talking about.

My dad came on some of the trips, but I tried to avoid involving him. He had been an Eagle Scout, such a standout, when I could barely tie a bowline. Instead, I delighted in rebelling by frequently, and loudly, labeling my fellow scouts as a group of "dickless wonders." I had heard the words somewhere—maybe in a movie—and took to repeating them in an attempt to show my independence and what I believed was my great capacity for humor. (I can't say the other scouts appreciated it.)

I liked the idea of learning to be capable and resourceful, but I realized that I liked it a lot more on the wrong side of right. I bombed at the Boy Scout jamborees, with their competitions for archery and knot-tying and teepee-building, where boys with flashy red neckties and bandoliers marched to the sound of trumpets. I enjoyed wallowing in my manifest inferiority. I liked plotting in the quiet of the forest, with a few fellows, the sabotage of some imaginary evil empire. But I wanted to do it alone, to hog the glory. I failed in the communal world somehow.

At a local jamboree that spring, Paul and I grew bored. So while the other scouts were preparing for an evening "roll call," we snuck off into the woods with a younger kid from our troop. After walking for a while, we stopped to rest. Paul and I lit up. Go ahead, we said, proffering a lit cigarette to the kid. He refused. We puffed on our own and laughed.

When Toot found out, he kicked us out of the troop. My father stopped talking about the Eagle Scouts. He grounded me again, this time for two months. But I wasn't having any of it. I began to smoke pot, as most of the older kids did. I was only twelve, but some of them were into cocaine and guns, so my transgressions didn't seem so bad.

When the spring of 1986 rolled around, I had tired of living in the strange, forested land of Camp Peary. The thoughts of running away coalesced into an idea that maybe I should get out from under my father's controlling eye for a while. My mother and her air-force tyrant had divorced, and she was living alone in California. She had been depressed. She had many problems with her parents. And for the last six years, although I had spent summers and some weekends with her, my relative absence from her life had taken a toll. She had wanted to have me around more, she had told me the summer before. So I called and said I wanted to come live with her. I thought I heard her sob.

That summer my father drove me back up Interstate 64. He was kind the whole way. But when we got to my grandparents' house in Maryland, where he was to drop me off, he turned off the engine and broke down. I had never seen my father cry before, but he did then. He sobbed like a child; his whole body shook. I don't know how I made it out of the car, but I did, into my grandparents' basement, where I slumped in a chair and closed my eyes.

CHAPTER 5
Southfield, Michigan, 1987

One lazy Saturday morning, my father took me with him to his office.

He picked me up in a light-blue Buick, ugly as hell, and started down Ten Mile, just one of a dozen—or a hundred—parallel streets that stretched across that vast grid of the north. We could see the Detroit Renaissance Center on the horizon, looking like some lost and gutted metropolis, which it just about was.

I didn't like that damn Buick. It was beat-up and broken. Even I, never a connoisseur of cars, knew that it was meant for mechanics and fishermen and longshoremen with beer guts and wife-beaters and a permanent five-o'clock shadow. But he turned the classical music up, and we just coasted along.

My decision to leave my father the year before had turned out to be short-lived. By the time I had started high school, I was back with my dad.

The year with my mother hadn't been easy, for anyone. She was working full-time, but she was also still sorting out her own problems, and being a single mother didn't make it any easier. She wanted to keep me there with her—to have a chance at raising me. But I didn't like the guilt of depriving either parent of me and it began to seem easier, or less painful somehow, not to deprive my father. So I had left my mother again, and gone to live with my dad.

Once he had served his time at Camp Peary, my father had settled in gray old Michigan. Maybe it felt safer to be in the middle of America, where the bleak, urban anonymity was comforting—as if those long, gray streets and mini-malls and endless plains of suburbia could camouflage us more expertly. Maybe it had just become necessary. I was fourteen, old enough to be asking the kinds of questions to which my father's answers—or sleight-of-hand that masqueraded as answers—no longer sufficed. I think, too, that he knew the ordinariness that permeated most aspects of our life was corrosive, and that I craved something more; he may have suspected that his hold on me was tenuous, and that making me complicit in his secrets might be a way of staving off my inevitable revolt. Perhaps this was why he took me to his office.

We pulled into an office complex, and he tracked across to the mostly empty lot, past a Dalton's, a Baskin-Robbins, a CVS pharmacy, a laundromat and video store, and a pizza joint, easing into a parking spot in front of a drab-brown two-story building. The blinds on the second story had been shuttered. He put the car in park and turned off the ignition, leaving the engine to tick down. Then he shifted to look at me. When I reached for the door handle, he said gently, "Wait."

I turned back to look at him. His normally confident mouth slackened. He was stuck between apology and pride, which morphed into a mischievous grin, and then again into gentle certainty.

"Wait," he said again, and placed his hand on my shoulder.

The windows had started to fog from our breathing.

"Scotty," he said.

The warm seat was between us, an open space where the latticed wall should have been to transform it into a devotional bench. I was half-expecting a lecture about my bad behavior at home or my middling algebra grade, but these didn't materialize.

My father sighed, and then smiled. "I need to tell you something," he said.

"Okay."

"It's nothing bad," he said. "But it's serious."

"Okay."

He let the pause go. Then, "Do you know what I do for a living?"

I stared at him. I stuttered and began to laugh nervously. "The Foreign Service?"

But even as I spoke, I knew I was wrong. I looked around. We were in a mini-mall, sitting in a Buick, and that was our life.

He was straightforward, blunt. "Scotty," he said, "I'm a spy."

His face twitched. He grinned.

I didn't know what to say, so I said what anyone might. "Like . . . like James Bond?"

But he was nodding already, anticipating me. "Yes," he said simply.

And there it was, that feeling, just a glancing thing in my belly: impunity. As a boy, I had loved those movies in such a proprietary way: *Goldfinger* and *Dr. No* and *The Spy Who Loved Me*. I had wanted him to be like those dashing men, and I imagine he did, too, and that's why he encouraged the connection. The slightly bushy eyebrows that arched up at their corners, the charming wink, the dark Scottish gloom—there was a slight resemblance to Sean Connery. Other people commented on it, he sometimes said, or thought he looked like Clint Eastwood in *The Good, the Bad and the Ugly*: all low-slung and severe, as flat and hard-bitten as some desert butte; except in the eyes, which twitched with the glee of ambiguity.

"A spy." I repeated the word a few times, testing it out. "You mean, like in the CIA?"

But there was no wily Q providing a poison-darted pen, no desert hideaways, bad guys, or shark-infested waters—nothing even remotely similar. Nothing that I could see, anyway. And the Buick seemed like it was beginning to overheat.

He nodded and crinkled his brown eyes at me.

"Just like that," he said.

The clues had been there: the moving, living in strange places, the secrecy, the different jobs he had told me he had had, the various languages he had learned and now forgotten. But whereas before there had been only suspicion, now there was proof. He had released the truth like a genie from a bottle.

We sat in the car for a while. A few people strode across the parking lot. It was cold outside, and gray, the trees barren. My father looked at me sideways and smiled. I sniggered. He chuckled. Then, like two maniacal idiots, my father and I laughed and laughed. I was near-hysterical. My stomach hurt; my eyes watered. On it went until eventually we calmed down, and the laughter came in smaller bursts, faded, and finally subsided altogether. He took out the keys and opened his door. "Come on," he said.

We got out of the car and walked up a flight of stairs to a hallway lined with dirty beige carpet. To the left stretched another long hallway, and to the right there was an emergency stairwell and a small window. No one else seemed to be around—all the other doors were closed. Everyone was minding their own business, apparently. The door in front of us, which he opened, read "Apex Insurance." Inside, a portly blonde woman with glasses sat behind a desk with a tiny vase and a few pictures of her family—or what I assumed to be her family, although they could just as easily have been generic Hallmark faces. She greeted us with a chirpy "Hi."

He introduced me, and beamed. The woman beamed back, but her glasses were so small on her wide face. They shone and obscured her eyes, and I thought she could have been looking at me or right through me. She was too large for her desk, but it seemed not to have dawned on her until that very moment, as if she had just that day sat down at it for the first time. Another side door opened, and a dark-skinned man emerged, carrying a cup of coffee. He greeted my father enthusiastically, and I saw from his deference that my dad was the one in charge here. My father introduced the man as Marko, and they started to talk animatedly about something or other. Then Marko looked at me, and waved his hand. "Tell you later," he said, and my father nodded.

My dad's office was at the end of the room. We walked in, and he closed the door. There was a long, much larger desk, covered with paperweights and pictures: a wedding portrait of Janet and my father underneath blooms of bougainvillea and nasturtium—with a six-year-old me cradled in the crook of his right arm, holding a golden wedding band; and Duke and me somewhere in Yugoslavia, probably on the stoop of our house in Belgrade. Several of his own photos hung on the walls, too: a Hindu Brahman on the Ganges, praying; and the afternoon sun on a field of snowy wheat Out West, his home—or that was where we told people he was from. "Out West" was enough for people Back East. I walked over and peeked through the venetian blinds. Five yards below was the humble Buick. It didn't look so shabby anymore, that spy car.

My father was standing across the room, watching me. He wore a handsome suit, dark-brown loafers, and an elegant tie. His hair was combed smoothly over his head, and I could smell his aftershave. He fiddled with his ring finger.

"So," I asked, "what if someone comes in who wants insurance, Apex insurance?"

"No one does," he said.

"Ever?"

"Nope."

"Don't other people get suspicious, like, 'What kind of business are they running in there?'"

"I don't think so," he said.

I walked around, looking at the pictures, and the trinkets on his shelves. There was a long, steel letter-opener, and also a few knives he had picked up in Pakistan—maybe when he had lived there briefly as a boy, or maybe just a few years ago, when I had lived there. There were some plaques that I guessed had been given to him by foreign dignitaries, and a diploma from the University of Michigan. At home, I loved my father's secret things—his rings, cufflinks, tie clips, and collection of handheld stopwatches, none of which told time. I loved going through his menagerie of silky ties, or his jewelry box, in which he kept pins and eyeglasses and delicate shoehorns, and small, polished stones he had gathered from all around the world. I touched the desk, the heavy oak wood with its polished writing surface and dead weights along its edges. These were his public things.

We talked idly about life for a while. I told him I didn't want to go to college, and he mocked me gently for my intransigence. He asked what I wanted to do with my life, and I said I had no idea—maybe a park ranger, or a sporting-goods–store owner. We were quiet for a while. I couldn't tell anyone, he said suddenly. He looked at me from across the room, and the distance was the distance of adulthood. What he had just told me—I had to keep it secret. Everything else was okay, he said; everything else could be worked out in due time. I was not to worry, and he was sure I would figure it all out. But this was different. He walked toward me and put a hand on my shoulder and squeezed. He said that he trusted me.

The world out there, the one we had just come in from, the cold and gray one, was the illusion we had to wade through. And although I didn't say it, the feeling of familiarity with the truth of this moment, with all that was spoken and unspoken, was thrilling in the way that nakedness is thrilling—never old, never dying, endlessly regenerating.

What he didn't say, but what was understood, was that he needed me to lie for him from then on, and lie like a professional. I had license to dissimulate, fabricate, invent, cover-up, and deceive if necessary. There was a greater good. There was no need to know before, he said, no pressing urgency. But now, apparently, there was. I didn't know where that need originated, whether from him or the men who controlled him, only now it was upon us both, much like the cold outside—just a simple fact of life. From then on, the world and all that was in it would be different, especially with other people.

"Deal?" he asked, offering me his hand. I took it.

"Deal," I said.

I think my father thought that might have been the end of it. Of course, it was only the beginning. His double life was mine now, too.

For a long time, I wasn't allowed to mention my dad's work, his double life, at all. But in those first few years the learning curve was steeper. Telling anyone the truth probably wouldn't have resulted in treason charges, but it was, I was convinced, illegal. More to the point, he had asked for secrecy and I had agreed not to talk about it to others. Our next-door neighbor designed cars for the Chrysler Corporation and lived a typical suburban existence. To him, or anyone else that asked, my father was a Washington, D.C., bureaucrat on loan to the local department of commerce.

I had a friend in those early high-school years, an older boy named Jeff, who knew damn well, somehow, that my father was in the CIA. Jeff was smart, and he believed the story of our life history—the overseas postings, the vague job descriptions—had too many red flags. Jeff harassed me about it regularly. "You know your dad's a spook," he'd say, as he was giving me a lift to school, or in the locker room after swim practice. "Just admit it." When I weakly demurred, he'd shake his head and grimace because the lies coming out of my mouth were so transparent, so weak and spineless.

I'd shrivel away and try to change the subject. "No," I'd say, "he's a diplomat." He worked for the State Department, whatever; I reached for something, anything. Sometimes I just said I didn't have the slightest idea.

I used to look people in the eye when they asked about us. But I stopped doing that sometime after I learned the truth. One day, probably after someone pointed out my skittishness, I realized that I was acting furtively. So I started to make an effort—I looked people in the eye. I even held their gaze. But that didn't change much. I kept lying for my father.

A simple explanation was usually enough for most people. Why did I move around so much as a child? What did my father do? "Oh," I might say, "he worked for the government. He was a diplomat."

Now and again, someone wanted to probe a bit further. Which branch of the government? "Department of Commerce," I'd say, "commercial officer."

My father made a good story. That's what my friend Ray thought, anyway. He was a reporter at the Southfield High newspaper. And like Jeff, he was another nonbeliever. Ray was slower to come to the conclusion Jeff had reached almost instantly; but he was also a closer friend, and too much suspicion probably would have seemed disloyal. In those days of 1989, Ray would come over to our little townhouse and sit with my father in the kitchen for hours to talk about foreign policy—America's involvement in Iran or across Central America.

I usually tried to creep away from the encounters between Ray and my father. I didn't want to give anything away inadvertently. I knew my skittishness and discomfort must have shown. The truth was, it was difficult to have to keep my father's big secret—even more difficult when I saw how easily he did it. I watched him elude questions, gently laugh away inquiries, downplay it all.

Sometimes when Ray and my father were talking, I'd sit in the living room with my back to the mirror and listen through the wall. I suppose I could have taken part in the conversation, but how? I knew my father was occasionally lying and concealing, and for good reason, but I couldn't call him out on it, however much I wanted to. I knew Ray wanted answers, but I couldn't give them to him. They each had their roles in those instances: pursuer and pursued. My role was to pretend not to know anything.

Despite their suspicions, Jeff and Ray got along really well with my father, and he adored their company. That was the thing of it: my dad was such a likable guy. He followed their accomplishments as closely as he did my own. But at other times, when my friends and I were alone and I wanted to talk about girls or sports, they would inevitably probe me for the truth. Was my father really just a diplomat? Why was he living in suburban Michigan?

I never had any good answers for these questions. And I was too proud of all the other places we had lived, India and Pakistan and Yugoslavia, not to mention them whenever I could, which probably inflamed my friends' curiosity more than anything my father said or did. Part of me thought what my dad did was cool, and I wanted the cachet of this in my teenage survival kit. My dad was too much a professional, and I wasn't. I probably did more to blow his cover than hide it. While I never told Ray my father's secret, I let my hints about my dad's exoticism linger.

But our suburban house, my fresh-faced stepmother Janet, our golden retriever Duke, our walks in the nearby park, and our over-the-fence afternoon chats with the man who worked for Chrysler—all of those things aided his cover. My father liked to point out that they were the reality, too. But that's what made them such good cover—the utter believability of them all. All you had to do was play along as unobtrusively as possible, and keep quiet.

Yet I was also becoming curious myself—I was starting to wonder exactly what my father was doing. Spies did things, after all, in addition to pretending they weren't spies. One of the first things I learned about Michigan was that there were a lot of Lebanese and Iraqis living there. Lebanon was where American hostages were being held, Americans who worked at the CIA like my father. Iraq was next door to Iran, he reminded me, which was where, in the 1980s, U.S. Marine Ollie North had gotten up to so much mischief. As a result, Iran and Iraq and Lebanon became in my imagination the lands of the zealots, both Middle Eastern and American alike—a kind of Mordor. I started to wonder whether this place had something to do with what my father was working on. There were Chaldeans, Iraqi Christians from an old Syrian sect, in my high school. The hirsute woman who cut my hair was Chaldean, and so were a couple of the boys on my swim team. Zealots believed in things too strongly, I remembered my father saying. Better to keep it cool, distant; to devise a middle way. Was that what he was doing in Michigan—devising a middle way?

Around this time I first heard about The Farm.

"You remember the Pembrokes, from The Farm," my father said.

"The Farm?" I asked, thinking that it might be our old family place Out West that my great-grandfather had settled, where my grandpa had been raised, and where my cousins now lived in a sort of splendid rural squalor.

But it wasn't. It was the other name for my previous home, Camp Peary. My father told me that The Farm was where the CIA trained its people, and when the trainees got older they returned there to train the next generation, and so on, year after year. That was what my father had been doing there—teaching spies their trade. The Farm wasn't that secret, it turned out, but few people knew what went on there: the paramilitary exercises, the helicopter runs at all hours of the day and night, the vast tracts of uncut forest that hid bunkers and schools and classrooms that no one could see. Officially, Camp Peary was the public name for a place that otherwise didn't even exist. I had been living in a black hole, an unmarked spot in the world where the façade at the gate was the only thing most people ever got to see.

I found out that during World War II, the U.S. Navy had

annexed the land that would become Camp Peary and drawn up the broad outlines of the base, which it named after the renowned Arctic explorer Robert Edwin Peary. At first it was used as a boot camp for Navy Seabees, mechanical and civil engineers who could double as soldiers, or soldiers who could double as construction workers. In the winter of 1943, the navy transformed the base into the U.S. Naval Construction Center. As World War II dragged on, Germans and Japanese were captured and brought to the United States for interrogation, and The Farm was used as a prisoner-of-war camp. After the war, it became the Armed Forces Experimental Training Activity. The Office of Special Services, the precursor to the CIA, eventually annexed the land. When the OSS became the CIA in 1947, Camp Peary became the CIA's principal training facility. Specifically, it was given over to the Directorate of Operations, the Agency's clandestine service, for which my father worked. Camp Peary's history as a POW camp was erased, the stockades destroyed or dismantled. Sometimes it was called a "special training center." In 1987, our first year in Southfield, Nicaraguan rebels had been secretly flown into The Farm for paramilitary training to fight the Sandinista revolution back home in Central America.

When I learned this, all of my forays and discoveries with Jeff and Reid began to fall into place. I remembered the missile silos, the bunkers, the long roads to nowhere, and the men skulking around that campus whose qualities of studied nonchalance I now began to recognize in my father. Of course they acted like him—he had been teaching those young American men how to spy. And he'd been teaching me the same thing for years—quietly, surreptitiously, and almost unconsciously. I was starting to see that now.

I began to learn other things about my father, things I never could have imagined. One day, talking about Iran, he told me the story of the 1979 hostage crisis at the American embassy in Tehran. Some of the hostages had been spies, he said, like him. One of them, a friend of his, was a military type and skilled survivalist. As a matter of course, he wore a belt he had purchased through *Soldier of Fortune*, a magazine that catered to mercenaries. It had a knife secreted between two strips of leather. After the embassy was taken hostage with him inside, he had rifled through desks until he found a hacksaw blade. He used this to rip out telephone lines, and quickly wrapped them around his midsection. So before the enraged hostage-takers even reached his floor, he had a knife, some rope, and a hacksaw.

Of all the hostages, he was the only one to eventually make two escape attempts. Both failed, but they were escape attempts all right. Escaping from terrorists who were aiming to kill you was just about the coolest thing I could imagine.

Other stories my father told me weren't so heroic, however. The CIA station chief in Beirut in those years was William Buckley, who held the same position that my father now had in Detroit. Buckley had been kidnapped as he left for work, and murdered. I wondered what could these people, like my father, know and do that would make them important enough to want to kidnap or kill?

"What happens if you get tortured?" I asked, because I didn't know what torture was, in the real world. I knew what it looked like when Rambo got beaten silly in *First Blood*, or when Sean Connery was tied to a table, squirming as Goldfinger slowly and methodically set a laser beam on a collision course with his crotch. But what happened if my father was taken away? What would happen to him, to me?

"I don't know," he said. "I just don't know what that would be like."

I remembered us walking in an autumn forest, surrounded by the soft scratching of leaves; a long footpath down the middle of a blaze; peat and moss underfoot; the smell of leaf rot in the air; the slight chill that he fended off with a brown trench coat, leather gloves, and a wool beret; and how our breath had swirled around it all. We were two small beings moving through a canopy of brightly dying trees.

"But I'm not going anywhere, Scotty," he said. "I'll always be here for you. I love you more than the sky 'cause the sky never ends."

He was trying his best to allay my fears. He wanted me to be part of his whole life, not just a fraction of it. That's why he had taken me to his office, shown me his world, and told me his secret. But I still had the thought: what if he disappeared? When my father had first told me about his work, he said it was just like James Bond. But that clearly wasn't entirely true. It was another convenient tale—or shall I call it a layer of truth? Because what did I know about tradecraft, other than the word itself? He had explained that it was what spies did, their bag of tricks, their secret skills. It was their art. But he still had to hide huge parts of his work from me, which left gaping holes in my understanding of him and, to a certain extent, my relationship with him. In James Bond movies, there was never a son who came along, or got left behind.

The interior design of our house seemed to have been modeled with my father's profession in mind—it was a veritable hall of mirrors. One wall of the living room was a floor-to-ceiling mirror. The dining-room walls had been obscured by full-length, billowy red curtains that emanated from a large chandelier and mirror, blooming down from the ceiling like a tent. Our dining table was made of glass. We ate there when the Pams came over for dinner.

The Pams, so-called because her first name was more fun to say than his last, were the couple from whom we had purchased the townhouse. He was an elderly Detroit lawyer called Irving, she his young wife. Dinners with the Pams were always exciting occasions for me. Pam was so beautiful and full of life, and she promised me that someday, when I grew up and Irving was gone, we would marry. But her fascination with my father was the driving energy of our dinner parties. "Is Keith Really a CIA Agent Masquerading as a Government Bureaucrat?" very quickly became the most fun game to play around the dinner table, and time and again I watched how my father did it—how he smiled his way out of the truth with these close friends; how, with the slightest nod of his head or twitch of his eyebrow, he managed to keep the suspense going, all while leaving no doubt that it was just a game. The whole point of the night's exercise seemed to be to test my father's abilities to navigate the minefields of truth and deception with the people closest to him; to see how far others could push him, or if they could trap him in a lie. At least that's how it seemed to me at the time.

But no one ever did catch him. I remember looking down through that glass table during dinner, at his hands in his lap. He picked gently at his fingernails, rubbing their sides, smoothing them out one by one, massaging his thick ring finger, where a star sapphire shone in a band of gold. In hindsight I think they, like Ray or Jeff, might have known who, or what, they were dealing with.

The questions came again and again, every time the Pams came over, and I struggled with the idea that there was something fundamentally illusory and maybe even shameful about our life. It wasn't that my father lied about everything; he didn't. But the lie about his work was enough because it informed everything else. The deceptions that followed cascaded down. Again and again he'd say no, he was not in the CIA, or lie about the work he pretended to do at the Department of Commerce where, he said, he was just a bureaucrat. And the accusations from our friends and acquaintances, not just the Pams but also my schoolmates, shot back with equal force. At the center was this fundamental question about my father, and by extension about the rest of us: but who are you, really?

Okay, so people didn't have a right to know these things about us. National security dictated that it must be so; I knew that. I knew what was at stake. I was not naïve about it. What I was, in fact, was a little bit scared.

One night Irving brought up the subject of alien abduction. His former brother-in-law, a Harvard professor and author of several books about alien abductions, was staying with them, so aliens had been a big topic of conversation in their house lately. Irving was a rationalist, but he didn't discount the possibility of other intelligences operating out there. I loved this idea and told him so. I had been reading about alien abductions and had devoured a book called *Contact*, written by a man who claimed to have been victimized. I thought I would make a good candidate for abduction, and fantasized constantly about being swept out of bed by green men with huge eyes and spirited up to a spaceship where experiments would be performed on me (and from which vast amounts of secret knowledge would immediately accrue to me). Irving was the first grown-up I had ever met who seemed even remotely open to the idea. And he was smart—surely he would know. Even Janet and Pam didn't dismiss the idea.

But my father wasn't having any of it. He laughed so hard that tears came to his eyes. My dad didn't mean to be nasty, but I still felt bad for Irving. I felt even worse for my father; I wished he had been able to believe in aliens, or at least the possibility of aliens, like the rest of us. But he couldn't, or wouldn't.

I wondered whether he felt like the alien sometimes—opaque, all-knowing, and living by a different set of rules. Maybe the familiarity was too close. This predicament of ours reminded me of the 1980s television series *V*, in which lizard-like aliens from another planet had come to Earth and disguised themselves in human form. Who were they really, under their human skins? I couldn't quite put my finger on the reason for others' unease. But I felt people around us were looking for something dirty and untidy and illicit. I was one of those lizards.

At the end of the night, there was always a moment that came after the public part of the game was over, when the Pams had taken their leave amid a flurry of kisses and hugs, because it was then that the truth of our life became so naked and apparent. It wasn't just idle dinner-party chatter or a parlor game after all. The secret was real, and it had to be kept. I knew it, and so did Janet, who seemed now diminished to me by the toil it involved. So we'd clean up the dinner table in silence, walk to and fro by the mirrored wall and under the billowy red curtains, and know that at the end of the day we were alone with each other. No amount of joking or teasing or self-deprecating humor could ease the isolation of our secret.

My father often came up to me after the Pams left and told me he loved me. I think he knew, or at least suspected, that it probably wasn't altogether right somehow, this morality play. An odd assemblage of lessons would inevitably be drawn from these encounters. There was in our lives an unpleasant but necessary organization that had an ironfisted grip on our loyalties, and we could no more betray it than we could each other. There were really no easy answers to this reality, and this sometimes led to doubts about what and who we were to each other, or even to ourselves.

Those doubts began to wriggle within our family dynamic in different ways. My father's secret loyalties made it easier for Janet to justify her growing sense of discomfort. She believed my father had tricked her into a marriage in which she had no place other than as the adoptive mother to his child and keeper of his secrets. She began what would become a three-year affair with a friend from her past life in Michigan. The trust my father had placed with her began to break. She might have been just as happy to let it go.

She let her temper run wild. She threatened to leave us time and again. One day she would be stony and cold, the next solicitous and full of charm. Each time she yelled at me, or delivered some cutting remark about my weaknesses as a boy, I swore to myself that I would never, ever forgive her. But then she would

apologize and cozy up, and I would be drawn in again. I did forgive her.

One day, while driving me to school, she was in a particularly good mood. I tried talking to her, and to my great surprise
she responded in kind. I can't remember what we were talking
about exactly, only that suddenly I said something that displeased
her, and she snapped. She glared at me and pulled the car to a
stop. "You always fuck things up," she hissed. "You always just
fuck things up!" At the time, of course, I blamed her. But I think
somewhere in there, sometime during those long Michigan win-
ters, we simply stopped trusting each other under the strain of the
many lies.

On a day that winter, the Pams invited us over to their house
for an afternoon of ice-skating on their pond. They had a large,
modern place with a bay-windowed living room that absorbed
the pearly winter light like a solarium. Out the back was a pond,
where we spent a couple of hours tottering around on the ice.
At some point, back in the house, when the four of them were
talking, I wandered down into the basement, where Irving had a
library. He had a lot of great books, I thought, but I kept brows-
ing until I realized what I was looking for. I didn't know what
it would be, exactly, but I knew I would recognize it when I saw
it. And then I did see it. The book was called *Her*, four hundred pages of lurid sex written by Anonymous. Perfect. I slipped
it into my pants, pulled my sweater down low, and wandered back
upstairs. When we all hugged and kissed goodbye, I made sure to
keep my stomach from touching anyone else's.

A few days later, my father wandered into my room. I was
sacked out on my bed. I had slipped *Her* into my bookshelf backward, with the pages facing outward, trying to make it look hap-
hazard and uninteresting. My father walked around the room
commenting on this or that, and eventually wound up at the
bookshelf. I knew what was coming. Without drawing too much

attention to his gestures, he inoffensively slipped *Her* out of the shelf and started flipping through the book.

"Where did you get this?" he asked, innocent as could be.

I said I had found it somewhere.

"Huh," he said.

We were quiet for a moment.

"The Pams mentioned that a book of theirs was missing."

"Really?" I asked, genuinely surprised.

"They didn't say what it was, though."

"I don't know," I said. "Sorry."

"So this isn't it?" he asked.

I lay back on the bed and stared straight at him. "Nope."

"Nope?"

"No," I said. "That's mine."

He looked at me. Then he laughed. He put *Her* back in the shelf, but with the cover, the title in effusive scarlet cursive, facing out. "Okay," he said. "Good night, chum."

CHAPTER 6
Madrid, 1992

I had just graduated from high school the next time my father was posted overseas. After two years in Michigan, he had moved us to McLean, Virginia, near the CIA headquarters in Langley. I had finished my last two years of school where he started his career. By then he was desperate to leave Virginia, and couldn't wait to arrive in Spain, where he would be the third in command at the CIA station. He had worked on mastering Spanish for a year.

The following summer, after my freshman year of college, I arrived to visit him and Janet. He seemed so at home in Spain—so comfortable with the language, so in love with the country—that I had trouble imagining him ever being able to shed his new identity.

My father wasn't crazy, but he was a man of appetites. The older I got, the more I began to see that. I was eighteen that summer in Madrid when my father introduced me to a woman named Irena. Irena was slight and delicate, which was odd, because she was a bullfighter. She was also a horse expert, and she and my father used to go riding in the country outside Madrid, through the verdant olive groves and rocky hills encircling the city.

Soon after I met Irena, he introduced me to her children, a guy and a girl about my age. I liked them well enough. One afternoon, the three of us went to the circus together. We padded around the Ferris wheels and shooting parlors. My rudimentary Spanish wasn't as good as the English they spoke, but only by a hair, so we muddled through, trying to have fun. They were more polite than me, more composed, and more adept in the chaos of celebration. There was a frenetic absurdity to the circus—the big-top rings and stuffed bears; the real bear, which was in a cage; the cotton candy spinning in the sun; and the Americanness of all these Spanish teenagers in their skater T-shirts and high-tops.

The girl was slim and delicate, like her mother, with sloping brown eyes and waist-length dark hair; her brother was kind and gentle and solicitous in the most gracious way. I remember them looking at me with a kind of pity, as if they were waiting for me to understand something that I, in my bigger, more exposed frame, had not had the ability to make room for yet. Every now and again they flicked quick phrases or words back and forth, a lubricant to keep the day going, the conversation flowing. And yet I got more and more tired, wading through the circus with them—all the horns and sirens and cycles of gypsy polka just got louder and louder until I couldn't hear anything at all. And suddenly it was all over, and I was back in Irena's apartment—sitting on a linen couch laced with some dead relative's embroidery, with the boy and the girl next to me, and the lady bullfighter on a wooden chair across the room, under some small gilded mirrors and finely sketched portraits of caballeros and toros, and my father in a wooden chair next to the door, smiling at me.

All eyes seemed to be on me in that moment. Yes, I liked it, I thought, this sophisticated little parlor with its wrought-iron equine statuettes and leather whips, faded black-and-white family portraits in wooden frames, and the five of us inside like figurines in a snow globe. The city was so hot, and this apartment, above the crowded streets, so cool.

"What did you think of them?" he asked me a bit later when we were walking home.

"I liked them," I said. "We had had a good time at the circus."

"I really like those two kids," he said, rather casually.

My father lived in an upscale apartment on Miguel Angel, near the Metro Rubén Dario. One night, we threw a cocktail party. Janet was very fastidious about parties, and went to great lengths to make sure our stress levels were on high. Appetizers had to be prepared and set, serviettes wrapped, drinks cooled and prepared. My father tended to give her as much room as she needed; I also avoided her as much as possible, knowing that the slightest deviation would bring down the full wrath of her temper. But I was also starting to understand that these out-bursts had little to do with me. Our apartment was her realm, her last refuge, and she took great pride in making everything in it perfect. It had big salons with tall windows and little French balconies, and when the guests arrived it would fill up nicely. My father always played classical music in our house, but shortly before guests showed up he changed the music to something slightly more upbeat, something like Clapton or Baez or Coltrane.

Soon it became lively. Many of the guests were CIA, although no one seemed to be talking official business. A man that I knew worked in administration was there. He was of Irish stock and gregarious and liked me, though he didn't much like the CIA, and had no real problem saying so. There was a well-groomed dandy with a lithe young blonde on his arm, who looked like a Hollywood version of a spy. He even wore a red-and-black ascot. I felt a tinge of jealousy at the attention he garnered in the room, even from my father. I thought he was too slick, too polished—and I suddenly wondered whether other people saw my father in that way.

I sidled over to a well-built man who was hanging around

the dining-room table, where Janet had laid out a festival of hors d'oeuvres on her favorite Talavera pottery dishes. I introduced myself as Keith's son, and the man smiled and nodded. He said his name was Mike.

"Mike?" I said with a raised eyebrow, to show I doubted it was his real name, but my attempt at creating a sense of complicity went nowhere.

"So, you just visiting?" he asked.

I said I was and we both sipped our wine. I wanted to size him up. I wanted to be able to do that. I wanted to get his information without him knowing that I was doing so. "So," I asked, "you work with my dad?"

Mike nodded. "Something like that."

We were silent for a while.

"So what kinds of stuff do you guys—"

But before I could finish, Mike nearly choked on his wine. Then he swallowed and began to laugh, a belly-shaking guffaw, right in my face. "Unh-uh, no, no," he said, and shook his head. He downed the last of his wine and put the glass on the table. Then he walked away.

Later, I asked someone else about "Mike" and heard he was apparently part of some special CIA paramilitary group, sort of like the Navy SEALs, only more secret and with much greater resources at its disposal. I was told that Mike had done a lot of "work" in Central and South America over the years, flying into hot zones under cover of darkness, parachuting out of planes into the open ocean, and swimming ashore to carry out night missions in the jungles of God knows where—Colombia maybe, or Panama. Pick a country, Mike had probably been there. He certainly had the build—and the discretion.

I asked my father about Mike.

"Oh," he said. "He helps out now and again when we need some technical assistance on something."

I didn't know what that meant. And now I was of an age

where vague answers weren't just confusing; they were aggressively irritating.

Not too long after the party, my father and I went out for dinner. He had to make it an early night, he said. There were some things he needed to get done. No sooner had we gotten home than he headed out again—back to the office, he said. It was around 11:00 p.m.

A few days later, he told me that he hadn't gone to the office at all. Instead, he and some members of a technical team, along with a host of Spanish intelligence officers, had gone to bug a house. It wasn't too far from our apartment on Miguel Angel. Somebody needed watching. My father had accompanied a team of Spaniards who had broken into his apartment, searched for incriminating documents, and tapped his phone. My dad was away all night.

"Geez," I said. "Really? That's exciting! That's what you were doing?"

He smiled at me. "It wasn't that exciting. It was pretty routine, actually."

"Bugging someone's house is routine?"

"Yeah," he said. "I mean, it's not that exciting."

"What if you get caught?"

"We don't."

Later I learned that the Spanish and American teams were concerned about a North Korean who they believed might be supplying weapons to Middle Eastern terrorists, using Spain as a transit point. During the operation, my father had stood on the sidelines, watching. I imagined him doing this—observing, analyzing, clutching at the darkness of a foreigner's life. I imagined the unfamiliar smells, and the creaks and groans that could herald an unwelcome visit. In my mind's eye, I saw my dad quietly absorbing the darkness and felt how his pupils might have dilated, and wondered what feeling, if any, he had in his stomach.

I had to find out more.

When I was alone in the apartment, I rummaged through my father and Janet's things. Naturally, I gravitated toward their bedroom. It was, by and large, a sterile and uninteresting place. The sheets on the bed were dark red, and the comforter seemed too big somehow, as if nothing could comfortably survive under its weight. The bed seemed as if it was slipping off the frame, too, crowding the room. And it wasn't made, although everything else in the house was neat.

The closets were filled with boxes, most of which had been heaped to the top with family photographs—our years of life in different places, the recording and classing of which, I realized, had become one of Janet's obsessions. The photos were randomly piled and grouped, some of them spilling out onto the floor, as if every spare moment of her time was taken up with the retrieval and examination of these varied past experiences. (I had sometimes passed by her bedroom on the way to the kitchen and seen her sitting on her bed sorting through the random pictures.) There were also letters among the photos, but I could not bring myself to read these. I only snatched words or phrases here and there as I sifted nimbly through their contents. Sorrow, love, romance, desperation—all of those words were in this room at Miguel Angel.

My father's bedside table was filled with books, newspapers, and a spare set of reading glasses. His side of the closet was loaded with clothes, and I stuffed my head into the bulkiness of his coats, ties, and jackets and smelled the odor of him, of years of him. But every other part of him lived somewhere else. Maybe that's why Janet kept all of those pictures, aching to recover and contain some part of him that only lived in the boxes and frames and letters.

Toward the end of my stay, my father told me he had a surprise for me. The Summer Olympics were being held in Barcelona and he had gotten tickets for a couple of friends and me. On the last night my dad and I went to see the closing ceremony. We were seated at the far end of the stadium, about halfway up, and we had a perfect view. It was soon the most raucous display I had ever seen: giant paper dragons, baton-twirling tigers, and troops of girls so beautiful I wanted to rush down from my seat and join them. And in the midst of all the celebration, my father caught my gaze and pointed up to a window on the farthest side of the stadium from us, above the announcers' box, that was shaded entirely black. Inside that box, he said, was the CIA, monitoring things from above. The CIA was there to inform the Spanish state services that were providing security for the event about possible terror plots.

One after another, Olympic processions continued to fill the stadium, people dancing and gyrating. The music swelled, moving everyone with a steady thumping, and my father and I began to dance alongside everyone else. Confetti swirled in from every direction. Wing-like flags rose and swept over the green carpet as their bearers rolled and twisted across the floor. And then the dancers began to motion to the crowd, and soon the whole stadium of people had descended onto the floor, turning it into a giant swirl of humanity. I rushed around snapping pictures as fast as I could manage, hugging people, singing, chattering to anyone who would listen. It seemed the whole world was gathered.

Irena had come up for the party in Barcelona, too. The next day I saw her and my father; we met up at midday for ice-cream and walked through the Olympic grounds. She was happy, my father was relaxed. But little by little they edged back behind me until I was walking alone, several yards ahead of them. It was hot that day, and I had to lick my scoop assiduously to keep it from melting off the cone. Now and again I'd look behind me to see where they were. I didn't want to lose sight of them, lose them in the crowd. I kept looking back and eating my ice-cream and walking along with everyone else until the flow of people became even thicker. When I looked back the final time, my father had disappeared altogether, and the crowd had closed in around him.

It was really none of my business. But the terrain had already been cultivated, by him and by me. There was so much I didn't know that I began to lose sight of what I did know about my father. When I thought about it later, I thought that maybe he showed me the private side of his secrecy in spite of himself. You've got to protect your own, and maybe that's what he was doing. Maybe he wanted to prepare me for these moral hazards, knowing that I was headed in that same direction and hoping to inoculate me at an early age. Because the rules that governed his secret world must have been so uncompromising. How can the man keep them at bay, away from everything else the boy has ever known?

Well, he couldn't.

The first time I met another Camp Peary boy was in Spain that summer. Our fathers worked together. He was a couple of years younger and had lived on Camp Peary after I had, but we had been about the same age while on the base. He spoke fluent Spanish from having spent years in various South and Central American countries. One night, he invited me to sleep over at his house. We were both adults by then, but I remember the thrill of lying in the dark in his room. I had been so looking forward to this, I realized. The idea of talking to someone like me about my father had been festering. This boy and I were going to confess to each other. So I told him my story, such as it was, the childhood of moving around from place to place. His life had been the same. We talked about Camp Peary: the bucolic isolation, the strange restricted areas, the jobs our fathers shared. We both knew older boys on the base who were strung out on heroin or cocaine, or dealing drugs at the Williamsburg High School gymnasium. We talked about what we knew, and then suddenly, it ended. Within a few steadily collapsing moments, everything that could be said had been said.

"It's so weird," he said, and I agreed.

But I knew that we hadn't really said anything at all. The boy just a few feet away was in so many respects like me, and it dawned on me that neither of us had anything to say, nothing to which we could cling except this vague notion of belonging to something neither understood, but knew was important.

And because I didn't understand to what or where I belonged—and would not for years to come—my childhood started to ebb away in that moment. But I could not see adulthood anywhere.

Part II

The men of my own stock,
They may do ill or well,
But they tell the lies I am wonted to,
They are used to the lies I tell;
And we do not need interpreters
When we go to buy or sell.
        —"The Stranger," Rudyard Kipling

CHAPTER 7

Roaming, 1995

I didn't really begin to consider the scope of my father's life until I was finishing college in Seattle. One of my earliest confidants was my girlfriend. Sara had asked about the relationship between my father and mother—why they had gotten divorced—and I tried as best I could to explain it to her. I hardly understood it myself though, for it was complicated. They had loved each other, but that hadn't been enough. The reasons for the divorce sprang in part from deep-rooted problems within my mother's family that affected the relationship—but that is another story for another time. At this point in my life, I was still more focused on my father, and what his life said about my own.

By the time I had met Sara, my father had been retired for about a year. He had taken a buyout and moved to Spokane, Washington, into the house that his elderly parents had bought; they evacuated upon his return. I took her to this home so that she could meet him. I told her what little I knew of my father's life as a spy, adventure stories of derring-do and espionage and subterfuge that took place all around the world—in Mexico and India and Pakistan and Yugoslavia, many of the places of my childhood. These were the missing pieces, I thought, the most important fragments of his life.

Over time, I started to tell her the stories that had stayed with me over the years. I told her that my mother's best friend during those years in India, a cousin named Raffy, had been married to a UPI journalist named Bob. Whenever my parents came back from India on home leave, Raffy and Bob pestered them with accusing questions. Bob thought—knew, somehow—that my father was a spy. "Bob just suspected it," my mother told me. "And I had to say, 'No, he's a commercial officer' again and again. I was having to lie to my best friends and my family."

Sara thought the situation problematic because love was all about trust, and how could you ever trust someone whose life involved so much deception and fabrication? But when I thought about it, I erred on my father's side of the equation. She was so naïve, I thought. She didn't understand what had been at stake. How hard could it be, I said, to let go of the subterfuge? How hard could it be to become another person, shed the skein of illusion, the grip of the organization? Easiest thing in the world, I told her. I'm not that man; I'm not my father.

I told her about what it had been like growing up with my father because that was the most important fact about me. I told her these stories of geographic transience because I thought I wanted to claim, or calm, the constant motion: the countries and schools, the reasons, true or not, for being somewhere, for staying awhile, and then for suddenly leaving. Yet despite their constant flux, the years with him had felt oddly stable.

All of those adventures that bound my father and me together were the things I clung to, and not because we were so very different from everyone else—because I don't think we were all that different. What we were, though, from the very beginning, was separate from the rest of the world. My father's need to have me near him was inexhaustible; I was a talisman for him to keep the forces of evil away. The fierce possessiveness had always been there, this push to have me at his side, as if I was something pure and true to which he could cling, and be close. His work was frightening: trying to navigate through situations where it wasn't clear who could be trusted, and where the consequences of not knowing could be severe. It must have been an incredibly vulnerable feeling, knowing that he was alone in a psychological battle where his own best instincts were his only weapon. In such a world, where loyalty could be bought and sold, I think I became a vassal of sorts for what he wanted to keep close, cherished, and unspoiled. Possessing me became, perhaps, something stable in an otherwise frightening and unstable world.

Sara wanted to be close to me. She took me to her family's house every Sunday. I felt more comfortable around her grandfather's dining-room table than my own: they had no special gloves for me, and there seemed to be nothing that couldn't be said. Her father had been a heroin addict. Her aunt was a writer in Hollywood. They repeatedly fought and made up over the table, in front of everyone. Surrounded by the warmth of her imperfect relatives made me realize how perfectly screwed up the silence that lurked in my own home was. All of the things that hadn't been said through my childhood, whether out of necessity or convenience, began to trouble me. I wondered why we didn't talk to each other like this in my family. In my house, conflict had almost always been dealt with by icy silence, or by a raging of the furies that left us weakened and shaken to the core.

One day I told Sara about Irena, my father's "friend" in Barcelona, while we were sitting on a cliff somewhere, on the shores of the Pacific.

"Scott," she said, when I told her. "Was she . . . ?"

I looked at her. "What?"

"Nothing." Then she said what I knew she was thinking. "You didn't realize?"

"Not then." I grinned ruefully. "It took awhile."

"Oh, Scott," she said, punching me playfully on the arm as if I had made a bad joke.

Sara and I dated for three years. But that summer of 1995,

when I was twenty-two, I broke up with her. I wanted to leave her mainly because I was young and immature, and wasn't ready for the responsibility of a serious long-term relationship. When I told her, Sara spluttered, "You remind me of an . . . an animal. A rat! Just like your father!"

But I had never thought of my father as a rat. What did a rat embody, anyway? Filth? Stealth? When I asked her, she said that a rat was always skulking around in some corner, but ran away once spotted. What surprised me was that Sara had given my father's infidelity and behavior toward his wives more than just a passing thought. Jesus, I thought, I must have talked about him a lot.

There was also something else that made me run away. I was scared because a few months earlier, out of the blue and apropos of what seemed to be nothing, I began to hear a voice. I thought if I ignored it, it might go away. It wasn't a voice of the sort that schizophrenics endure—another's giving advice, punishment, or comfort. No, it was my own voice, and I couldn't figure out how to silence it. It was predatory, a sliver of evil I couldn't dislodge. It said to me, over and over again, that the devil was in me.

I thought it would go away eventually, but it didn't. Each night I fell asleep hoping, but when I woke the next morning it would still be there. It lingered for days, and then weeks. And weeks dragged into months. Every moment was laden with the same words: the devil was in me. When I eventually dug up the courage to tell Sara the words I was telling myself, she laughed, joking that I was crazy. But I was sure she was right. Finally, I went to see a psychiatrist who told me not to worry; I was symbolizing an internal conflict. It wasn't entirely clear to me what that meant, but I had neither the wherewithal nor the courage to ask.

So I decided to go away, to Alaska. I thought that if I went somewhere else, the words might leave me. I got a job on a purseseiner, and sailed north from Seattle to Canada along the Inside Passage. We started hunting halibut as soon as we crossed into

Alaskan waters. I was the least experienced man on the team, and my job was in the stern, butchering and cleaning the fish, many of them the size of a human. They rose through the sea and up to us on hooks, like white balloons. When they came up to the surface, I pulled out a hammer; and sometimes I prayed for them as I beat their heads until they lay still. I opened their gills and sliced their jugulars and let the blood seep out over my gloves.

I was seasick for days, and threw up on the fish even as I cleaned them. It rained and rained. I tied the fish to the runners with lanyards and gutted them with a spoon, and their bones tore holes in my gloves. I broke a rib when I slipped on their spilled innards. I packed whatever of them remained on the boat—their huge, white bodies and lopsided mouths, and their eyes like silvery beach stones—with ice and stuffed it in the container hold. At night, I slept in the foc's'le with an ex-convict who yelled in his nightmares and carried buttons of methamphetamines in his ass crack. He threatened to kill more than one man that summer.

After three weeks, the boat dropped me off and paid me $1,500. But nothing had changed. The voice had only gotten worse.

I got a job working the night shift at a cannery in Petersburg, on the island of Mitkof. I was on the slime line with a crew of Mexicans, gutting salmon for caviar and tossing the bodies into containers on wheels. I scooped giant blobs of pink caviar and loaded them into buckets bound for New York restaurants. Then I packed cardboard boxes full, and threw the boxes into freezers. After that I de-boned the worthless pinks, filleting them into neat rows. At the end of my shift, I hosed the blood and accumulated guts off the floors. Then I walked home, two miles to a tent city where I shared sleeping space on a wooden platform with two other guys. I hardly ever changed my clothes or brushed my teeth. In the morning I lay down dirty, covered with scales, and woke six hours later, in the haze of the afternoon, for the return walk.

The island was lush with alpine forests that glowed dully in the midnight sun. Heavy black crows often floated just overhead.

But instead of being rejuvenated, all of it—the long hours of day-light, the numbing sameness of each day's routine, and of course the words repeating in my mind—conspired to accentuate the feeling of being trapped. At the cannery I got a supervisor job and became a mini-tyrant, shouting orders at the other workers and berating them if they weren't fast enough for me. My broken rib pained me. I had developed an infection from being so dirty. *I am the devil*, I kept telling myself, and with each day that passed, I became more convinced that it was true.

One morning I left the cannery as usual and began walking back to the tent city. The town was quiet; only a few fishermen and stragglers from the night before were out. Gulls floated into the harbor and back out again, as if being pulled by invisible wires. The darkness was beginning to lift, and the frost on the marshes was thawing quickly. Instead of going home, I mean-dered down a street, passing a diner opening its doors and a dol-lar store with blacked-out windows. I turned onto the highway and got a glimpse of the rising plain that led to the other side of Petersburg Sound, and from there jagged rose-colored peaks, including one called Devil's Peak, lifted impermeably into an egg-blue sky. I stopped. A lone pay phone sat on the edge of the road, as if the city planners had thought the town would one day encompass this stretch of road, and then those plans had died. Frost dripped down the panes of glass. I stepped inside the box and called my father collect.

He accepted the call. His lonely voice mirrored my own, which was unusual. I asked how he was. I hadn't spoken to him for several weeks.

"Oh . . . ," he said, and didn't say more. I knew he was having trouble with Janet again, although not the details. I was too preoc-cupied to want to help. Something was wrong with me. All of my life my father had been able to fix me when I needed it. He buoyed me, and pulled me along toward life. I wanted him to do that now. I didn't know how to fix myself, or even what needed fixing.

I thought my father should be able to read my mind. It was his job. He had always known when I was angry or upset before. I wanted him to look into my mind, to see what I was thinking, to hear my thoughts and purge me of them. Or make me forget them. He had always been able to make it seem as though problems didn't exist, and therefore didn't need fixing. I wanted that, too. I wanted a new life, like he had always been able to give me every couple of years. I wanted a new life into which I could disappear.

I asked him what was wrong. He wasn't forthcoming. I wanted to know about my mother, about their divorce. He couldn't answer my litany of questions. Finally, I exploded. "Why do you have to be so secretive?" I shouted. "Why is everything hidden?"

He sounded exhausted when he answered. "It's not secret," he said. "It's just complicated."

The phone connection was terrible. He sounded as distant as he had when I had spoken to him as a child, when he was away on business, halfway around the world. But psychologically he was even farther than that—as far away as he had ever been. He was deep inside himself. His career was over; his marriage to Janet was in trouble. And his son was making demands about the past that he wasn't able to satisfy.

For the first time, I started to believe that I didn't know my father at all. All he had told me now seemed tainted by my doubt.

There was little dexterity to betrayal. It was crude and impatient. In our family, we had kept ourselves safe with plenty of lies. But they were catching up with us. First Janet, and then my father, had lied to themselves about their marriage. I had lied to others to help protect my father and his work. And we had all lied to ourselves about what this had done to us.

An eerie, palpable quiet settled between my father and me; it was scary. I didn't know how to get around it, and neither did he. If there had been a moment in the conversation when he thought he could have spoken freely to me, it had passed.

"I'm not doing so well," I said.

"I've told you all I can," he answered.

I abandoned my line of questioning. I didn't tell him that I had a secret: I didn't tell him about my voice, or that I thought I was going crazy. For the first time, I didn't tell him anything. We stayed quiet for a while, paralyzed by distance and our inability to talk. All I sensed from him was a tired wish that his life had somehow turned out differently, or that the problems he was facing would just go away. He couldn't help me, which wasn't his fault, but it felt like the worst betrayal of all. I had kept his secrets, but now I believed he couldn't handle mine. I had lied to my friends for him; I had watched him lie to his. What had brought us together for so many years now sat like an ocean between us.

I arrived back at his house unannounced a few weeks later. The rib was healing; the infection had dried up. I was $5,000 richer and freer. I still had the voice. But for a while it was as if nothing had happened between us while I was in Alaska. I told him stories about fishing and the cannery, how the skipper had been a drunk and the first mate was a suicidal meth-head with an outstanding warrant. We went on long walks with his new dog, Tucker, up into the wild-grass hills behind his house.

He was still having problems with Janet. During the days they disappeared for hours into the guest bedroom, where she was staying, I heard their low, strained voices if I stopped on the stairs. On these occasions, I took off with Tucker for hours at a time. When exhausted with walking, I sat on a log, closing my eyes and praying for the voice to stop. I listened to the hum and crackle of the electric wires overhead. I let Tucker lick my face and bury his head in my chest.

One night, sitting with my father in the basement, I asked how he was, and soon enough he was telling me about his marriage problems. I listened, but what I really wanted to do was scream out my secret to him. And I couldn't. I began to cry. Then I stood up and just bolted. I was tearing down the street when I heard the front door slam open behind me.

"Scotty," he yelled. "Scotty, wait!"

Around the corner, at the end of the street glowing with the wet, I stopped. The Hale-Bopp comet shone in the sky, a dandelion in a field of tiny daisies, streaming upward at a million miles an hour yet not going anywhere at all. I wanted to look up and see it gone—see it shoot out of my world like a slingshot. But it didn't. It continued to linger, staring back at me like the gleaming eye of an Alaskan halibut.

"I don't want you," I yelled at my father from the darkness.

"Scotty," he shouted back. I could hear him panting, and searching for the source of my voice. I had hid in a thicket of bushes beside an abandoned house. I tried to stay quiet. I saw him standing in the middle of the street. He had briefly emerged into the cone of a lamplight. The comet above was boundless, amorphous, hurtling over itself with the speed of its own momentum. I watched my father plunder his way back into the darkness.

"Scotty," he shouted. He was shouting at the sky. We paused. The comet burned another inch further to the south. He was out of breath. I could hear him panting like an animal.

Then, "I need you," he croaked into the night. His voice was the only thing I could hear. "Scotty, I need you."

After this incident, the urge to run began to well up in me very quickly. I would have gone anywhere, but I chose Morocco. I left very soon.

In the early winter of 1998 at a café in Fez, I received an email from my father. The subject line said "hello from your dad." He was writing from a cousin's house in Seattle. The next day he would board a plane for Hong Kong. He had gotten a job as a tour manager with a company called People to People, which organized trips abroad for American professionals. I hadn't spoken to my father for months and, judging by his email, wouldn't for another long while.

"And so, dear Scott," he wrote, "I am off tomorrow, and won't be back until the first week of June, so don't try to respond to this before then. If I'm able to get to a computer somewhere en route, I'll try to send you another note—maybe less serious but, I hope, with some stories of my adventures as an international Willy Loman."

I sat at the little computer table for a long while, staring at the screen, as the theme song to *Titanic* played over and over on the stereo. The movie had come out that summer and Moroccans—at least the ones who ran this café—couldn't get enough of it. While Celine sang about enduring love, I thought about my father.

"I love you, Scott," he had written, "as intensely, but more complicatedly, than ever."

I had no recollection of a Willy Loman, nor did I make an effort to find out who he was, even though I was in front of a computer. I briefly considered the possibility that he was a character from one of the spaghetti westerns my dad had been in as an extra when he was in his twenties—a roguish gunslinger, maybe, or a hired deputy run afoul of the law. That he had attached the word "international" to the name suggested an American original, and I imagined Woodie Guthrie meandering his way through a Steinbeck novel, with my father picking up the trail when the story left American shores. After that I let it go, filed away the email, and returned to the afternoon heat.

I did look up Willy Loman a few days later and was reminded of who he was: the down-and-out protagonist in Arthur Miller's play *Death of a Salesman*. I had never thought of my father as a salesman, much less considered the possibility that he thought of himself as one. But he clearly saw traces of the familiar in Willy Loman, whose optimism has been so tarnished and withered by the meanderings of life, by weaknesses small and large and dreams gone awry, and by the failures of those around him, including his son. Yet I wondered how plausible it was for anyone, especially my father, to conceive of living a second life resounding with adventure if he saw himself as Willy Loman. Was Loman something to aspire to?

I picked up *Death of a Salesman* in the library of the school where I was teaching English. Willy Loman tells his friend why he became a salesman:

> *I met a salesman ... His name was Dave Singleman. And he was eighty-four years old, and he'd drummed merchandise in thirty-one states. And old Dave, he'd go up to his room, y' understand, put on his green velvet slippers—I'll never forget—and pick up his phone and call the buyers, and without ever leaving his room, at the age of eighty-four, he made his living. And when I saw that, I realized that selling was the greatest career a man could want. 'Cause what could be more satisfying than to be able to go, at the age of eighty-four, into twenty or thirty different cities, and pick up a phone, and be remembered and loved and helped by so many different people?*

Twenty or thirty different cities, cities that could be countries—it was a life that could be measured in a daily accumulation of thank-yous and smiles of appreciation. I had never thought of my father's life like that. But when I thought about it, he had spent his career selling ideas: of himself, of his country, of an ideology that he fiercely believed in. He sold persuasion and the ability to persuade; he sold himself and his country with aplomb. But he also sold the seductive attraction of betrayal—he trafficked in loyalty and faith. And if there is an imaginary line that divides one's family from one's fatherland, he crossed it frequently, and with well-intentioned ease. I adopted that life as my own, as if there were no other logical choice in the world. I could sell myself as someone new every time the opportunity presented itself—and I did.

CHAPTER 8

Paris, 1998

Inscribed on the lobby wall of the CIA headquarters in Langley, Virginia, was a message from the Apostle John: *Ye shall seek the truth, and the truth shall set you free.* The lesson was as old as it gets.

I was convinced that I had lost, or was losing, my father—whether it was to the vagaries of my mind or the depths of his marriage problems, or to something else entirely. The thought scared me, and I wanted to mend our relationship.

He was in my mind on the day I first walked into a *Newsweek* office in Paris and naïvely asked for a job, unsure of even what sort of job I wanted. I had come to Paris after Morocco, to stay with a friend. I was seeking an alternative arrangement for my life. And I had no money. I had little idea what journalism was, but I desired the legitimacy to probe and the authority to question. Still caught in my existential crisis, I wanted my questions to have meaning.

My father had given me license to lie and deceive. I wanted sanction to do just the opposite. What I didn't know then was how similar the two professions, spy and journalist, are.

Those Paris offices had what I wanted. There were stories—exposed truths—all over the walls. Out of the windows, the Eiffel

Tower rose up gloriously in the distance, and Montmartre shone from its solitary hillside. The weather swept across the windows as the journalists toiled. I was twenty-five years old, a latecomer to responsibility. I wanted to find a means to seek out the truth, but I also doubted if I could. I could barely hold myself to account; I wasn't sure how I was going to successfully hold anyone else to it as well.

I was interviewed by a journalist called Chris. On his walls were pictures of Sandinista guerrillas. He had knives from Yemen, swords from Saudi Arabia, and a sash from parts unknown, and the room was virtually drowning in books. I sat on a couch and stared around. Chris leaned back in his chair and sized me up. "Why do you want to be a journalist?" he asked.

I had some pat answer, but really I didn't know. He pondered my response and wondered aloud, "What did your father do?"

I told him he had worked in the State Department or something similarly vague. But when Chris pressed me, my defenses broke.

"So," he said, "he was a spy."

I nodded, embarrassed, thinking this would lead to more questions. But he had moved on. "Journalism isn't so different from spying," he said. "You're not so different from your father."

I nodded.

"Journalism," he said, "is all about gaining people's trust."

That much made sense to me.

"It's all about gaining their trust because one day you'll betray them, and yourself."

I tried to understand, but failed. So I held on casually to the thought, because some truths are meant to linger, to slow-cook. My father had always told me how important it was to protect people, the sources and methods of his work. I didn't think he had betrayed his agents—although they may well have betrayed him. But if journalism was about telling the truth, how could I betray anyone?

Chris took me on as an unpaid intern, responsible for little more, at first, than gathering newspapers and making coffee.

A few days later, I was doing some such task when he called my name from somewhere in the office. I wandered down the hallways until I found him in a musty back room, an archive filled with old fifty-year-old copies of *Newsweek*. He was hunched over a computer, holding a long scroll of paper he had printed from an ancient machine. "Come look at this," he chuckled.

I walked over and looked at the screen. It was an old computer, the kind that didn't use a mouse, destined for rubbish. On the screen a green cursor flashed. He was on some database I had never seen.

"How do you spell your father's name?" he asked.

I hesitated, puzzled, and then spelled it out for him.

He typed the letters in. A few seconds passed. The computer whirred. Then the results flashed up in an alchemical glow. The lines started scrolling out as the green cursor blinked and moved. I read: "Smith, J. List of CIA agents. 1985."

"Holy shit," I muttered.

I had never seen anything like this. I wasn't very familiar with the Internet—I didn't even know how to type. This information made me feel vulnerable, and I momentarily hated Chris for finding it. I didn't want the world looking in on my dad like that. But there he was, defenseless. I felt like a thief.

But my own life was there on display, too. "India, 1970–1977," it said. "Yugoslavia, 1980–1982; Islamabad, 1982–1984."

We kept scrolling down. There were other names, familiar from my childhood: family friends, people we had had dinner with, men whose wives my mother once counted among her closest confidantes. This one had cheated on his wife. This one was a control freak. This one behaved like he was a movie star. This one was a genuinely nice man. I saw Reid's father there—Reid, my childhood friend. And Jeff, who was always the Dungeon Master in our games. And Paul, the boy who taught me how to smoke, and "what to do when you get some pussy." Their fathers were all there.

Chris chuckled again, and it quickly became a roaring laugh. "Cool, isn't it?" he said, comforting my uncertainty.

I nodded.

"That's what's great about this job. It's an excuse to ask pretty much anyone any question you want."

That felt vaguely illegal to me, but I thought the boundaries would probably become clearer with time.

"Well," he added, "it's a lot more than that, but you get the point."

Questions were all I had, though, and in between trying to do my job, I began to try out my new skills in other ways. I knew there was a colleague of my father's in Paris. I invited her to dinner.

We found a small bistro near my office, set back off from a long boulevard and sheltered from the traffic by trees. It was only moderately busy inside, and dark, but she chose a table near the back anyway. She quickly took a seat on the bench side and scanned the room. We ordered wine. For most of the night she sat stiff-backed against the wall, and we chatted about nothing in particular. I made a few game attempts to gauge her measure of my dad, but she didn't give anything away. She talked about her dog, about a painting of Janet's she had bought, about Paris. I grew bored.

"You know," she said finally, "the CIA once did a study to find out which jobs in the civilian world most closely resembled ours. Your father was a case officer. Guess which job came closest to his?"

I leaned in closer and shook my head.

"An investigative journalist," she said, looking around, nodding with her chin at the roomful of innocent diners. "More particularly, a foreign correspondent, since it's all taking place overseas." She sipped her wine. "We have analysts," she said, "Like me. And you have editors, like your bosses. See?"

"My dad's job," I asked. "Was it hard?"

"I couldn't do it," she said. "There aren't all that many people like him, who can do what he did."

I asked why. Cultivating people was an art, she said. What you did with what they told you was, too. They had lives and families. They had loyalties. There was no real handbook. And it never ended. She gave a little smirk and shook her head.

She was right; she couldn't have done what my father did. He would have entertained me all night. I would have left with nothing but excitement to see him again and the knowledge that it would be rewarding. The conversation was never really over—it would just pick up at some point on a vast, continually spinning ring.

The next day, I told Chris about the encounter.

"There's one vital difference," Chris told me. "Spies gather secrets and keep them to themselves and their governments. We gather secrets and tell them to the whole world."

I didn't yet know if I was comfortable with that idea. I wasn't used to that kind of exposure, and I wasn't sure if I ever would be.

Chris must have sensed my hesitation, but didn't say anything.

Under Chris's tutelage, I worked on all kinds of stories for the next three years—about NATO and rioting French farmers and Mad Cow disease, about European pedophiles and French socialism. I traveled to Belgium, Holland, Switzerland, and Italy. Chris sent me to Algeria to track down the family of an alleged terrorist, a man who had tried to sneak explosives into the United States through Canada. Back in the office, he spent hours teaching me how to write, how to report, and how to ask the right questions.

The more I learned about journalism, the more I realized there was only one kind that I really wanted to do, and that was war reporting. Occasionally I saw the war reporters come through the office. They were serious, hard and knowing. They immediately reminded me of my father. I wanted to know what they knew.

"Don't worry," Chris told me. "You'll get to go to plenty of shitholes. Be patient."

One day, after I had been working with him for a while, he stopped me at the door of his office. "Scott," he said, as I was leaving, "promise me one thing."

"What's that?"

"Promise me that you'll never go to work for them—not while you're a journalist. Okay?"

"I promise," I said. But I wasn't so sure. Making promises like this to anyone except my father felt a bit like betrayal. And in any event, it would be a few more years before I would get a chance to go where I longed to.

CHAPTER 9

Washington State, 2001

As a child I used to sit around the campfire with my father and tell him tall tales about how I could read the galaxies, and about the color associations I had with certain numbers. Four was green, I'd say. Three was blue. Eight was black, like the sky at night. The stars were zeros, or sometimes ones. I told him I could read the lines between the stars. I saw shapes there, and they had more meaning than humans could understand. He listened patiently and showed the keenest interest in my nonsense. He poked the fire with his stick and encouraged me to roast my marshmallow. "Make sure the chocolate doesn't melt too much; watch that cracker now, see that it doesn't break."

Now, thirty years later, during one of my periodic visits home, he sat behind me on the vinyl seat of our camper and got ready to change his insulin pump. Outside I could hear Tucker prowling around in the bushes, so I went to open the door to let him in, but he just looked up at me quizzically and wagged his tail. The fire glowed and vanished into a gaseous aureole.

I watched my father scrupulously. With great fanfare, he undid his shirt and ripped off the plastic tape that kept the needle in place. "Egad!" he shouted. "We open this, still smarting from the agonizing pain."

On the radio, *Madame Butterfly* had ended and John Coltrane had begun to wail. "Well, that little baby's out of insulin," he said. He prepared an alcohol swab and lifted his shirt up to grab a slab of his belly. "See that god-awful needle," he asked, tipping it into the little bottle of insulin and drawing out a small, clear dose. He tapped the syringe delicately, dispersing the bubbles as he hummed along to the jazz. "This one goes in my belly, this one doesn't." He ran the insulin up a long, thin tube, filling an auxiliary bottle. "I don't know what folks who don't get to do this do. What fun it is!" He pointed to a tube of clear liquid sitting on the table. "A whole vial of this in there."

Outside, the dog began to bark. My dad's fingers had turned bloody. He watched the monitor to get the correct amount of insulin into the machine. The table was littered with tiny vials, clear syringes, thin plastic tubes, strips that measured blood sugar, and machines that drew blood. He slid the needle into its holster and then attached the whole pump, which hooked onto his stomach. The ends of his fingers were blistery and hard from poking them again and again.

"Egad, Scotty!" he shouted again. His brows arched in mock agony, his face gleaming. "Somebody shot me. My dying wish is that you get the rustlers before they get away from here with all the cattle. And that varmint that shot me, go shoot him—well, maybe not shoot him, but don't ask him to dinner soon, anyway."

I sat back. The lamp glowed on the windows. He held a syringe in his mouth like a cigarette.

"Quick," he said, "maybe you better get some whiskey to splash over my wound here." He was suddenly viciously happy, momentarily relieved of his sadness.

A few days earlier, my father had arrived home in the afternoon. His eyes were red and he hugged me, and I found out that my grandfather had died.

The phone rang all day, and he sat in his den and answered callers and made calls. He played solitaire on the computer while

Janet fussed around the kitchen. "I fully intended the other day to take that chrysanthemum for my dad," he said to someone who had called. "Do you still have that? I'd like to pick it up. It's a perennial, so we can plant it in our backyard here."

He moved the phone to the other ear and looked down at the floor. "Oh," he said, "you probably sensed how important my dad was to me." His voice sounded choked with emotion, and his fingers grabbed the phone tighter. "Yeah, my mother is staying here with us, and of course my son is still here."

A few days after his father died, my father and I went for a walk together. He led me to the edge of the Little Spokane River, on a grassy bank that overlooked a pool where the waters twisted into curls. He sat down on a rotting stump, talking through his fingers. "I can just see myself through the years. You kind of transport yourself—you think about something fifty years ago and you remember vividly what it felt like. I see those memories differently. And when a father dies, it kind of all rolls together so that your emotions get sort of skewed." He looked out at the water. "All of us tend to control our emotions."

He was trying not to cry, but every time he started to talk he would lose control. He looked confused and sad. I couldn't stop watching him. The thought occurred to me that he was acting. Then, as he cried, I berated myself for thinking his emotion was less than genuine.

"My father, maybe more than others, treated me like a mature person early—he didn't exert a lot of control over me. I tried to be a mature person early. Where he had expectations, it was easy to know what those expectations were, and it was comfortable living up to them. I inherited from him a love of the land—a love of stewardship of the land—so there was never any question of doing anything that would be irresponsible or destructive to the land."

He began to play with a twig that he picked up off the ground. Right then, it seemed like it was a piece of himself. "I remember when I was eight years old and we had just moved to Colville. He was going to be going over to the coast for a few days, and I really didn't want him to go—I wanted him to stay with me—and I said something childish like, 'I hope the train has a wreck so you can't go,' or something, you know, something that if uttered by an adult would have been hurtful, but all I was trying to say was that I wanted him to stay with me. I think my mother scolded me for wishing ill on him. I didn't wish ill on him; I just didn't want him to go."

I waited for him to continue.

"He knew that his life, the quality of his life, was disappearing—his friends were gone, his brothers and sisters were all gone, his life was gone. He couldn't move, he was getting increasingly dependent on pills and doctors, and was in pain—and the dementia had started setting in. He said he wanted to go. He was close to ninety-five, and he always said he didn't want to live to be a hundred. In the last few weeks it clearly was time for him to go: his body was shutting down, his heart was shutting down, and he had no quality left in his life. It was selfish to want him to stay, and rationally, I wanted him to be relieved, but emotionally . . . I wanted my dad to stay."

My father put his face in his hands and cried, then he pulled himself together and continued. "And of course I have a lot of regrets. I regret that I didn't answer the letters he wrote to me when I was in college. He would write a letter every week; I would write one every three months, maybe. When I was traveling in Hawaii or India, or living in Yugoslavia or Spain and all those places, I knew he wanted to hear from me but I, um, didn't take the time."

We got up and kept walking along the river. He looked big to me, lumbering and sunburned, with ankles torn up from the brambles, and as he walked along the banks he stumbled and grabbed at reeds for balance. He picked up stones randomly, tossing them down the hill. He looked at the river, and I wondered if the currents made sense for him.

In the distance the green hills were bald, and skeletal armatures had begun to appear. We could hear the sound of four-wheelers on the dirt tracks, throwing up skiffs of powder. When the forests burned around here, the skies turned black and the timber cracked and fell.

We passed the church close to his house. There was always some new saying on the board outside—"Walk forgiven in the presence of the Lord" or "Kneel today and rise tomorrow." Usually when my father saw them, he scoffed and made up an aphorism of his own. The corny maxims and false sincerity made him wish the fires would creep to the churches and burn them to the ground. But when we went past that day, he stayed quiet.

Over the course of the next several days, talking with my father about his youth evolved into conversations about death. What kind of childhood led a man to the CIA? He told me about incidents in which people he had been close to had died. One was a boy named Roderick, my dad's best friend, who died when he was twelve. Another was a scoutmaster who died of pneumonia when his Christian Scientist wife refused to seek medical help for him. A third was his grandfather, who died on the very same day my father, only six years old, had taken the bold step of initiating the only meaningful conversation they ever had.

"That just occurred to me now," he said very suddenly. "That just as I reached out to them, they died. It's a coincidence that it never occurred to me before . . . I don't attach meaning to it, though."

"Why not?" I asked.

"I didn't bring on the deaths," he said.

There was a pause.

"Years later, I found Roderick's grave and went to visit him," he went on.

"Did you talk to him?" I asked.

"I think so."

"Do you remember what you said?"

"Yeah, I talked to him," he said, but didn't say more, and I let it go.

When we went on those long walks and drives in the days after my grandfather's death, I often brought a camera or a notebook to record my father. He had withered and recoiled at his father's death, and I had witnessed it.

Perhaps because he was vulnerable, or in a reflective state of mind, I sought a different sort of confession from him. I asked about his work in the CIA. I wanted to know what it was he did, exactly. I wanted him to confess to me the way confessors used priests to absolve themselves of sin, the way whistleblowers did it. I wanted to be the revealer.

I asked him what kinds of qualities were necessary to be a spy. He thought about it for a while. The conversation was a welcome distraction from his pain. "An agent might tell you at length about how he is fighting to preserve the free world," he mused, "when in fact what he really wants is a case of whiskey."

It was important, in other words, to be able to respond to the real needs of people, as well as their stated needs.

He meandered up an incline, through a stand of birch, and sat at the foot of a limestone boulder that left flakes of chalk on the ground. "There's a lot of myth about the CIA," he said, "the Agency, espionage, and so forth. It's not a world of guns and arrests, like most of the books. It's more about counterespionage—trying to find the spy within."

The spy within. I thought that it must be such a strange way to pass the hours—always looking for the whisper of deceit among your own kind, a shadow of your self.

But it turned out that it wasn't that easy to shed only one part of one's identity, at least as far as the rest of the world was concerned. A couple of years earlier, my father had tried his best to emerge from the shadows intact. He had run for public office when a Washington State Senate seat came open.

The day before he announced his candidacy, an article appeared in the *Seattle Times*. "A Spy in the Senate?" the headline asked. The paper wrote: "Johnson said his job experience—primarily spying on the Soviet Union—should transfer nicely to Olympia law-making. 'The whole time I spent as an intelligence officer I was trying to get important information for our decision-makers. I was working with foreigners, identifying problems, agreeing on solutions. I also developed a heightened sense of patriotism.' Johnson said he didn't consider challenging [Jim West] until he grew disturbed by the senator's behavior. 'He is known to be angry, mean and a hip-shooter.'"

"A Senator Spokane Can Be Proud Of," my father's blue-and-white campaign brochure proclaimed. People seemed to want to listen to him. He hired Janet as his campaign manager. They put tickets up in their front yard, and bumper stickers on their car. He embraced his spy persona as much as he dared. "Keith Johnson: committed to country and community," said his posters. There was a shot of him sitting, listening patiently to prospective voters. His posters told his life story in quick, bite-sized abbreviations:

> *Keith Johnson was born in Spokane. He became an Eagle Scout, and he graduated from North Central High School. His early years growing up in the Inland Northwest taught Keith important lessons about duty, service, and commitment. For twenty-five years, Keith Johnson served our country as a foreign intelligence officer. He risked his life to ensure liberty and freedom for others. His efforts helped to tear down the Iron Curtain and spread democracy throughout the world. Now, Keith Johnson is running for the State Senate.*

He had vocal support from the Democratic establishment. Yards across town filled up with his campaign posters; bridges and lampposts and the sides of buildings all carried his picture. There were strategy meetings downtown and swanky fundraisers uptown. Phone calls poured in. Money did, too. He started canvassing door-to-door. "Hi," he'd say, "I'm Keith Johnson and I'd like your vote."

He had launched his campaign on my birthday, which was also the anniversary of his marriage to Janet. It was late in the political season to join the race, but by October polls showed him in a dead heat with his contender. Most forecasts said he was going to win.

Many people liked the idea of my father as a senator. He was handsome, intelligent, and articulate. Knowledgeable about the issues, he had, at times, an indefinable sense of bearing. He could be charismatic. Sometimes he was angry, too, and anger was good when it translated as political passion. He wanted to change things, shake them up. He was quick to choke up and become sentimental, and that too translated well as political theater.

By the summer, my father had emerged as the favorite of the two Democratic primary contenders—the other was a registered nurse. He began publicly criticizing the Republican incumbent, Senator Jim West, for some allegedly threatening comments West had made on the phone to a lobbyist the year before, and for which he was facing a misdemeanor charge. West had apologized, but the telephone threats became good political grist for my father. "People are disgusted by bad behavior in public office," my father told the local paper, the *Spokesman-Review*. "The best example of bad behavior in public office in Washington State is Jim West."

In a brief profile of my father, the *Spokesman-Review* described him as a "Spokane native" who the CIA had recruited in Mexico City in 1969. "He tracked Cold War Soviet activity in Yugoslavia, Southeast Asia and Spain," the article noted. "Fluent in Spanish, he worked on counterterrorism operations prior to the world exposition in Seville and the Barcelona summer Olympics. He said he was also a trade representative for the U.S. State Department and worked undercover, but declines to provide specifics."

"I can't get into operating procedures," my father told the reporter.

The paper described some of my father's campaign positions as "populist," and noted that he had received most of his campaign funding from labor unions and the state Democratic Party.

"The big danger, it seems to me, is when professional politicians want to stay in politics and climb the ladder," he told a reporter. "When that happens, they start collecting PAC money at a furious pace and the PAC money compromises their beliefs." Increasingly convinced that my father could defeat Jim West, the state Democratic Party gave him $8,000.

In another article, the paper noted that my father's criticism of West had taken on a "moral tenor." "I went out in the world and came back to Spokane and became increasingly convinced about abuses of power in many places," he said. "Jim West abuses his power." Soon, my father had more than $20,000 in funds pouring in from state supporters and local Democratic Party headquarters. Later, he told another interviewer, quoting the U.S. Constitution, "I've done my part to provide for the common defense. It's time to promote the general welfare."

Two days before the elections, the residents of Spokane opened their mailboxes and looked down at their doormats and saw, tucked between the webbing on their screened-in porches or scattered willy-nilly across their lawns, an eye-catching flyer filled with provocative imagery. Across the city they sat down at kitchen tables and leaned in their doorways and stood befuddled on their front lawns unfolding this piece of paper. Almost all of these people were registered Democrats, fully intending to vote in the upcoming primary. What they read was disturbing.

"Who is Keith Johnson?" the flyer warned ominously in white block letters set against a black background. It gave an answer in red lettering: "Johnson is an ex-CIA agent with some secrets he doesn't want you to know." A red question mark loomed over the page, opposite pictures of a firing-range target and a world map in the middle of a radarscope.

"What is 'misinformation'?" the flyer warned. "The CIA calls it misinformation when they spread information that is false or deliberately misleading. They do it to overthrow governments or remove politicians from power. They are forbidden by law from doing it in American political campaigns. When someone does it in America, it's just plain old political hot air pumped up by the political bosses. Don't be fooled."

The flyer went on to criticize my father for not voting in three of the four most recent elections, for getting most of his financing from groups on the other side of the Cascades (outside of the electoral area), and for being unqualified for office. "You might not guess it from watching his television commercials and reading the brochures his campaign has put out, but Keith Johnson is a newcomer to Spokane," the flyer noted. "Don't be tricked by Johnson."

My father and Janet went all over town tearing down posters, ripping them off lampposts, and collecting them from people's front lawns. They called Jim West's office and complained. They appealed to the media. They counseled each other. Privately, my father raged.

The next day, the *Spokesman-Review*, although widely viewed as Republican-leaning, ran an editorial titled "Republicans Owe Johnson an Apology":

> *Plumbing the depths of dirty politics, the Washington State*
> *Republican Party committed a drive-by sliming last weekend.*
> *It mailed a flier to residents of the 6th Legislative District in*
> *Spokane, suggesting with sinister imagery and sneaky rhetoric that*
> *a Democratic Senate candidate was a CIA assassin out to overthrow*
> *our government. The mailer arrived in voters' homes on Saturday*
> *and Monday, too late for the victim and the media to respond in an*
> *effective way. This timing, of course, was intentional. Apparently, it*
> *worked. Keith Johnson, targeted because the GOP thought him to be*
> *the stronger of incumbent Jim West's two Democratic challengers, lost*
> *in Tuesday's primary. How sad.*

Now, as we sat under the trees on the river, his father dead, his attempt at public life a distant, painful memory, I asked him if he thought he was good at manipulating people. "Wouldn't that quality make you a good case officer?"

"I don't think I was an extremely good case officer," he said, "and I don't think I had any particular insights." But he talked about the history of adventurism in the CIA and of Teddy Roosevelt's son being a high-ranking officer. He told me about his love of languages and strange places, and his thirst for history, and how he chafed at the chain of command and wanted independence. He said it was important to be on the right side of the law, but also not to betray the promises of fealty and friendship to the people who were deceiving their countries for you.

"Did I answer your question," he asked, "or does it seem like I've skirted the issue?"

"Well, doesn't it take a certain kind of person?" I persisted. A certain kind of person who could cajole and persuade, and wrench if necessary; who could extract information but convince that extraction doesn't hurt—and who could go even further, to convince someone to switch ideologies?

A few days later, toward the end of my visit, my father took me to Colville, where he had grown up. On the way, we passed a restaurant with big black-and-white signs that said things like "buffalo" and "salmon" and "big screen." There was a store called Depot, and the train tracks where Route 292 crossed, heading north to Colville. We passed old barns, and solid brick warehouses no one seemed to be able to find use for anymore. I asked where he had lived as a boy, and he drove me to 820 N. Elm Street, a squat yellow house with blue trim, a tidy front lawn, and an elm tree. He told me how he used to spread a blanket out on the lawn and read comic books. He had lived here when his dad had unexpectedly told him he would be moving to Pakistan to take a job as an agricultural adviser to the Pakistani government.

He parked the car on the empty street and we just sat there for awhile, watching. "It was the beginnings of the Cold War," he said.

"They were working up to a fever pitch of Russian Soviet scare, and they enlisted people to go to designated high places and scan the skies for Russian airplanes that might be coming to bomb us—this was slightly before the Russians exploded their first atomic bomb. So my mother dutifully signed up, and there was an American Legion place up on that cliff, up on that bluff, that high point.

"So they went up there and they had all these charts and pictures and profiles—silhouettes of what these Russian planes looked like—and they'd sit up there looking at the skies, looking around and around, listening for airplanes. If they saw one, they'd quickly identify it."

He watched the skies in imitation. A smile came to his lips. "Not a single Russian plane."

I asked if she got paid. "No, no," he said. "This was done as a volunteer, for patriotic duty. She did that for a while."

On another of my last days, we went down to the beach of the Columbia River. He sat down beside me on a big piece of driftwood. He was wearing a pale-blue shirt and jeans, with his insulin injector attached to his belt like a cell phone.

A couple of years earlier, on a drive back to our house, he had told me that he was "sad" most of the time. He was cutting an apple with the pocketknife he always carried around, and he had looked at me skeptically, wondering, perhaps, what other answer I had been after.

Now, I asked if he was happy.

He shot me a hard look and shifted his position. He had begun to whittle on a stick with the knife. He was silent, and his mood seemed to shift between anger and amusement—he seemed to me to stifle a grin, but his face twitched with what looked like fury.

"Well," he said, "I will try to answer that question with a caveat. I know from past sessions that these questions really weren't a conversation, an exchange. Nor were they just interview questions. They became an interrogation, and I don't want to be interrogated."

But because neither he nor I could get around the conventions, we couldn't figure out what rules to obey. He wanted to answer me truthfully when I asked questions. I could see him struggling with it as he sat there. He worked on the stick as a distraction, a way to keep from looking at me. I sat behind the camera I carried, hidden and secure. We were at an impasse: he refused to answer me in the way I wanted him to, and I refused to accept his answers passively. All the journalism I had done, or thought I had done, and I was failing dismally at the story I most wanted to understand.

I watched Tucker walking along the beach, as if giving us space to figure this out. I had never been afraid of looking at my father, the way I had been with other people. I had never shied away from his face or his gaze, his love or his anger. I felt an endless capacity to soak it up, to take from it what I could.

"What interests me," I commented to him later that day, "is that you're lacking all religious affiliation and any traditional notion of faith, and yet you had total faith in the ideology behind that process of bringing people to your side."

He didn't understand. "According to traditional religion, you mean," he said, "am I an amoral person?"

I went with it. "Well, do you think you are?"

"An amoral person?" he said, hurt. "No." He had stopped smiling. "The Soviet Union was a formidable enemy. It had a declared purpose to defeat us, to undermine us, and I did not have any sort of moral repugnance at trying to counter that."

I asked him, "Don't you think to be a spy you have to be able to justify your actions, to view things from an appropriate angle, to be morally flexible?"

"Not any more morally flexible than the average priest who speaks out against sin, but deals with, listens to, helps, and treats the sinner," he said. "I think there are very few professions where one can live by some stern creed of righteousness. The world is a flexible place. I mean, do you run to report every violation of law that you see? No. We live with it. I was not going to hold out for some absolute, politically correct version of the government before I would let myself go to work for them."

He looked at me for a while, and then broke out into a grin.

I asked him if he got a thrill out of the idea of secrecy—if he was attracted to it, if he liked having the ability to lie with impunity and institutional backing.

"Well," he said, "the point is, sure, there were elements of that. I found those things exciting. But it goes back to psychology—not lying or cheating or stealing. I was not betraying the things I had pledged to uphold."

I thought of the many things that he had upheld without pledging to—his love for his family, his devotion to me, his commitment to the land—and those that had required a pledge seemed pointless.

"It has to do with nationalism," he said.

I told him that some people, those with a more objective view than us, might just see it as lying and cheating and stealing.

"I hesitate to call it an objective standpoint," he said. "The Soviet Union knew full well who I was and they didn't like what I was doing, or trying to do. I mean, I was on their list as somebody to thwart, which they tried to do very hard. And it comes down to this: when there are two sides, are you going to choose one or the other, or are you going to stand aloof and apart and say, a pox on both your houses, I'm above this, I don't deign to live in that world, I'm pure? Or, I'm a priest, I just listen to everybody and try to help them as individuals? I was trying to help my country."

I probed further. It was almost against my will, but I was dragging myself there. Something was taking the conversation there. "So you were willing to get your hands dirty and let your conscience be sullied for a greater cause?"

"Give me an example," he shot back. "Not generalities. Where should I have had qualms of conscience?"

"I don't know," I said. "Do you?"

He was silent for a while.

"Was there a border?" I asked, and hesitated before continuing. "Between your work life and your private life, I mean?"

He sighed and stood up, and I joined him. As he walked away, he began telling me a story about India. A long time ago, an Indian man had come to my father with an offer of help. The Indian had been spying on my dad for the Soviets. He had broken into our house, planted bugs in many of the rooms, and stolen one of my mother's photographs, which he produced to prove he had been in our house. Once, on his way in, the Indian had spoken to one of the servants, telling him he was from the government and had authorization to be inside the house. He had asked the servant what kind of man my father was, and the servant had said that he was a good man, a very good man.

The Indian spy had pondered this. Unhappy with his Soviet employers, he decided that he was working for the wrong people. And, just like that, he determined to switch sides. It was a betrayal brought about by little more than a passing character judgment. "I learned a great deal about what the Soviets were up to from this guy," my father said as we walked along the riverbank, "and there wasn't any deception on my part."

He then told me about one of his first spy teachers, a Russian case officer who had been the principal CIA handler for Oleg Penkovsky, a Soviet military officer who had defected to the United States with vital information about the weaknesses of the Soviet nuclear arsenal. As my father spoke, he looked at me with a crooked eyebrow and I knew I was to understand something; I had known my father all my life and some languages will always be unspoken. "You're never going to be able to recruit a Soviet by cajolery or coffee-table books or Sears Roebuck catalogs on the living-room table," the teacher had said. "Soviets recruit themselves. They decide when they want to come over to our side. So all I can tell you is, get to know as many Soviets as you can. But just be a typical American. And be the kind of person who, when they decide they want to come over to our side, they decide they want to come to you."

As that summer ended, I left my father and returned to Paris. When terrorist planes hit New York and Washington two months later, I spoke to him on the phone. He was having nightmares about bodies falling out of windows, he said. He had tried to come out of the shadows, but the world didn't seem to want that. And now he didn't want it any longer, either. He wanted the shadows back, and the shadows wanted him.

"I wish I was back in," he said. "So that I could know what's really going on."

"What do you think is really going on?"

"I don't know." He added that he intended to find out.

I left it there. His mind was working; I would have to wait and see what came of it.

CHAPTER 10
Afghanistan, 2001

A few weeks after 9/11, I was standing on the Afghan border, gazing into the country I would call home for the next several months. I felt a little bit ridiculous, an imitation war reporter—nothing close to the real thing. What I did have, though I told no one at the time, was a dim awareness of somehow coming home. To what, exactly, I couldn't say—only that memories of standing with my father peering at a version of what I was seeing now were pulling me back. For here I was looking at Afghanistan from the other side of time; and still, like the child of years before, I longed to know what was on the other side of the hill.

From Tajikistan, a group of Russians ferried me across the Amu Darya River on a flat metal barge equipped with an outboard motor. They wore blue coats and smoked, and took my money and stuffed it deep into their pockets before drifting back across the water toward Tajikistan. I hired a driver and we traveled all afternoon in the back of a Nissan pickup truck, passing hundreds of refugees who flowed haphazardly over the hills in every direction. Small groups of them had stopped, looking at the ceaseless undulations of reddish desert. Here and there a single man sat or stood alone, trying to figure out how to rejoin the flow.

Above, B-52 bombers circled. The planes arched in huge

figure-eight loops, and dropped their payloads on the curves. Sometimes we didn't see the planes until they were at the closure of an eight, when their contrails—thick, cotton ropes—suddenly emerged. We could see the impact of an explosion long before the boom, so a hill out there on the horizon, maybe a mile or two away, suddenly disappeared in a raft of dust, and moments later we felt in our skulls the shattering crack arriving from across the desert. I wondered if whole towns were being obliterated. All across that endless terrain was the slowly moving wreckage of a war, like goods spilled from a freighter, floating and shifting on an open sea.

I had no experience of war reporting, so I latched on to friendly colleagues who did. That night we all slept in a squalid refugee settlement called Howja Bowdin, on the floor of a house the Associated Press had rented. The Americans bombed all night. It was a low and terrible rumbling, and packs of dogs outside howled at the sound of it. Two Russian photographers huddled with their computers under sheets of plastic and pored over images of the people they had seen killed that day. They smoked and drank vodka, and their sheets grew steamy and wet until the water pooled onto the floor.

I called my dad on the satellite phone. He told me he had a fire going in his study. I pictured the walls, lined with etchings of the Raj and the houses of the Moguls, a muzzle pistol and knives, and a wooden panoply of the Hindu deities whose oiled crevices had always reminded me of a bed of snakes.

I told him about the bombing and held the phone up for him to hear. He was proud of me, scared for me, and curious. "I wish I knew what's really going on right now," he said. He still couldn't stand to be out of the action. He desperately wanted to go back to CIA work. If he did, he told me, it would mean that he would probably be coming to this part of the world.

"Great," I said.

It'll never happen, I thought to myself after I hung up.

I wanted to see the fighting. It was taking place along a series of ridges on the other side of the Kotchka River. The Taliban were there, black-turbaned, bearded, and gaunt. They wanted to be men of God and they had swept across the country in a feverish rush. I had only ever seen them in pictures. They looked simple, and they were—just like the Northern Alliance soldiers fighting them.

I hitched a ride in a truck and then on a donkey, crossed the river with an Uzbek horseman, and began to wind up toward the front through a warren of small, dusty streets. A few children watched us pass and shouted greetings, and not long afterward that sound was replaced by the low thudding of artillery in the distance. It sounded like a strange clock chime—regular, beating in time. There was a bend in the track, down which came refu-gees and fighters carrying rifles and rocket-propelled grenades. On the sides of some of their donkeys, long, gray missiles had been slung like stalks of bamboo or firewood.

The Northern Alliance troops were gathered on the Qaleqatta Hills. Years of fighting had scarred long trench lines that wound over the hilltops like worms. There were men scrambling up inclines, falling into the dirt, digging into the baked earth. Several tanks had been positioned in formation there, with their turrets all facing toward a silky expanse of grass-covered hills. It was quiet, and a few journalists walked about among the soldiers, sunning themselves in little patches of dirt. Every now and again one of the cannons thundered, jolting a tank backward, and everyone scurried for cover.

A general stood behind one of the tanks. I asked him where the Taliban were. He swept his camouflaged arm out toward the glowing fields. He had a collection of Taliban bodies, he said, and wanted money for them. "Dollars," he shouted, rubbing his fingers. "Dollars!"

I left the hill in the early afternoon that day. It was a Sunday, too late for one week's deadline and too early for the next, and there didn't seem to be much of anything happening anyway.

But after I left, something did happen. The general I had spoken to decided, on a whim, to mount a surprise attack against the Taliban by rolling out across the hills with several of his tanks. Several European journalists hopped on top of a couple of the tanks, thinking, possibly, that they would get a front-row seat to what must have seemed like nothing more than a lazy-afternoon show of force.

The general made a great show of it, preening for the assembled cameras, and then they trundled out into the green pastures. The Taliban ambushed them almost immediately, firing on them and dropping missiles and mortars in their path. That lazy afternoon, three of the journalists died in the ambush. I was safely back in the refugee camp before I heard the news, but I was sure that, had I been there when the general made his offer, I would have been right alongside those others on the tops of the tanks. It would have seemed to me at the time like just the thing to do.

I never saw their bodies. But that was my first full day in the war, and already three of my own kind had been killed.

I didn't relish the idea of my father following me to Afghanistan. If he did, and we met, it would simply place us in an impossibly close and uncomfortable position. It might force us to lie even more. Everyone lies, but I didn't want those particular lies to be part of the world I was carving out for myself. But he had said he intended to find out what was happening, and I knew he would.

In those first days of the war, everyone was trying to move south, so I did too. There were lines of advancing Northern Alliance troops, and I and the group I was with tried to stay behind them as best we could. We camped out in abandoned villages as we moved, sleeping on roofs or in front yards. The road south wound across the backs of hills scraped so bare by wind and erosion they were almost white. A gray cover of cloud, filled with dust and smoke, hovered above. Below were valleys filled with aspen trees whose tops sagged heavily. Sometimes the roads petered down into tracks or rutted ditches, or finally into nothing at all, and our line of cars crept slowly along through the dust because the hills were filled with mines. Now and again we saw a wreck off in the distance, a burned chunk of metal, the cause of destruction never determined. We followed the rising dust trails of convoys that had passed before us. When they disappeared, we followed a few bare trees on the horizon.

Sometimes bodies lay by the sides of the road. One day we found six of them. One after the other they had fallen, and by the time we got there they were cold and rigid. Our jeep pulled to a stop at the first of the bodies, and I saw he had a young man's face. I had never seen a dead man this close before. He lay in a ditch, and his left leg was splayed out. His arms were stretched out above him, as if he were still carrying his weapon. His eyes were closed, almost like he had been caught in repose. One of his lips had just the faintest hint of a curl—the beginnings of a rec-ognition that the end was at hand, perhaps.

Here he lay, on this ordinary stretch of road. He had come this far, and only this far. I stood over him for a long time, half-expecting him to move, but he was stiller than anything I had ever seen. I walked around, to see him at all the different angles. I wanted him to whisper to me—I wanted one more word out of him. He looked as if he were about to embark on a ballroom dance, his arms up and away like that. Just a little twitch of the fingers, and that frozen music could begin again.

Another jeep idled up and came to a stop. The engine went quiet, and out of the cab came the sounds of an Indian song on cassette—a mournful wailing.

More bodies lay further down the road. One was headless. A driver pulled over and walked up to the cadaver, hocking a giant gob of spit down at him, and at that he and another man hugged. "Shall we run them over?" they laughed. Our drivers were Tajiks from the Northern Alliance and the dead men were Taliban, their sworn enemies for the last decade. The enmity was deep and unforgiving, like the war that had divided the country.

Another mile or so on, a group of Pakistanis was being forcibly marched back toward a tank position and a prison. Their guards prodded them with the butts of their guns. The captured men kept their heads down. I wanted to talk to them. "There's no time—we have to deal with them!" said one of the guards, which was to say they had to kill them. Off they trudged, stumbling along the broken ground.

That night, we were to sleep in Taloqan, the capital of Takhar Province. The Northern Alliance had recaptured the town from the Taliban a few days earlier. Nearly every man we saw carried a weapon of some sort. A single road bisected the town, and down it roared pickup trucks full of haggard-looking soldiers, coming and going from the front lines.

After I had eaten, I went out to the front yard, sat in a patch of cropped rose bushes, and called home on the satellite phone. I told my dad about the fight on the hills, and the dead bodies. "I hate sitting here watching it on the news," he said.

I asked him how it was in America. He said the war was all anyone could talk about. "Where are you now?" he asked.

I looked around. "Sitting in a bed of roses."

We talked for a long time. He had always wanted to come to Afghanistan. He had had the chance, twice, but turned both down. Before I was born, the Agency had asked him to come to Kabul on a one-year assignment as an NOC, or "non-official cover"; there was an American airline that was ready to take him in Kabul. But a colleague told him that it wouldn't be "career-enhancing," so he turned it down. The NOC assignments were dangerous, often to countries or war zones where bringing along a family was unquestionably risky. It usually meant going in as a regular employee of a legitimate business—the ranks of many an American business have had their share of NOCs. Some senior person in the company always knew, but apart from that, NOCs did their spy work on the side. And if they got caught, the American government couldn't come to the rescue. NOCs wouldn't

have a diplomatic passport, or the protection of immunity conferred by association with the embassies. They were on their own.
It was about wits.

NOCs required extra training and were paid more. The CIA
gave them special priority and took extra measures to make them
invisible. They gave those NOC jobs to the best, the brightest. Or
was it just the craziest, those with the least to lose?

After I was born, the Agency again asked him to come, this
time as the chief of the station. But accepting the assignment
would have meant sending me to live with my mother, or to
boarding school, and my father wasn't willing to do that. So he
declined, and gave up on the idea of Afghanistan. For a number
of years, at least.

But now it was October 2001. I had been in Afghanistan for
a couple of weeks already. People believed the war was going to
drag on for months. Kabul was still under siege by the Americans
and the Northern Alliance. The CIA had been there for many
weeks already. But they were short-staffed. Old, retired hands
like my father were being asked to come in from the cold.

"I put out some feelers," he said. "I'm working on a way to get
back in."

On the second day of Ramadan, I was on a hill in northern
Afghanistan with Luc, a photographer with whom I was working. The hill was nothing more than a dust mound with a view out
into a desolate no-man's-land. Nearby, soldiers were lying in the
dirt begging for food, and said they'd give anything for a bottle of
whiskey. The Taliban were there, they kept saying, pointing to a
copse of trees on a distant hill.

I questioned our presence in the country. We were simply waiting for the fighting to begin. It was easy to be brave when I knew
that someone else was being brave for me; I was just following. I
asked Luc why he went to war zones. He had spent many years
in wars just like this, and also very different, and much worse. He

had seen so much killing, so much horror and evil. It was more real, he said, and it led to greater understanding. But what happened here didn't always necessarily have to do with the rest of the world. "You can deliver it later, or interpret it, give it to the rest of the world," he told me, "but for the time being you're all alone." And there was nothing wrong with that, but I should keep something of myself in reserve, to maintain a distance from the rest of the world, from this, if I was going to survive it all. It was an exercise in restraint as much as anything—restraint in seeing, and in understanding, and in my own enthusiasm or dismay about the world.

Luc chewed on a root he was using to stop smoking. He grinned. "It's okay," he said. "Everything is going to be okay. Just keep going forward, keep trying to see with your own eyes."

Those days on the front were exhausting, not because there was constant fighting but because there wasn't. The soldiers on the hillsides were tired. I looked around at these men, wearing turbans and carrying their Kalashnikovs on their backs, their children running through the dust. Thirteen-year-olds smiled through broken teeth. They'd tell me they were much older, but no one really knew their age. They walked alongside their fathers, uncles, and brothers. They carried rifles, and the barrels reached down past their wobbly knees, scraping the ground.

The hills themselves were vast and barren, ridged like the skin on pigs' necks, and refugees trudged across them endlessly. Now and again a cannon or tank's gun would go off and some distant hillside would collapse into dust, and then slowly drift off in fragments with the wind.

I eventually made it to the capital, Kabul, where I stayed for many months. At the start of winter the snows began to fall, and in the mornings bicycles made fresh tracks through the drift. By afternoon, the famous kites were sailing. Sometimes we made fires in the evenings.

My father was waiting for his security clearance from the Agency, he told me when I spoke to him.

One day I drove south, toward a town called Gardez, a few hours away on the main highway that continues on to Kandahar. The war was moving in that direction generally. What had once been a decent highway had been reduced by years of war and neglect to a mass of rocks and ruts, some of them a yard deep. The Taliban had rejoined society in a normal fashion since their inglorious defeat by the American bombers; they had returned to families, slid back into communities. Journalists often said they had "melted" back into the fabric of the country, or even away altogether, and I thought of the Wicked Witch of the West, melting on her broomstick with her army of loyal and demented monkeys at her side.

The snows were a permanent feature of the landscape now, and the long broad slopes of the Hindu Kush, which ran in imposing lines along the horizons, gleamed in the morning sun. The mountains were always most visible on the ride south, as the altitude rose and the plains dropped off into a hazy expanse of rural splendor. Gardez, which lay on the other side of a high mountain pass, had been under attack for several weeks by a warlord whose loyalties were suspect. Pacha Khan Zadran professed to be part of the government, but his fighters had rained terror down on the town repeatedly, and his hunger for more power had made him form temporary but disturbing alliances with the Taliban and even, some said, Al Qaeda.

I was traveling with a friend, a reporter for the *Washington Post*. That first day we roamed through the town, which seemed deserted. The NGOs had fled, and the detritus of war was very recent. People asked us for food because their families were starving. We visited a house that the Americans had bombed because they suspected that one of Osama bin Laden's deputies lived there. Neighbors were still milling about in the wreckage, looking for some lost thing—a shoe, a Koran, some remnant of those who had died.

Like everywhere in Afghanistan, the men in Gardez had guns, but they weren't the Northern Alliance soldiers we had grown accustomed to seeing in the north. These were Pashtun, the ethnic group from which the Taliban drew the majority of their recruits.

A few miles south of Gardez was a walled mud fortress that blended into the landscape and was unremarkable in most ways— except for the checkpoint at its entrance, the heavily armed guards, and the white Nissan pickups filled with American Special Forces soldiers that routinely raced in and out of its gates. Helicopters came and went with regularity. Everyone in town seemed to know what it really was: a CIA and special-operations base.

From the outside the base looked primitive in the extreme: four walls and a rooftop lookout. My friend and I tried repeatedly to get access to the base, but were denied every time. Instead, we saw the work of the men who lived there. The Special Forces guys or the CIA were always working on psychological operations in and around Gardez. These psy-ops missions included paying visits to important locals to ensure their support in hunting down Al Qaeda. They distributed leaflets with pictures of wanted figures, which we picked up whenever we were out, and nicely printed entreaties about the good work that the Afghan government was doing, the evils of the Taliban, and the need for local people to cooperate in bringing the perpetrators of violence to justice.

Some of their efforts didn't go over well. They were constantly providing MREs—meals ready to eat—to locals, but often did so when the menu, always in English, explicitly stated that the meal contained pork.

From Gardez, we traveled on to Khost in two cars. Khost was even farther south, and served an even larger base of Taliban and Al Qaeda. Even the road to the city was a testament to the admiration people felt for bin Laden and his loyalists. There was a cemetery on the roadside with prayer flags that had been strung up for each of the Al Qaeda figures killed when the Americans had bombed the mosque. We meandered in, and I walked underneath them and felt them flap against my face. They looked almost pretty, all those death flags fluttering in the wind.

There was an American base in Khost, too. We drove through groves of beautiful eucalyptus and aspen, along small riverine settlements, up to the gates, and peered inside. The base was right next to an old Soviet airfield, and it was strewn with the wreckage of old Russian and Afghan planes that had been blown apart and brought here to rust away. The Americans inside, an assemblage of Special Forces and spies and other assorted weirdos, ambled about nonchalantly; they were part-soldiers, part-hunters, part-futurists. They stared at us and didn't once nod, and turned away when we raised our hands in greeting. The Afghan man who had come to find out what we wanted told us to move on because the area wasn't safe. We left.

As we continued, we saw women in bright orange burqas walking along the small banks of nearby tributaries. Grain peeked through the snow—stalks that should have been bright yellow, but the lack of sun had made raw and weak. And on the horizon was the low winter sun, like a slug moving through the spring mud. When it dipped behind the mountains in the early afternoon the sky got dark so fast, and the headlights of our cars bounced along and revealed the dust rising off the ground like steam. The streets emptied and we raced to make it to whatever shelter we had for the night—raced to the gates of the city, where a guard and a gun, familiar by now, nodded and saluted, and ushered us to safety.

I was in Khost when I received an email from my father. He had been accepted back in to the CIA as a contractor. He'd be doing psy-ops. I called on his birthday to congratulate him, and he was thrilled. "How long are you going to be there?" he asked.

I didn't know.

"See if you can stay," he said. "I'm going to be coming over soon."

"To do what?" I asked. I felt the anxiety mounting in me.

"I'm not sure yet."

I pondered this.

"Won't this be a great adventure!" he exclaimed.

My immediate thought was an emphatic no. I wanted to tell him that I wasn't a child, and that Afghanistan was no place to have father–son adventures. I didn't want to be part of his psychological operations. And, I realized with vehement force, I didn't want him following me into a job and a life that I felt like I now owned.

The CIA was active in Afghanistan; they had bases in the countryside and hotels in the capital. But there were plenty of journalists there, too. And these two camps weren't always friendly. During an interview with a provincial governor in Khost, we heard about "journalists" representing nonexistent media outlets conducting "interviews" that later proved impossible to find in print. A hotel manager told us that several Americans had come by offering to keep us, the real journalists, away. The Afghans we saw often assumed that we were either CIA ourselves or, if not, had such close relations with them that we could pass messages along without any trouble. Tell your people that we need such and such, they would very often say, weapons or money or phones, to which we would defensively reply that they were no more our people than the Afghans were, a lesson in semantics that went entirely unheeded.

But underneath my attempts to be professional, my secret felt dangerous. The CIA, "those people," were in fact my people. The knowledge that my father was going to be conducting psychological operations here took on a very personal significance. There had been years of watching him operate with friends and family—with me—and now all of it had a name: psy-ops. When I looked at the men standing on the other side of that chain-link fence around the base in Khost, or watching us from behind the mud walls of the fort in Gardez, I knew I was looking at my father's tribe, the tribe that I had been given entrance to as a boy.

Now I was on the outside looking in, but I knew what it was like to be the other way around: to be on the inside looking out, to be the keeper of secrets and the blockade against inquiry. I knew how important secrets were to survival. For me, psychological warfare had another meaning—the battle to keep the rest of the world as far away from you as possible. One wrong answer and it went up in smoke.

That night, I went to the roof of the guesthouse where I was staying. Two Afghan soldiers were huddled there, and they greeted me customarily, with their hands on their hearts. From the distance came sounds of shooting, dull and sporadic, but the men paid it no heed. They sat on their haunches, blankets wrapped around their shoulders, smoking cigarettes and watching me fiddle with my phone and computer, trying to get good reception. They clicked their tongues and smiled and talked softly. Meanwhile, green tracer fire arced up and across the city.

My translator came up a while later and sat down with me. He began talking with the soldiers. The men felt sorry for themselves, they said. Because they didn't know how to read or write or use phones and computers, because they didn't know how to speak English, because all they knew how to do was use Kalashnikov rifles. They said they were pitiful and condemned. They seemed willing to acknowledge this state of affairs, which was surprising. The four of us watched each other and smoked. Clutching his rifle, one of them said he had told his children never to look to a gun for guidance. He held the barrel and placed the butt on the ground. He didn't want them to use him as an example of how to behave in life. He gestured to my translator to make sure I understood. I nodded. But hearing this, I told him I thought his children should look to him because he was obviously a decent man. "My father is coming here," I wanted to say. "He'll help you." He was coming to wage war, or peace, or love—I wasn't sure which.

My father wouldn't know when he could come for a while longer, he had said during our phone call in Khost. He had to get the necessary security clearances. He would have to take a lie detector test. If accepted, he would receive weapons training. Still, it looked like they were going to let him back. The career he had ended so abruptly a few years earlier was now alive once again. It felt to me like a game of upside-down hide and seek: I had set myself the task of seeking out the truth about him, and was dissatisfied with what I found; but when he came searching for me—when he caught my trail like this—I wanted him gone. I felt immensely guilty.

Suddenly, shooting erupted a few streets over. Tracer fire arced up nearby, and I moved closer to the door and crouched. The men stubbed out their cigarettes with their slippers, shoul-dered their AKs, and went to take up their positions on the edge of the roof.

As I crouched there, I felt my father again, urgently, only now he was gesturing at me from the distant past—he was sitting on another roof like this, with armed men nearby, motioning me to look. As I waited on that Afghan roof, peering down into the night and the uncertainty, I recognized the familiar.

CHAPTER 11

Mexico City, 1968

My father's rooftop was in Mexico, and it was a long time ago—at a university almost forty years earlier, in 1968. The Cold War was at its height when my father, twenty-eight years old—the same age I was in 2001—got caught up in its midst.

Mexico was an expansive battlefield in those years. It attracted spies and oozed espionage. Embassies in Mexico City were huge, lumbering affairs. The Soviet Union had made great strides across Latin America during the 1960s. Just over a decade earlier, Fidel Castro had launched an insurgency against Cuban dictator Fulgencio Batista, leaving from Mexico's eastern shore in a boat, accompanied by Che Guevara and a rowdy band of revolutionaries. Mexico had been trying, with varying degrees of success, to quell its own peasant uprisings in poor, rural areas like Guerrero and Chiapas, where communist sympathies ran high and hatred of the Mexican government was widespread. At the same time, the government, ruled by the Institutional Revolutionary Party, tried to style itself for public consumption as the party of workers, revolutionaries, and landless peasants when, in fact, it was little more than a coalition of monied interests.

Many of the most virulent antigovernment protests had originated with the thousands of students in Mexican universities, and throughout the spring and summer of 1968, the protests and marches gained momentum. The students' complaints would have been familiar to the rest of the world. They wanted more freedoms—of the press, of expression, of political activism. They wanted a voice in their own governments. The demonstrations often turned violent, as students and police clashed in the streets of the capital. The locus of the political unrest was at the National Autonomous University of Mexico (UNAM), in Mexico City.

But Mexico City had been chosen as the site of the 1968 Summer Olympics, and the government, keen to portray a positive, stable image to the rest of the world, was prepared to ensure that the games, set to take place in October, would come off without a hitch. Worried that communist guerrillas could wreck Mexico's chance at the spotlight, the government began to crack down. In April and May of 1968, the Pentagon, still consumed with the expanding war in Vietnam, supplied the Mexican military with radios, gunpowder, and mortar fuses. Later that summer, the Mexicans would ask for riot-control gear. And America, predictably concerned about the opportunities the protests would provide to communists, was happy to oblige. By the end of that summer, Mexico's president, Gustavo Díaz Ordaz, fed up, decided to put an end to it. In September, as the summer rains began to ebb and the jacarandas bloomed, Ordaz ordered Mexican Army troops to occupy UNAM. The soldiers followed orders, beating and arresting scores of protestors on campus, and fueling the tension that had been building in the city for months.

The army occupation of UNAM came just three weeks before the Olympics. But the students were undeterred by the attack. Early on the afternoon of October 2, ten days before the opening ceremony, fifteen thousand students from across the country converged upon Mexico City. They carried red carnations to symbolize their anger. Their destination was a middle-class neighborhood called Tlatelolco, home to the Plaza de las Tres Culturas, a colonial-era public square. As they marched, they chanted: "We don't want Olympics; we want revolution!"

My father was the dean of men at the University of the Americas, just outside of Mexico City. He was in charge of helping students in trouble, organizing their schedules, and meeting parents, as well as teaching a few classes. One day in early 1968, one of his students, a young man named Matthew, had asked his permission to invite the famous Soviet poet Yevgeny Yevtushenko to the school for a reading. Sure, my father said, go and ask the Russian embassy.

Yevtushenko was an intriguing character. He was openly critical of Joseph Stalin who, while no longer alive, remained a towering figure of fear within the Soviet Union. Stalin's purges, during which up to twenty million people were murdered, were by then becoming well known. Yevtushenko traveled widely in those long, hard years of the Cold War. In 1968, he appeared before twenty thousand enraptured Chileans at the Forum de Mexico in Santiago to read, in Spanish and Russian, a selection of his poems. Such public performances were immensely popular. They fueled speculation about where the poet, and the war, would move next. It didn't take long for rumors to spread across Mexico City. The Soviet embassy wanted to capitalize on Yevtushenko's stardom by promoting a cultural tour, with him as the central attraction. For while Yevtushenko was sometimes critical of the regime, he was still a great Russian poet. On the leafy campus of the University of the Americas, Matthew was inclined to believe that Yevtushenko, who would be in Mexico in the coming weeks, might be available soon.

It was on one of those bracing spring days when my father ran into Matthew again. The boy looked haggard and distraught. My father wondered if he was on drugs; so many other kids were. "What's wrong?" he asked. Had he gone to the Soviet embassy, as my father had suggested? What had they said?

Matthew had gone to the Soviet embassy, yes. He had enquired about Yevtushenko. A young Soviet embassy official going by the name of Ivan, who represented the cultural section, had greeted him warmly, with a handshake and a smile. Ivan was interested by Matthew's idea of bringing the poet to the school, and agreed most enthusiastically to that proposal, but said he couldn't make an immediate commitment. He would, of course, have to look into it first. There would be protocol and scheduling to finesse. The two men had stood in the dim foyer light of the Soviet compound, shaking hands as they concluded their conversation. Matthew left the embassy with the feel of the man's grip on his hand, and in his mind a promise to revisit the matter again.

Matthew and Ivan met repeatedly, very often at Ivan's request, and every time they did Matthew pressed the issue of Yevtushenko's visit. But there never seemed to be any news of the poet. He was elsewhere, his words elsewhere, which meant the war and the sense of urgency must also be elsewhere. As the possibility of the poet's coming began to fade, lost to obscurity and protocol, Ivan began to show a much keener interest in Matthew. He began to insist on more frequent meetings, to discuss a wider range of topics. He wanted them to get to know each other better. One day, Ivan wondered aloud whether Matthew had any other friends who he would like to bring along to their discussions, friends who might be interested in the same kinds of things as Matthew: peace, culture, poetry, and discussion. Another day, Ivan proposed that together they form a cultural discussion group, ideally to include other peace-loving students. There seemed to be no obvious forethought, no apparent malice in the gesture. Surely, Ivan said, Matthew should consider some of his own friends. Might there be some whose fathers worked for large American defense contractors, like Lockheed Martin? Or IBM? Or Martin Marietta? They might be particularly interested in discussions of peace and prosperity, perhaps more than most. Matthew should feel free to bring them along, too—should they, of course, desire such a thing.

My father listened to this tale and felt a shudder of something within him waking up. He had never thought much of Matthew, but now he stared at the boy as if at a key. This American redhead, large and impolitic, was offering him a gift. He felt his heart thump.

Matthew knew that Ivan was not really Ivan. He had realized that some arm of the KGB, the Russian intelligence service, was reeling him in, and he knew it was folly—suicide—to be taken in. It was so far from his purpose, so far from simple poetry. It was a mistake. So Matthew explained that he had gone for help. He bussed the long, slow descent from campus into Mexico City, to the American embassy. He arrived at reception. He asked to speak to someone from the Federal Bureau of Investigation. It was urgent, he told the receptionist. Then he sat down to wait.

Only when a man appeared, proffering a warm hand and a smile, did he allow his gaze to relax. The American was friendly, familiar, and benign-looking—even bland. His name, he said, was John. How could he help?

Matthew said he was a student. He wanted to continue with his uncomplicated student life, but the meddling of a Russian was preventing him from doing so. He explained how it had all started when he asked for the help of the Soviet embassy, but so much time had gone by without any word, any progress—time that had instead been devoted to other, frankly more sinister, probing—that he now had concerns about being manipulated by the KGB, and in particular by a man who said his name was Ivan.

John listened patiently to Matthew's story. He asked questions now and again, intently probing this or that detail of the story. There were no guarantees in a business such as this, he undoubtedly warned himself. It could be a ruse. The Soviets could have put the boy up to it. Because this genial bureaucrat, "John," was a spy we'll name Timothy Irons—a man who spoke fluent Russian, a junior case officer in the Mexico City station of the Central Intelligence Agency. Irons showed no outward signs of emotion, but in his mind there was naked glee. As he listened to Matthew, he began to fashion a counterplot. He decided he would use Matthew as bait.

Irons's intention was to recruit Ivan. Like any case officer worth his mettle, Irons was trained to hunt for pliable Soviets ripe for recruitment—few achievements were more coveted. It was notoriously difficult to recruit them, he knew—particularly those working in Mexico City in 1968, where opportunities for advancement were high, progress on the path to communism had already been made, and the shadow of the enemy to the north loomed large. But even failing recruitment, he knew that if his plan was successful, it could guarantee that Ivan would be sufficiently embarrassed that he might agree to cooperate with the Americans to avoid further humiliation.

Irons realized that recruiting Ivan, who undoubtedly worked at a reasonably senior level of the KGB apparatus, would require a meeting. His plan was simple: he would lure the Soviet into an even more complex relationship with Matthew. Then, Irons would set a trap and reel him in.

After another one or two meetings between Irons and Matthew, the spy explained his plan. Together, they would organize one of the cultural-discussion meetings that Ivan had been pursuing. During one of those meetings, Matthew would introduce Ivan to Irons, who would pose as a disaffected and peace-loving student eager to establish an underground newspaper publicizing American war crimes being perpetrated in the name of democracy. Irons, of course, would go by the name of "John."

Matthew, having finished his story, looked at my father. The two of them stood up and away from the others, on a shady hillock underneath a blooming tree where a slight wind blew. My father stared at Matthew, his mind racing. Matthew, really just a boy, stared back. On the footpath was an array of indigo blossoms, falling and drifting, disappearing into the crowd. A bell rang, marking the beginning of classes, and it seemed to ring for a fraction too long.

My father began to formulate his own plan before he even realized he was doing it. He wanted to be part of the action, while Matthew, realizing he was in over his head, wanted out. The plan he proposed was efficient and mutually beneficial: it would enable my father to meet Timothy Irons and sell himself to him, and at the same time, allow Matthew to make a graceful and necessary exit.

Once again, my father gave his student instructions—only this time he was very specific. Matthew was to go back to Timothy Irons. But he was to deliver a story of my father's making, a lie that, once set in motion, would give Matthew an out, and at the same time open a door for my father. He used a metaphor of fortune when talking about it: luck. He relied on the fate of the cards. But then, my father was a gambler by nature. By dealing Matthew out, he dealt himself in.

On my father's instructions, Matthew lied to Irons the next time the two met. Matthew said that in order to be as thorough as possible in concocting the story of a student who wanted to set up an underground newspaper, he had decided to find the name of a real student. And to do that, he had sneaked into the university's filing room to peek at the student files. The dean of men, a man named Mr. Johnson, had caught him. The dean had reminded Matthew of his failing grades and his poor attendance, and told him that if he didn't provide a written explanation of why he was sneaking around trying to get someone else's file by Monday, he would be suspended. Matthew pleaded with Irons: please, go and talk to the dean. He added that the dean was basically a good guy. Moreover, if the dean knew what the two of them, Matthew and Irons, were actually doing with the Soviets, he probably wouldn't kick him out of school. The dean graded papers in his office every Sunday afternoon; that might be the best time to reach him.

This was how, that very Sunday afternoon, Timothy Irons came to see my father at his little office on campus. Behind a broad metal desk, my father was waiting patiently. Irons delivered a long and sincere explanation of what he and Matthew had been doing. My father sat back in his chair and listened, no doubt exuding a certain professorial cool. He played the part: he was now concerned, now curious. Their apprehensions, he assured the diplomat, were his as well. And certainly, if there were anything he could do to help, well . . . in other words, should he be able to, say, contribute in any way, he would, he supposed, be willing to consider it. In fact, he mused, it might make more sense for him to be more involved than he had been up until then. As for the unfortunate Matthew, mightn't it be better to relieve the already overburdened student of some share of what was obviously a very complicated and serious affair? He cocked his eyebrow at Irons. In a situation where numerous parties were being duped, my father was not, at least this far, among them. They sealed the deal that lazy afternoon.

A few days after they made their pact in my father's office, the two of them met again to hatch out the details of their plan. Over the next few days, they conspired to orchestrate a series of treacherously manipulative encounters to trap Ivan and recruit him as a CIA mole. Their plan, such as it was, had been designed so that Timothy Irons, aka John, would be the primary contact for Ivan. My father's role would come later. For the moment they worked at drawing the Soviet in as deeply as they could.

As the spring of 1968 rolled on in Mexico, the student protests gathered momentum, and the Ivan plot began to take shape on the grounds of the otherwise calm University of the Americas campus. In several private meetings, Ivan was introduced to a student of truly remarkable potential. John was not only anti-American by temperament, but he was also interested in setting up anti-American discussion groups, and seemed generally keen on propagating a view that would serve to undermine American interests abroad.

My father and Irons met separately to evaluate their progress. They brainstormed new ways to ensnare the Russian. The spring wore on. Temperatures in the valley soared, then cooled with the moisture that flowed off the mountains and spawned blooms of bougainvillea and jasmine and lavender. The air began to fill with the anticipation of a long rainy season.

By early summer, Irons and my father were convinced that the plan they had hatched would deliver Ivan into Iron's hands. Ivan didn't seem to suspect anything. Irons scheduled one more meeting with him to review some of the latest, much more virulent, anti-American material that Irons had been collecting and showing to Ivan. The plan now was to set up the sting. But for the sting to work they needed a secluded place, away from the student halls and restaurants they had been using until then. And they didn't have such a place. Irons, of course, didn't have a real student residence. But my father did, and ever accommodating, he offered up his own small cottage. Irons agreed. My father knew that if the operation didn't go off as planned he, as the occupant of the house, would be compromised—he would be exposed as a co-conspirator in a nefarious American government plot. But he gave Irons a set of his house keys anyway.

The afternoon of the sting was unusually clear, although a wind snarled through the city. On the horizon, the cones of the volcanoes Popocatépetl and Iztaccihuatl were luminous and imposing. Irons let himself into my father's cottage and sat down on the sofa to wait. It wasn't long before his quarry, Ivan, drove into the gravel driveway in a Chevrolet. Ivan parked in the shade of some trees and low bushes, got out of the car, and walked up to knock quietly on the door. Letting him in, Irons went on the offensive almost immediately. He fixed a stern gaze upon Ivan.

"Look, Ivan Ivanovich," he said in Russian, "would you prefer to speak in Russian or English?"

Ivan, immediately aware of the trap, tried to back away, but Irons blocked his path. "You've made a bad mistake," Irons said.

The American thought that it would be better not to mince words or waste time. Besides, there wasn't too much time to waste; Ivan would get frantic. Irons managed to keep him there long enough to deliver a message: if Ivan agreed to cooperate with the American government, Irons would make it worth his while. The Americans, he said, would make sure that Ivan had enough authentic sensitive U.S. intelligence material to keep his superiors in the KGB contented. And there was the possibility that he would be given prepared intelligence from future trips he might take back to the United States. His bosses would no doubt consider him a success—but only if he agreed to cooperate. If he refused this generous offer, everyone knew that his career as a rising star in Soviet intelligence was doomed.

As Ivan recoiled, digesting this, Irons's threats continued. He became increasingly aggressive while Ivan grew more anxious. But while the CIA may have duped Ivan, he was no traitor. It didn't take long for him to refuse Irons's offer. Cooperating with the Americans was simply not an option, and however difficult it would be to wriggle out of this mess with his superiors (who would no doubt consider Ivan's stupidity a significant security breach), he wasn't going to play along. When Irons could no longer restrain him, Ivan rushed out of the cottage and ran to his car.

But it wouldn't start. While Irons had been working at wrangling a deal from Ivan, outside in the driveway two men had been discreetly removing the distributor cap from Ivan's Chevrolet. The men were from the CIA's technical services division. Having successfully removed the cap, they had disappeared into the nearby bushes to watch and wait.

Dusk was approaching, and Irons walked out to the car and continued to pressure Ivan while the Soviet stared disconsolately under the hood, and then into the trunk of his car, as if the answer to his engine problem might be found there. Eventually, he turned and walked resolutely to the highway, leaving his Chevrolet in my father's driveway. He caught a public bus that was headed into the city. After he was gone, the American team emerged from the bushes, replaced the cap, hotwired the car, and drove it to the parking lot of the University of the Americas, where they abandoned it, carefully locking the doors and wiping away fingerprints.

It was dark when my father drove home from work. He was aware that the operation had gone down that day, but not how it went. He was nervous and excited. He slowed his Karmann Ghia to a crawl as he approached his driveway, where he saw several strangers, some of them uniformed, milling about. A Mexican policeman walked to and fro, his pistol drawn. My father drove past and had just begun to pull around at the end of the lane to make a quiet retreat when a shot rang out. As he turned around to see where the shot had come from, he saw the Mexican policeman take aim at his car. He slammed his foot on the gas, and managed to make it around the corner before a second shot was fired.

Still unsure about what exactly was transpiring at his home, and too curious to leave, my father drove down a couple of side streets and parked in an alley behind several other cars. He lingered for a moment, pondering his options. He was reluctant to return to a scene that featured a Mexican policeman. And yet he had committed no visible crime. Above all, he was just plain curious, and he was willing to risk the danger to satisfy his urge. So he stole back to his house on foot. He hopped over a low wall beside the house and made his way onto the roof, where he lay down flat and slowly lifted his head to peer over the edge. From there he was able to spy on the police.

The scene was chaotic. There were several more Mexican police than he had thought, and all of them had weapons. And there was also Ivan, who was impatiently demanding that the Mexican police break into the house immediately. The police, however, justifiably confused, were reluctant to follow the orders of an agitated Russian who seemed to have no good reason to be loitering around a house that wasn't his. My father, excited and bemused, watched from the shadows of the roof until, finally, all of them left. He returned quietly to the alley, retrieved his car, and went home to sleep.

But the next afternoon, when he returned home from work, the police were there again—this time with Ivan and two unknown Russians. And this time, my father didn't flee. When he pulled up, the policemen brusquely ushered him into his house and began to interrogate him. The pair of suit-and-tie Soviet bureaucrats stood nearby with looks of contempt on their faces. As far as my father could tell, they were directing the interrogation, demanding answers and giving directions to the Mexican cops in Spanish.

"Where were you last night?" one of the policemen asked, prodded by one of the Soviets.

"I was working," my father answered.

"Where do you work?"

"At the university."

"Can you prove it?"

"Sure I can. Ask anyone who I work with there."

As the questions came, so did more details of the story, and my father was able to fill in the gaps. Ivan told the Mexicans how he had been in the house the night before. The Mexicans wanted to know why, and what my father had to do with it. My father played dumb. The police got frustrated, but the Soviets weren't finished yet and, dissatisfied with my father's story, forced him to open up a large leather case sitting in a corner. They believed it held an assault rifle of some sort. When it turned out to be a movie tripod, the police got even more impatient with the Russians.

Sensing that a shift had taken place in his favor, my father tried to turn the tables. What had this Soviet communist been doing, by his own admission, in the house the day before, and who had he been with? The Russians seemed not to have a satisfactory answer for this. The Mexicans were nominally in charge of the situation; they had the guns, and it was their country. But they were also beginning to realize they were in over their heads. My father became even more aggressive. How could a Russian, he asked, much less a communist, dare to show his face around Americans after one of them had killed President Kennedy?

Until now the police had shown some sensitivity to my father. But this latest bit of self-righteous anger on his part was too much. They decided to cart him off to jail. Inside the prison, the police continued to harass him, telling him he'd better start talking or else. But my father fell into a stubborn silence. The police grew bored and eventually let him go. They didn't even give him a warning. He took a taxi home that night, where he slept like a baby.

The CIA paid my father a few hundred dollars for his assistance in the Ivan plot. After it was over, the station learned from a friendly contact that the Soviet embassy had been discovered to be trying to infiltrate the University of the Americas, and had been seriously discredited in the eyes of the Mexican government, including the president. As far as the recruitment of Soviets was concerned, however, the operation wasn't successful. In the larger scheme of things, what good came out of the weeks and months spent massaging such intricate and convoluted intrigue? A small plot to infiltrate the University of the Americas had been disrupted momentarily, but it would no doubt start again. A Soviet had been compromised, but he was replaceable. This was an aborted throw of the dice in the Great Game. This list of caveats was of little or no consideration to my father, however, whose appetite had been thoroughly and definitively whetted.

The Ivan plot came to an end just as the student protests were gaining momentum that summer and fall. For over nine weeks, the protests had been getting bigger and more unruly. As preparations for the Olympics continued, activists from elsewhere across Mexico had begun to converge on the capital. Yevgeny Yevtushenko had by then vanished off to some other front, almost as if the swirling storm that was gathering over Mexico was too much even for him to calm. The Mexico City station of the CIA was buzzing with activity. Throughout the summer, they sent memoranda back to Washington detailing the increased frequency and vigor of the protests, and warned that the situation was becoming harder for the Mexican government to control.

Throughout the long months of that rainy summer, the CIA kept a close watch on the vast student population in Mexico. Their main focus was the radicals on the campus of the UNAM, the university that President Ordaz had targeted in September when he sent in troops. But the events at the University of the Americas came under close scrutiny as well. Which was why, even once the Ivan plot was over, my father's involvement with the CIA only deepened.

Timothy Irons left Mexico shortly after the Ivan plot was over. But before leaving, he turned my father over to another first-tour officer at the station. My dad's new "handler" was Robert. Tall and handsome, Robert was also young and ambitious, and to my father, the epitome of the smooth elegance that until then had existed only in the pages of spy novels. Robert assiduously cultivated my father's friendship. He invited my father to CIA parties with other members of the Mexico City station and exposed him, casually at first, and then more forcefully, to an inside look at the world he was trying to get my father to join.

My father was a useful asset. Robert began to use him as an "access agent"—a handy go-between when a quick meeting was required with an unknown person. The two of them would arrange for accidental run-ins when my father dined or drank with somebody Robert was particularly keen to meet. After striking up an acquaintance, Robert could work the target at his own pace and on his own terms.

After each of these meetings, Robert gave my father more access to his world. They often went for lunch together, in Roma, or Lomas, or La Zona Rosa ("the pink zone"). They talked about politics and power the way men with dreams do, with camaraderie and complicity. My father was not a great connoisseur of automobiles, but on one occasion, when he saw one he liked on the street, he exclaimed on its beauty. "Well," responded the older man, "if you join the CIA, you'll be able to afford a car like that."

My father and my mother, Lee, met that same year. Her father was a diplomat stationed in Mexico City. She had come to visit that summer and had gotten a job as my dad's secretary. They married in March of 1969. The wedding took place in the Union Church on Reforma. Afterward, at the reception, the band played mariachi and she danced on the cool patio tiles with my father. When the clinking of glasses rang across the verandah and the long-leaved plants quietly ushered them along the floor, she was able to think serenely about the future, and the way the two of them both seemed to fit together, and the eagerness they had in common. She imagined the beaches they would lie upon, the oceans he would fill with her image while he was traveling—all of it laid out in a neat and glassy panorama. She leaned into my father's chest. They must have spoken softly to each other. I can hear her giggling, and his deep bass voice, reassuring and comforting. I can also see Robert standing on the sides, happy to see his protégé now, finally, coming into the world.

Soon after, my father and mother boarded an American Airlines flight from Mexico City to Washington. As the wheat fields and purple mountains rolled through his mind, he looked out the window, down at the country he had left but loved, and would leave again and again.

He took classes in Washington, and later at Camp Peary. Within a year, he had been hired by the CIA's directorate of operations, their clandestine service. He was a case officer. A spy.

CHAPTER 12

Mexico City, 2002

I moved to Mexico when I was twenty-eight, to run *Newsweek*'s bureau. One day soon after I arrived, I took a taxi up the old Toluca highway that rose out of the city. I hoped to find his old house, the one in which the Ivan plot had reached its dramatic denouement. The road wound past a giant, stadium-sized trash dump over which highrises had been built. There were shopping centers and movie theaters and fast-food joints. An exit ramp led to a cul-de-sac and a gated community. A guard inside a hut, armed with a rifle, peeked out.

At the location I got out of the car and walked around a bit, peering up and down the streets, wondering whether I would recognize his old house immediately, and whether the image in my mind would correspond to what was here, for there appeared to be nothing more than overdeveloped suburban homes—the blandness of America in a Mexican neighborhood. I tried to picture the roof my father had clambered onto, trying to spy on the Mexican police. But all I could see were delicately trimmed hedgerows, some hydrangea, and a little blue Opel parked near the guard's hut. The city extended below, smoggy and expansive. A curtain of rain drifted slowly across a distant hill. The whole megalopolis of over twenty million souls was quiet in the silvery afternoon.

I took out my phone and called my dad at home. He answered at once. "I can't find your old house," I said. "I think it must have been demolished. Everything here looks new."

"Can you see a big house and a little house at the end of the driveway?" he asked.

I couldn't. The confluence of so many disparate elements of my life seemed to swirl around me here on this Mexican hill-top. It was the city where my parents had met and then married, where my grandparents had lived, and where my father found his calling—where all of our lives were rooted somehow.

I wandered some more, listening to the static. But the more I looked, the more I realized I was lost: on the wrong side of the highway, or too far up the hill. And then what I knew of the little house—the decorations my mother had put on the walls when she and my father were dating, the comfort and intimacy they had shared there, the happiness I imagined it contained—suddenly overwhelmed me. It was the first house my parents had ever shared as a couple: small, but huge in my imagination. I wanted, suddenly and not entirely consciously, to leave that bit of memory to my imagination alone. I wanted not to find it at all.

"Well," he said.

"Well."

Shortly after I moved to Mexico, I met a woman named Sofia. She was a photographer, also working for *Newsweek*, who had showed up at my house one day with a large portfolio of black-and-white pictures she had taken of Mexican prostitutes. We sat on a patio outside at my house, which was also the office, and flipped through the images. I found myself fawning over them, and, soon enough, over her. She had blond hair and huge brown eyes that had an overwhelming softness. She was shy and curious and observant, and she beguiled me with her quiet intelligence. Before she left, I got her to agree to see me again.

Sofia was a committed leftist. Her father, Carlos, had been a Stalinist. In 1968, Carlos belonged to an armed guerrilla movement that wanted to overthrow the government. He was often underground, hiding in safe houses in Mexico City, or in jungle redoubts where rebel sympathies were strong. He married a young American woman named Gilda, who had studied ancient Mayan civilization at the University of the Americas in Mexico City during the same period my father taught there. Gilda gave birth to Sofia, their first child, in 1967.

Sofia spoke of her father in vague but reverent tones. I knew he came from a prominent Spanish family that had produced at least one military general loyal to the fascist dictator Francisco Franco. Other members of the clan had splintered off. Some became hardened communists, including Carlos's mother, who had initiated her son into radical politics in Mexico—where they had fled to safety in fear of Franco's terror.

Sofia told me these things in the backs of ambulances on trips we had started taking around Mexico City with the Red Cross. I wanted to do a story on the medics, and gaining access to their world meant spending a lot of time in ambulances. Soon after I had told Sofia about these trips, she was coming along too. I liked to think this was more for me than the photo opportunities. We spent hours poking our cameras in the wreckage of car crashes, or sneaking around crack-infested slums, or watching medics wash blood off the ambulance floor. We went several times a week, mostly at night. We made out on seats in the back, and the medics sniggered and made fun of us, and I imagined them to be jealous. She laughed when I sang along to the English pop songs on the radio, and teased me that I knew all the words. I don't know why it was so comforting to explore with her the misery those trips seemed to yield—broken bodies and drug-addled crack whores, beaten wives and alcoholic gang fights. Maybe it was because I had just come back from Afghanistan, and so the wretchedness of what we saw seemed reassuring and familiar. It made sense, seeking refuge in other people's sorrows. And it was surprisingly easy to fall in love surrounded by the ostracized, the wounded, and the dead.

One day Sofia told me that her father had been imprisoned for four years when she was young, starting in 1968. Student leaders much less strident than he had reportedly been thrown out of planes at miles over the Gulf of Mexico, or shot in the head in dark alleyways, or beaten to within inches of their lives with lead pipes. Others had vanished. Even now, over thirty years later, those years were still an open wound for her. She had been raised on legends of her father hiding in jungles, running from the law. But she never saw his ginger hair and pale eyes and mustache for herself until she was four years old.

Mexico, in those months, was entering a process of self-examination, and a deep sense of recrimination about its past. The same month I moved there, in June 2002, the government of then-president Vicente Fox announced it would open and declassify thousands of documents from Mexico's spy and security services from the 1960s and 1970s, an era which had become known as "the dirty war." The killings and disappearances of left-wing radicals, students, and intellectuals in Mexico had continued throughout the 1970s and 1980s, but an aura of intrigue remained around the year 1968, as if time and history had simply stopped then; as if everything that came afterward only served as an epilogue.

I had not expected to see myself in that history, and yet here it surrounded me. The campus of the University of the Americas, where Sofia's mother had been a student, was under constant scrutiny. Nineteen sixty-eight was significant because it was the year of the Tlatelolco massacre, on October 2—and now, a quarter of a century later, it served as the lightning rod around which journalists and investigators began to swarm.

Carlos's history had shaped Sofia in profound ways. Because he was a renegade, I imagined Carlos being interrogated and tortured by thugs from the Mexican secret services. As I began to picture his life, I also saw how closely it could have hewed to my father's life, there at the university, among the students and the demonstrators, in the intrigue that flowed so powerfully through the city and its people. He was a silhouette in reverse, a shadow my father could easily have been chasing.

Carlos didn't seem to be doing much in particular in 2002. Sometimes, his name would come up innocuously in my conversations with Mexican politicians, and it opened doors. But Sofia revealed so little about him that I soon hesitated to ask. Yet everything about her seemed to lead to one place: an eerie Mexican past filled with regret that no one wanted to talk about.

My only hint was that my father had been there, too, on the other side of Carlos's world. And now, the idea that he knew more than he had told me began to grow within me, as if I had planted it. Had I buried a seed of mistrust years earlier—mistrust of him and his motives, and perhaps mistrust of my own gut feelings? Was it now coming to life? An unintended consequence of, or unintended lesson from, my childhood was that what may appear to be so is not, in fact, just so. That general sense of distrust was never meant to be focused on my own family, and yet here I was, questioning my father. It was difficult to avoid. I didn't want to think of him that way, but I was unable to keep my suspicions in check.

One night, sitting in my darkened house in Coyoacán, I summoned up courage and called him. I was halfway through a bottle of red wine already. But I found alcohol made it much easier to talk to him, given how treasonous I felt. That I was even considering whether he had told me the truth about something so important made me hate myself. I can't recall how I sounded when I asked him where he was the night of the Tlatelolco massacre, only that I felt like a police officer asking for an alibi: "Where were you on the night in question?" And his answer was almost immediately suspicious to me. It was a long time ago, he said, and there had been so many protests, so many riots and demonstrations. He was having difficulty remembering which night that was, and so I reminded him that it was at the Plaza de las Tres Culturas, that thousands of students had gathered in the early afternoon and entered the plaza, only to be locked inside by tanks that were stationed at the entrances, and then mowed down by government soldiers rampaging about inside. It must have been a bloody, chaotic scene, I said. Did he remember anything like that?

No. What followed was a vague description of an uneventful night.

I was nervous throughout the conversation, unable to shake the idea that I had stumbled upon something he was hiding. I wanted to believe him. I had by now accepted that selective nondisclosure was part of the deal with him; he couldn't tell me everything, and I didn't need him to. But this wasn't as much about information as loyalty. I had always wanted to believe I came first. But what happened, I wondered, to spies when loyalty to their loved ones conflicted with their loyalty to their masters? Who, in the end, would win? Whose loyalty was more important?

So you weren't there, I thought. You weren't there, and didn't see anything, right? And I don't have to worry anymore about who my father is, or what he's capable of. Am I going to have to dig this out of you? Am I going to have to ask you again, later on?

But disbelief and mistrust are so corrosive. How was it possible to believe so selectively—to know that his personal iteration with me was more truthful than what he told the world? Somehow, before all this questioning, that had been okay. But now I felt that the whole concept was beginning to unravel for me, to come unhinged. Spies had two masters—their families and their epic secret. I felt like a counterintelligence officer—searching for the mole within my own organization, the lie at the core of myself or my father, the fundamental untruth, the spy within.

On the afternoon of October 2, 1968, thousands of students had begun their march toward the city's dingy Tlatelolco neighborhood. It was a hazy, warm afternoon, the low sun casting needles of light across the rain. The protests had gathered such momentum that the people now thronged the streets by the thousands. Many of them carried red carnations, which symbolized the tears Mary shed upon Jesus' crucifixion, and thus, the sins of the world. There were mothers and fathers, children, brothers and sisters of students, the old and the young alike. They chatted as they headed toward the site of the protest, a spot where archeologists had discovered Aztec ruins and a pyramid. At that place almost five hundred years earlier, on August 13, 1521, Hernán Cortés, encountering local resistance to his arrival, had killed some forty thousand Aztecs in an epic battle. That day, as the protestors walked toward the ancient square, some of them might have noticed Mexican Army units gathering nearby.

During another conversation, long after my drunken interrogation, my father would tell me he was in his office at the university that morning, finishing up some paperwork. It was a Wednesday. When a journalist friend came by asking to use his tripod, my father, always up for a new experience, said he would come along to the rooftops himself. Later that afternoon, as dusk was beginning to settle, he apparently sat overlooking the plaza as thousands of students began to flow inside and chant, to raise their voices against the state.

Outside the plaza walls, the Mexican Army was gathering its forces. Earlier that summer, President Ordaz had authorized Mexican special operations troops operating outside the city to fire upon students whenever necessary, and without explicit permission from higher headquarters. The same mood of permissiveness prevailed that evening. Outside the arena, Mexican Army tanks had taken up positions. Soldiers sat lazily astride their hulks and cleaned their bayonets as they waited. They had received orders not to allow the protest to take place at all.

So, when, around 5:00 p.m., protestors began to arrive by the thousands, the army didn't wait long to move in. Cordoning off the entrances and exits, and securing them with tanks, armed soldiers advanced into the crowd.

At the same time, about a dozen officers from a civilian unit called the Olympic Brigade took up positions on the roof of a nearby apartment building called the Chihuahua complex. These men each wore a white glove on one hand.

Suddenly, a flare went up. Shots were fired. The first bodies fell inside the square itself. The shooting seemed to be coming from all quarters at once. Some witnesses reported that it originated from the government soldiers. Others said that the first shots were clearly coming from the roof of the Chihuahua complex, and still others that students armed with automatic rifles on different rooftops were the instigators.

Wherever the origin, the shooting was intense, and very quickly erupted into a full-scale riot. Soon, bodies were lying in pools of blood inside and outside the plaza, as squads of soldiers rampaged through the crowds, beating protestors and bystanders indiscriminately. Stick-wielding men dressed in civilian clothes beat people senseless and left them to die, while rifle fire rained down on the crowd from on high. The trucks that arrived in the aftermath reportedly carried the dead away to secret locations. In the years to come, it was said that pilots had taken to the skies with some of the bodies, flying out high over the Yucatan Peninsula, opening the cargo doors, and letting the bodies drop. The dead, it would later be said, were uncountable.

My father, it seemed to me, was on those same rooftops that night. But he had told me he left before the shooting started. I began digging for information. I scoured the Internet for documentation about the Dirty War, and came across a large, recently released trove of memos from American officials on the National Security Archive website (the Archive was a Washington, D.C., think tank that made freedom of information requests to the CIA, FBI, and other national security organizations). Another search turned up a memo from the American embassy that listed some fifteen differing—and sometimes flatly contradictory—versions of what had happened at Tlatelolco, all from either "generally reliable sources" or "trained observers." I also searched in bookstores for information about the period, and talked to older Mexicans about what they remembered.

Had my father been there after all? Was he just not telling me? Had he, simply and conveniently, forgotten?

One night, over dinner with Sofia, I asked innocently what she knew about the CIA in Mexico. I hadn't yet told her what my dad did. And she said that her grandmother, the political refugee from Spain, had often told her stories about CIA spies working with the government to abduct and maybe even kill troublesome students. There was certainly some precedent: Guatemala, El Salvador, and Nicaragua. Central America was where the CIA's dirty tricks had been most visible.

The more I heard these things, the more anxious I became. But much as I entertained these ideas, I chastised myself for even considering them. There was simply no way that my father could have been party to something that would have resulted in a massacre, or anything even remotely like it. Everything in me revolted at the idea. But his recollection of that night didn't seem to square with every recorded version on the public record. It was during those weeks, when I started going back to things my father had told me, that I discovered for myself Yevgeny Yevtushenko, the poet whose travails had ushered my father into the CIA. A poem called "Later" caught my eye.

> *Oh what a sobering,*
> *What a talking-to from conscience afterwards:*
> *The short moment of frankness at the party*
> *And the enemy crept up.*
> *But to have learnt nothing is terrible,*
> *And peering earnest eyes are terrible*
> *Detecting secret thoughts is terrible*

In simple words and immature disturbance
This diligent suspicion has no merit.
The blinded judges are no public servants.
It would be far more terrible to mistake
A friend than to mistake an enemy.

I wondered about my suspicion and its merit, as Yevtushenko warned. But I was also face-to-face with a woman who I cared for, whose personal history seemed to me to be evidence that what was known or admitted about Mexico in 1968 was only a fraction of the truth. It seemed to me clear that there was another, much more disturbing truth to be ferreted out. I didn't want to make mistakes, as Yevtushenko had said. But I didn't want to be blinded, either.

Others seemed to feel the same. All that fall, the papers were filled with stories of how the noble prosecutor's office in Mexico City was going after generals, spies, policemen, and ex-presidents who had been involved in the events of 1968 to finally put to rest one of the worst chapters in Mexico's history. The prosecutor was hoping to indict some of them for war crimes, crimes against humanity, and even genocide. But the generals weren't having it. That October, in an interview with the Mexican daily newspaper *La Jornada*, a retired general named Alberto Quintanar said, "What fucking dirty war? This was a clean war. We were ordered by the president to cleanse the country of Communism." And what Latin American country, I thought, had ever undertaken such a vast and purifying task without the help of the CIA?

I became increasingly wary of my father as the autumn came and went. Images of him thirty years earlier, crouching on a rooftop with a trained sniper, crowded my mind. At first it had been difficult to imagine, but once I made the initial leap it suddenly became much easier—and also much more frightening. Still, I didn't know exactly what the CIA's role had been. Had they been working with the military? Or were they just watching from the sidelines, gathering intelligence? Perhaps they were secretly working with the students in a bid to overthrow the fifty-year-old sclerosis of Mexico's Institutional Revolutionary Party with something even better.

My father had been sympathetic to the protesting students, he had said. But he decried communists and Stalinists—all killers, according to him. Stalinists, in particular, as Yevtushenko had pointed out, had killed millions. And Sofia's father had been one of them—dedicated to revolution by any means necessary. It wasn't too much of a stretch to imagine my father involved in an operation to bring people like Carlos down. No matter how much I rebelled at the idea, I couldn't shake it. In those weeks, that wall of secrecy grew and grew, and wondering about what horrors lay on his side of it began to consume me.

I went to visit him over Christmas that year. One night, we sat at the kitchen table. On the refrigerator was a CIA magnet. In the hall was a CIA cap I had bought him somewhere. There was a mug, a T-shirt, pins, a coaster—our house was filled with the Agency's knickknackery.

I told him that I had met a woman whose father had been imprisoned in Mexico the same year he was recruited. He asked for her name. He pondered the information. "It sounds familiar," he said eventually.

"Did you ever meet him?" I asked.

He shook his head.

I asked about Sofia's mother, who had been a student at his school, but he didn't seem to recognize that name. I told him I wanted to write something about the two of them, Carlos and him, and the two of us, their children. "Sofia could make a movie," I exclaimed.

But the enthusiasm he usually showed for my projects didn't seem to extend to this.

The coincidences that bothered me most were the proximity of our parents and the symmetry between their lives during the years of conflict. The possibility that the Ivan plot, and Robert's careful ministrations of my father, had extended to other initiatives I'd never heard about was now foremost on my mind.

Back in Mexico, I began to sift through more of the documents from the online National Security Archive. There was speculation among American officials that the government had allowed the Tlatelolco rally to take place in order to round up suspected agitators in one place and arrest them or mow them down. The pathways of two lives—Carlos's imprisonment and my father's recruitment—seemed to be dovetailing. And there was no getting around the worst fear of all: that my father had played a role in the imprisonment of Sofia's father.

That autumn, I filed several requests under Mexico's Freedom of Information Act. In the space reserved for subjects, I wrote my father's name. And then I waited for a response.

Meanwhile, my father spent the autumn in Afghanistan. He gave me regular updates. He was doing "propaganda work," he said, which involved helping the Afghan government to craft and deliver its message of strength, tolerance, and unity with greater appeal and efficiency. Propaganda, he told me, was a misunderstood word. In its true sense, it simply meant the dissemination of information. To me, it was a distinctly dirty word—the great obstacle for journalists, the ubiquitous tool of governments and bureaucracies. The creators of propaganda were the enemy. They were worse than the individuals who peddled it. The latter, at least, may have been brainwashed. But the message itself, when it smacked of the Big Lie, was always the most revolting presence in the room precisely because it could not be ignored, ever. It had to be investigated, cognized, rebutted, and rehashed, and still it managed to return in some other form.

I looked it up just the same. It came from the Latin: *congregatio de propaganda fide*. Congregation for propagation of the faith.

One day, on a reporting trip, I was standing in a splendid hotel room in Baja, Mexico, looking out at an infinity pool and the blue waters of the Pacific when my phone rang. The number didn't register. I answered, and there was a long pause. I heard the static of deep, long distance.

"Hello?. . . Hello?"

"*Salaam alaikum*," came my father's voice eventually. The joy there was unmistakable. "Guess where I am, Scotty?" I didn't have to answer. "Khost," he said. He was beaming; I could hear it.

He said he was standing on the roof of the Special Forces base. I remembered the craggy men I had seen there a year earlier: long-haired, bearded operators with cargo pants and M6 assault rifles. They were the men who came before my father. And now my father was one of them. "I'm on the roof," he said. "The reception's better."

I knew it was. My roof; my country.

He was calling me from a satellite phone, as I had called him so many times when I was there. I asked him if he was carrying a gun and he said yes, a 9mm pistol, but he had never used it, which came as a relief. I imagined him standing there with his pistol on his belt and an Afghan *pakol* on his head and I could see what he was seeing exactly: the pink and blue mountains and the dust on the plains, the low scrub hills, eucalyptus trees, and the roadside ditches where the sewage water lay stagnant.

The Afghans called him "white beard," he said, a sign of respect. Because he was older and his beard had filled out handsomely and properly, he could walk among them with at least that sympathy on his side, something that I had never been able to do. He was doing some interesting work; he couldn't say too much, but the men he was with were "really neat guys." He told me they went out on a long patrol, hunting for an insurgent lair. Every now and again, the Taliban would lob a mortar their way. "They always miss," he assured me.

Even as I wondered about what had really happened in Mexico decades ago, I listened to my father tell me how he was meeting all sorts of Afghans, befriending them and trying to help, and

I believed him without hesitation. His enthusiasm and exuber-
ance were resounding. I thought his reasons were right. I had
spent time in Afghanistan, and had seen America's mistakes up
close. But part of me still clung to the notion that it would be a
better place if my dad were allowed to breathe his life and his
sense of right into it.

For several months, my father traveled back and forth from
Afghanistan. By the spring of 2003, he was back in Kabul, and
he had been put in charge of psy-ops for the whole country. His
career was coming full circle. The chief of the station, whom my
dad liked and respected, had once been a student of his at The
Farm. He also befriended an Afghan who became a tutor and,
ultimately, a friend.

Shortly after, he started taking regular trips out to Bagram
Air Base, where much of the American military was based, and
where a vast prison network had been set up to hold the "detainees" that the Pentagon was insisting were a continued threat to
America's national security. He had started talking to Taliban
prisoners, he said. But he didn't call it an interrogation. He liked
the prisoners, and he felt sorry for them. Their captivity made
him deeply angry. The overriding philosophy of the war—if you
aren't with us, you're against us—was antithetical to his beliefs. It
placed him in an uncomfortably difficult position.

During those months, my father took a special interest in several men who had once been influential in Afghanistan. One of
these was a man whom we'll call Abdul Malek. When the Taliban government had been in power, he had been one of its more
thoughtful representatives. Like the Taliban spiritual leader,
Mullah Mohammed Omar, as well as the president, Hamid Kar-
zai, Malek was an ethnic Pashtun. But unlike so many of the
Taliban rank-and-file, Malek was a moderate. Over the years he
had consistently urged Mullah Omar to reject the steady charm
campaign staged by wealthy Arab Al Qaeda figures like Osama
bin Laden. Malek made the case to Mullah Omar early on that

the Taliban should kick the Arabs out of the country, lest their alliance bring down the wrath of the west. But Mullah Omar was a simple man, and he believed that the Muslim Arabs deserved the hospitality that the Taliban were in a position to offer. So he rejected Malek's counsel.

After 9/11 and the invasion of Afghanistan, Malek, like many other senior Taliban figures, fled to Pakistan. During the siege of Kandahar in 2002, Malek sent a message to U.S. forces through an intermediary—he wanted to surrender, and work with the U.S. alliance and the emerging Afghan government to restore peace. A meeting was arranged. Malek returned to Afghanistan, where he was put in touch with a CIA official named Al, who would become a close friend of my father's. Al told Malek that the United States wanted to work together with him, and would not incarcerate him.

At the same time, the U.S. military, having learned of Malek's arrival, asked to take custody of him. As it was wartime, they had primacy. They said they only wanted to talk to him briefly about tactical issues, but once they had him in their grasp, they kept him. Malek was moved to a prison at Bagram Air Base, outside of Kabul, where he was kept alongside hardened Al Qaeda prisoners—exactly the kind of people he had once urged Mullah Omar to abandon. There he lingered for over a year.

My father entered Malek's life about halfway through that time. My dad was convinced of the merits of Al's basic argument, that Malek represented a moderate wing of the Taliban regime with which it was possible and desirable to negotiate. Al and my father began to lobby hard to secure Malek's release from Bagram. But it was slow going, partly because Secretary of Defense Donald Rumsfeld had taken a keen interest in the case, and was adamantly opposed to any kind of settlement with a senior Taliban figure. At one point, the Pentagon ordered that Malek be shipped off to Guantanamo. The U.S. military put Malek on a plane, but Al learned of it and managed to intervene just in time. Malek was ordered to be removed from the plane during a refueling stop in Greenland, and was returned to Afghanistan.

One day, my father met a young American soldier work- ing at the prison who had gotten to know Malek well. She was distraught about his treatment. She had taken a keen liking to him, escorting him to the prison exercise yard whenever possible, including when she had time off, just to lift his spirits and let him have fresh air. They played checkers together regularly. She saw him as a terribly sincere and violated man. She told my father that Malek's hair was starting to fall out, and that he was slowly losing hope. My father passed the message along.

Malek and my father met one day at Bagram Air Base, on the day that he was to be released. My father wound his way past the identity checks at the prison, which the Soviets had built as an airplane-repair facility, to the second-floor lounge area, from where it was possible to peer down into the "pens" where the detainees were held. He was escorted to a small cubicle to wait. Malek eventually came in. He had lost weight while in captivity. He wore a round cap with a scarf draped over it.

Malek was eager to see his family. My father gave him a Thu- raya satellite phone, and he used it to call home. My dad also arranged for a family reunion. Without telling his boss, he had flown down to Kandahar in a small plane and picked up the fam- ily—two small children and Malek's wife. On the flight back to Kabul, my father walked up and down the aisles handing out candy and nuts to the kids. He winked at them. Three were shy, but one of them stared back at him intently. My father winked and made funny faces at the child until he started to mimic them back. None of the family had ever flown before, and my father arranged for the kids to visit the cockpit. I pictured him on the plane with the kids, and I could see perfectly how he would have been able to disarm them. He had done the same with me when I was a child—winking, teasing, and smiling until I played along. He had always told me that you could never be angry if you were smiling or laughing, and I was sure he had been able to allay those kids' fears, even without words.

The reunion took place at the airport in Kabul. "It was completely overwhelming," he told me later. He teared up as he told me the story. For him, it was a simple equation: a father reuniting with his sons after years apart. I knew he had put himself in the father's shoes and felt the longing, the missed opportunities; felt everything human about the man he had been sent to inform upon. This was but one effort by concerned Afghans to bring about peace and reconciliation in 2002. But they were systematically turned aside by zealots in the Bush administration, as well as by Al Qaeda, which was alienated from the Afghan public and from the Taliban.

My father is a committed atheist. He is among the righteous defenders of freedom, the propagandists of the patriotic faith. My dad may not believe in God, but his belief in good, and the propensity of evil to disrupt it, is undiminished by a lack of religious faith. Somehow, my father reconciled a disbelief in absolutes with a life lived by the rules the absolutes created. He believed in evil, and positioned himself on what he thought to be the opposite side. But to do that, he had to become intimate with both.

There was, in Mexico, another man who had a connection to my father's past. Robert, my father's early mentor at the CIA, had a son, and that son had followed his father into the business—and was based in Mexico City. One night, he invited me out for drinks with another CIA man and their two wives. It was late when we met, and we sat outside on a patio drinking whiskey and smoking cigars. I felt a thrill to be in their company; it was notoriously difficult as a journalist to get access to spies, and I felt that my father had made it easier, opened up this door for me.

Both men's wives were from South Asian countries. They were pretty, unassuming women who seemed to accept their husbands' jobs with what I thought was a great deal of sanguinity. As we sat down to talk, the women disappeared quietly into the back room. That was also part of the game. Conversations with men like these—spies—are from the start an exercise in self-restraint, a game whose sides are apparent to everyone. If I asked a question, it had to be with the assumption that they could only say so much. Relishing the secrecy of it all, of what they could and couldn't say, was part of the game, too, and one had to demonstrate a certain degree of decorum and respect for the tradition.

During the conversation, they exchanged knowing glances now and then, as if weighing the options of disclosure in silent, telepathic communication. A look here, a smirk there—all of it a carefully orchestrated dance that was, I admit, incredibly seductive. I could see my father in me in that moment, sitting in Mexico just like this, with men just like this, plotting their subtle takeover of whatever situation called for their attention. I wanted to be swept up by it, too. I waited for them to try to recruit me, but it never came. I don't know what I would have done if it had.

As a journalist, there was plenty I wanted to ask the two of them, and I did. But I was more curious about what it had been like for the son of my father's friend, growing up in the CIA as I had. I suspected that there were a fair number of spies' children who went into the family business, but there were many, many more that did not. What was the difference between us? This man—I'll call him Sam—had had a real cloak-and-dagger childhood. At one point his father had been posted in an important Eastern Bloc country. The family had standing instructions that if ever he didn't come home by a certain time at night, they were all to hurry to a neighbor's house and wait there for further directions. It meant that something bad had happened—he had been kidnapped or arrested or detained. Perhaps he was dead. There was no telling where the danger could come from in those days of the Cold War. But it was worth it, he said. His father had been partly responsible for one of the most important defections of the Soviet era. It was a huge accomplishment. I could see that. I could also see how compelling it would be to want to replicate it.

I asked Sam if he had enjoyed growing up in that environment. "I guess I did," he said, "or I wouldn't be doing what I'm doing now."

Maybe I was mistaken—it was late, and I had been drinking—but I was startled at what I thought was a look of anger that seemed to flash across his face.

The night had grown colder, and we bundled up against it. The other man was silent. I didn't know what to say. Sam's wasn't the answer I would have chosen had I been posed the same question. But I didn't know what his past meant for him, and I couldn't probe any further. I had gone far enough.

I may have commented it must be exciting, or thrilling, to work in their jobs because the mood turned jovial again after that. Anyway, Sam soon sipped his whiskey and leaned back in his chair, and all seemed normal. Soon their politics came out. They were conservative. They said I was in the wrong business, and the media had it all wrong for the most part. They talked about bombing Al Jazeera because it was a propaganda machine for Al Qaeda.

Here we were, two sons of the CIA, and yet we had such different worldviews. My father had always imparted to me a judicious, temperate view of the world and of other people. Journalists were friends—or at least they were meant to be. I felt alienated from these men, who toiled in the temple of American intelligence alongside my father.

Maybe it was uncomplicated: there was good and evil in the world and it made sense to be on the right side of that equation. If they believed the sides were so sharply drawn, how could they take any other position? It was a compelling argument, especially in those days, a year after 9/11. But definitions of good and evil sometimes seemed so malleable as to be meaningless. Because for many people, including the woman I was beginning to love, the CIA was on the wrong side of that equation. Organizations being what they are—bureaucratic, amoral, and subject to the banal grind of the bottom line—that certainly made sense. But what of the people who made up those organizations? Were they more susceptible to becoming predators in the service of their jobs? Or would they simply be the first victims? Either way, they would always be the first to carry on the message to the next generation. They were, indeed, the propagandists of the faith.

In the following weeks, as I continued to dig into the National Security Archive, I discovered that most of the information that had subsequently emerged about Tlatelolco came from "raw" and "unfinished" reporting from the CIA's covert office—which is to say the Mexico City station, with which my father was in close contact back then. According to a confidential CIA memo released in 2002, students were the first to fire shots at Tlatelolco. I shivered when I read the description penned by officers at the CIA station—my father's friends:

> *The outbreak of rioting in the Plaza de las Tres Culturas which commenced at about 1800 hours was considered to be under control at 1915 hours, although as of 0000 hours on 3 October intermittent firing continued. A senior officer counted eight dead students and six dead soldiers, but there were many more fatalities. A nearby Red Cross installation had one hundred twenty-seven wounded students and thirty wounded soldiers, but the majority of wounded soldiers had been taken to the military hospital. The general officer commanding a paratroop battalion that was engaged in the encounter received a bullet wound to the chest, and he is not expected to survive. The first shots were fired by the students who had taken up positions in the Edificio Chihuahua, an apartment building in the plaza. Some of the students were in possession of automatic weapons. Army troops who later entered this building discovered many weapons and considerable quantities of ammunition. An American expressed the opinion that this was a premeditated encounter provoked by the students.*

The last sentence gripped me. Who was this American?

One night Sofia and I decided to go out for dinner. She had

asked me to get dressed up, so I put on a jacket and shiny shoes, and doing so felt something like adulthood. After we arrived at the restaurant, we started ordering shots of tequila, which was something we had always loved to do together. Soon the table was littered with little shotglasses. We were drunk and, looking at the table, the stout cups seemed almost comical to me.

I thought I had to tell her that night; I thought I owed it to her. I was scared and excited, and though it didn't occur to me then, I realize now that what I felt must have been something like what my father felt when he told me. I wanted this disclosure to bond us, but it had to be done in the right way. There had to be complicity, not coercion. I knew there was an element of betrayal in what I was about to tell her. So I ordered one more shot, raised my glass to her, and leaned in over the table.

"I have something to tell you," I said. And I whispered my secret to her.

She began to laugh. It sounded forced and overly loud, a persistent, cackling exhortation that shuddered out of her mouth and lay between us.

"*Que?*" She squinted at me with incredulity. "What?"

I told her again: that my father had been a CIA spy, recruited in Mexico City in 1968.

She looked down at her plate, confused. Her eyes were rolling as if they had become momentarily unhinged, and somehow, in my drunken state, I thought she was attracted by what I had said. In fact, she was scared, but I didn't know that yet.

For a long moment we both just sat there, unsure of how to proceed. I wanted the moment to build to more intimacy, but it seemed to be slipping away instead.

To cover our unease, we kept on drinking tequila, ordering shot after shot, and each one brought more kisses and more declarations of love, and with them, more hollowness. A couple at a table next to ours kept watching us. We grew louder and more frenzied. The waiters brought more food, more tequila. We bought a bottle of wine, then another. When she went to the bathroom, I looked out at the room with drunken confidence, waiting for her return, the woman I had wanted to win. But when she did, she crumpled into her seat with a deflated look. She looked distant and troubled. She smiled, but not with her usual wide-mouthed grin. Instead, it was a half-smile. And she looked at me with pity.

Then she began to cry, and I knew I had waited too long to tell her. I asked her to talk about it with me, but she refused. She said she needed to think about what I had told her. She was kind and gentle, but also distant.

The next day, we went for a walk and she was quiet. At lunch she sat silently, playing with her food and shaking her head. When I asked what was wrong, tears began to roll down her face.

Afterward, we wandered through rows of stunted and dusty hedges in a tree-lined park called Los Viberos near my house. She rolled a joint, and the smoke drifted into the gray day. On the way back to my house, she stayed close to the walls. She studied the cracks in the pavement to avoid speaking, and left me at the door.

"I'm sorry," I pleaded with her. "I didn't know it would upset you so much."

Later she called, but we didn't say much. I didn't know what she could be imagining. I had revealed my family secret to many people, and had been doing it slowly, carefully, for many years, but that was the first time it had ever hit me with any kind of force. Sofia's response wasn't a knee-jerk reaction to a vague and undefined threat, and it wasn't simply ideological or naïve. Her fear was rooted in her personal history, the arrest of her father and his absence for the first years of her life. The CIA had likely been involved in the arrests, the kidnappings and disappearances and deaths of Mexicans. Yes, it was true, so had the Soviet Union, and so had various corrupt governments, and militias and thugs, and all sorts of random assortments of people. But none of them had quite the mystique, the power, or the backing that the CIA had, and for that reason she was well within her rights to be suspicious. I wasn't one of "them," but I had committed the sin of omission, and prolonged the truth for long enough that my motives became suspicious.

But just a few days later, Sofia and I were in a jeep on a work assignment, climbing up verdant slopes into the maze of palms and long grasses and cloudy forest canopies of Chiapas. Our nerves were still raw since my disclosure about my father. I knew she was having trouble digesting it. I had miscalculated badly.

When my father had told me about his work, back in that Michigan mini-mall, I had been almost giddy with happiness, so relieved to discover that everything I had been imagining had a source, and that I was part of something bigger. The fact that it came from a man I loved and admired had made it more powerful. He had chosen to induct me into his world, and I had been able to accept his challenge. In hindsight it almost seemed like a rite of passage, and so far I had succeeded at navigating its treachery.

I had tried to do the same thing with—or to—Sofia. Maybe it was because I loved her, and wanted to meld the worlds we came from together in a way that made personal and historical sense, but I thought I could induct her into my world the way my father had inducted me into his. I had failed. All I had managed to do was isolate and terrify her, and tell her that a chapter of her past she thought closed had now been reopened—and not just by anyone, but by someone to whom she was getting close. This was how she felt as we sat in that jeep, getting further and further away from the safety of the known world.

We were working on a story that involved spending some time in territory controlled by a leftist rebel leader named Marcos, whose exhortations to revolution had galvanized a population of marginalized indigenous people and turned them into a potent political force in the mid-1990s. Marcos lived in a more neutral-ized universe now. Mexican president Vicente Fox's government had marginalized him; there were rumors that he had even been bought off by Mexican intelligence. His area of influence had shrunk to a few villages in an autonomous zone deep within the jungle, surrounded by Mexican Army patrols, and camps where every major artery inside had become as tight as a U.S. border crossing. It resembled a war zone with an endangered zoo creature stuck inside.

In the back seat of our jeep was Daniel, a priest who had agreed to help us out. As we drove, Daniel asked me what kind of journalism I did, and I told him all sorts.

"You don't understand the history down here, what we've lived through in Latin America," Sofia shot at me with a spit of anger, as if I had been partly responsible for the continent's woes. "Every single war, every single conflict that has come here, America has had its bloody hands all over it."

She talked about Guatemala, and the 200,000 people who had died or gone missing in the civil war that had erupted after the CIA had helped to put a right-wing strongman in power. She railed on about Chile and Argentina and Panama and Nicaragua. I was ignorant of the facts, she said. I didn't realize the nefarious things my government was doing. I might even be complicit.

I shot back lamely that communism was worth fighting, but I was outmatched in that car and didn't push it. I was suddenly more unsure of what I believed than I had been in a long time. I had been wrong about the effect my father's life might have on her, so maybe I was wrong about other things, too. The war with Iraq was looming, and even there I found profound resistance to ideas I took for granted. I didn't necessarily believe Saddam Hussein was going to develop a nuclear bomb, but I didn't discount the possibility that he would do something else, something terrible and deadly. But even this, Sofia countered—presciently, it turned out, but at the time with little more than the conviction of her story and the family history that overshadowed everything else for her.

"Weapons of mass destruction," she scoffed. "Please."

But she also seemed to be saying that the revolution her father was fighting had never really ended. We were right in the middle of it, in fact. Couldn't I see that?

Several days later, back in Mexico City, I found another CIA memo. This one said:

> *Several trained observers at the scene reported that the encounter was a premeditated provocation by the students, who apparently were well armed. Student strike leaders, perhaps believing they had already won a significant victory in their reoccupation of the national university, after the troops withdrew, pledged to continue the campaign against the government and broadened their demands. They now appear determined to try to force cancellation of the Olympics, which they recognize as of the utmost importance to the government.*

I thought about my father again, on that rooftop thirty years earlier, imagining Ivan the communist twitch with discomfort as his plan to infiltrate the university came unraveling before him. And then I pictured once again those "trained observers" peering down on the slaughter from their rooftop perches above the plaza. And the two images seemed to splice together, the one on top of the other, so seamlessly it gave me chills.

CHAPTER 13

Southern Iraq, 2003

In early February of 2003, *Newsweek* sent me to the Middle East. War with Iraq was brewing. I spent a quick ten days in Baghdad before the bombs began falling, and left when my short-term visa expired. Then I traveled to Kuwait to follow the imminent ground invasion. I found Luc, the photographer with whom I had worked in Afghanistan, living in an abandoned house in the Kuwaiti desert. Luc knew a colonel in the Kuwaiti military who had promised to help us find a way across the border into Iraq. Until he called, we had nothing to do but wait.

The desert in Kuwait seemed such a wasteland. Goose farms near the Iraqi border yielded huge quantities of shit, which gathered along the sides of the roads and in the yard of the house where we were squatting. When the sandstorms blew, so did the shit, smearing the world with its stench. That patch of desert already felt abandoned to the war. There was no question that it would slide in of its own weight; it was just a question of when. The border—the constant pounding of tanks, the hovering helicopters, and the military police patrolling—was a trembling faultline.

A few days after I arrived, the colonel called. A huge convoy of Americans would soon be moving across the border, he said.

He suggested we get ready. We arranged a meeting place and time. Luc and I each drove our own trucks, which we had rented in Kuwait City. We needed two to transport our gear, and also to have a backup in case one broke down.

On the appointed day, the colonel led us into the desert. The road quickly petered out and turned into soft, pliable sand that wound toward the west, through reeds and grass. He was following ancient roadways unused by all but a few shepherds. If we got separated, I would have no idea how to get back.

Eventually we arrived at a series of berms and loose fencing. The colonel stopped his car at a place where the fencing had come apart. The remains of a dirt road crossing into Iraq were visible. The colonel stepped up to the barrier and ripped the barbed wire away, tossing it aside with a flourish. He gestured into the void in invitation. "I stop here," he said, and chuckled. His sunglasses were low on his nose, and he looked over their tops at us. "That is Iraq."

He told us to follow the road, which ran parallel with the border, for another few miles, until we came to a larger berm and a bigger road. Within the hour, he said, an American convoy would come through there, and we could join it.

"*Viens,*" Luc said, and before I could even protest, he was through, skidding close to the fence and throwing up swirls of sand.

I could have left, but I didn't. I could have walked away from him, and the assignment altogether. Instead, I followed him in.

It wasn't long before we found the berm and the road. As the colonel had predicted, a massive convoy of American hardware was soon rampaging through the gap in the sand. We joined it, much to the surprise of the soldiers. When I stalled my truck in the middle of their invasion, an American colonel came back to investigate. I told him that we were journalists, and we wanted to join the march to Baghdad. He beamed. "Why not?" he said, and smiled. "It's a free country now, ain't it?"

Things went well with the convoy for a few hours, but by that night Luc and I had been kicked out. We weren't "embedded," which meant we hadn't signed up to any military rules about how to behave and what to report, so we were considered a risk and a danger. They worried that we might disclose information that would put them at risk. The major who shooed us away left us on a hill in the darkness and pointed back to the dark shapes where the rest of the convoy was tethered for the night.

"Stay here," he growled. "Don't come any closer to us. You can stay here tonight, and then you're on your own. Don't follow us." So I spent a freezing night huddled in my sleeping bag in the driver's seat, ready to pull away at any moment. Now and again the earth shuddered as bombs reached their targets. I slept only fitfully, waking every hour or so, waiting for the sun, and heat, and some semblance of safety to come.

The next morning, we sat on the dunes and watched the Americans' lurching crawl. Then we just drove, further and further north, into that morass of war. Minefields lay to the south and the north, and we skirted around them, sneaking past camps, sentries, lines of tanks, and rangers.

As we traveled, larger groups of American soldiers appeared out of nowhere. The desert swarmed with the lumbering shapes of those convoys. When they were close, you could hear their rumbling and see the life inside of them, like some uncoupled train from a lost world, carrying its survivors into the future. Some convoys were heading the way we wanted to go; others were detouring. Sometimes one group or another was clearing a field of mines, or securing it from looters. This way, some of the soldiers would tell us, when we asked where the most forward groups were. This way or that way, no one really seemed to know. But Luc had a GPS, and we used it to navigate toward what seemed like the right place to be.

For several days, he raced along and I followed. The sandy fields were filled with American tanks, and their turrets beaded on us as we passed, swiveling in unison and following us until we were out of sight again. We slept in our cars, in the lees of dunes, or on the open ground. At night, the far horizons glowed with bombing, and it became impossible to distinguish what manner of destruction was hurtling earthward—human-made or otherwise. Soon it just seemed to merge. The fighter planes flew over it all, racing in and out on bombing runs.

Some nights I wanted to leave—just turn around and go home. One night I called a colleague and told him so. Come on back, he told me. But I couldn't, really; I didn't trust my own navigation skills. So I kept going.

As we raced on to Baghdad, the world smelled tangy with diesel. Long hours passed when all I followed was the dust trail Luc's truck left for me as track. Helicopters sometimes thundered by above us, the bodies inside impassive. I had no idea where I was. But the small lines of the GPS led us north, toward a highway where we knew all the American convoys were gathering: Route 8.

Slowly, the land began to change. The desert started to give way to wet and muddy terrain. Marshes and reeds were visible, and past them, long fields of dark, tilled earth—the first signs of residents in several days.

One afternoon, around 2:00 p.m., we clambered up out of a long ditch in the four-wheel drives and emerged onto asphalt. The engines whined and ticked as the dust swirled off in the sudden stillness, and we came shuddering to a stop. We had come to an intersection and a bridge, and we were stopping to wait for an American convoy. They were going to move soon, we had learned, and we planned to follow behind. It seemed safer to be ensconced within the convoy, rather than drifting across the desert on our own.

Eventually, the road began to rumble. The convoy arrived, and we joined them. As we were doing so, dark figures appeared across the bridge. They waded knee-deep in water, carrying tools and bushels of grasses over their shoulders. Some of them looked at us, and then kept going about their work as if we didn't much matter.

We drove on, but when we came into a small town, massive crowds had turned out along the sides of the road to see the Americans. The convoy came to a stop. Soldiers milled around their tanks with their helmets unbuckled or under their arms. Children ran around screaming with glee, and bands of young people tittered nervously along the road's edges. We edged our trucks into the crowds.

Luc wanted to take pictures, so he stopped his truck and stood on the roof to get a better perspective. I stayed behind the wheel of mine. A nervous man came up to my window. He had a sickly smile and rotten teeth, and his mouth was twitching. I couldn't tell if he was dangerous, scared, or both. He put his hand through the open window, and I shook it. His eyes were wide. "No good," he said, motioning to the disruption all around us. "No good." It wasn't clear to me if he meant the invasion wasn't good, or the situation the invasion was in the process of altering. Then he leaned in quickly and hissed at me: "Bad people here, bad people." Before I could respond, he was away, trailing a flow of children behind him.

When the convoy left, we kept driving with them, toward Baghdad. A few hours later the convoy stopped again, and I thought we should too, but Luc wanted to push on. There was another convoy ahead of us, and he thought we could catch up to it before dark. We didn't know how far forward it was, so we raced ahead. Pretty soon we were going fifty, then sixty, then eighty miles an hour. The convoy watched us pass, and some waved, shouted, or cursed. And then, as suddenly as they had appeared, they were gone, and we were alone on that road.

It was a vast landscape we were in, and we the only things that seemed to be moving. The sound of the wind was furious, and I rolled my window up quickly.

Suddenly, I saw a man standing by the side of the road. He was wearing green fatigues. He was tall, bearded, and wore a green hat with a bill, Nicaraguan-style. He had a very big gun, and was holding it at waist-level. As soon as Luc's car reached him, the man began to fire. By the time I came within his range, it was too late to turn around. I had hardly realized he was armed until I was on him.

"*Ils ont des armes, ils ont des armes!*" I heard Luc over the walkie-talkie. Weapons, he was saying, they had weapons.

It all came at the same time, the sound of his voice telling me that the man, or men, had weapons, and the sound of the bullets as they began to hit my car. I realized that they were shooting at me too. I sped up. It had rained earlier, so the ground was wet and dark, including parts of the road, and alongside the road were ditches of mud streaked with shallow and putrid pools of waste. I heard the rounds as they hit my truck. They punctured the metal, penetrating the car and exiting on the other side. There was more than one man firing now. I ducked this way and that. I sped up; I slowed down. I heard glass shatter and figured the bullets were getting closer to me. Luc had gone silent on the radio. I saw his car tearing down the road in front of me, into the distance. And then it disappeared altogether. It just vanished; I was alone. And I collided with my fear—I realized that what I was in was much, much bigger than me.

I passed through the checkpoint, the gas station, which the attackers were apparently using as cover, but I was still under a fierce hail. The bullets were getting louder, more pronounced, and more frequent. Suddenly, the back of my vehicle caught on fire—I could smell it burning. They must have hit the gas tank.

I knew I had to do something. Or, rather, my body knew it, and it took over. As more of the windows around me began to shatter, I ducked. As I did, I swung the wheel to the right. But I realized almost immediately that I was going to run off the road, so I veered back left, without being able to see anything. I felt the vehicle begin to fishtail. Shit. Overcompensation of the wheel. I swung back up into the seat to try and regain control. But as soon as I was upright, I saw how far I had swung left, and thought I was going to crash. So I braked as hard as possible.

Luc was long gone by then. There was nothing ahead of me on that road except a long line of gray asphalt that led into a foreboding distance. Behind me were the attackers. And farther behind them still was the American Army, slouching along, or perhaps not moving at all. That stretch of road became, in those moments, my own purgatory—some seventh layer of hell, a *huis clos*. The possibility of death became real.

The next thing I knew, I completely lost control of my car. My erratic steering left me up on one set of wheels, and then the other. I could feel them shuddering beneath me, coming loose, tearing away, unhinging completely. I tried to regain control of the wheel, but it was too late. I was headed for the island that ran down the middle of the road.

I hit it with my right front tire and felt the car flip up and onto its side. There was a light pole on the island, and my airborne car headed for it, turning and coming crashing to a stop against it. The last things I heard were the clunking, crashing sound of twisting metal, and then the slosh of liquid.

When I came to, I was sitting upright. But the rest of the world was wrong. My feet were on a window, and the window was on the ground. In front of me was the windshield, now lengthwise. The smell of gasoline permeated the compartment. The car was on its side. I didn't know how long I had been out, but it couldn't have been for more than a few seconds because almost as soon as I woke, I heard the sound of pinging again. The attackers were still shooting. The bottom of the car, the hard metal section, was facing them, and whatever was hitting the vehicle was ricocheting off—pinging around me, but not penetrating into the cab. Perhaps they were far away. Perhaps they were bad shots. It didn't really matter why; the point was they were still aiming for me. I looked up at the window above my head, which was miraculously intact. It was like a skylight, a small square into which the dull light of afternoon poured. Terrified, I pictured one of the attackers popping his head into that beautiful frame and finding me. It was an image of unspeakable horror, that face looming into my life and blocking out the light. There would be two possibilities: the first was that he would lean back, aim his weapon through the window, and finish me; the second was that he would take me hostage. Neither was acceptable.

Realizing this, my body leaped into force. My feet lifted off the floor and began to kick at the window. I was wearing military-issue boots that I had picked up at a store in Kuwait City. I kicked, and the window didn't budge. I kept kicking. I kicked until I saw a crack, then another. A web began to form. I kicked as hard as I could; I kicked the shit out of that window. A small hole began to form, a tiny thing at the center of the web, and I kicked it until it became about as big as my head. I could hear the attackers shouting nearby. The firing continued. I heard feet. I heard the click of chambers, the dumping of bags, running, panting, breathing.

I wanted to put my head out of the window and appeal to the attackers in my father's calm voice: wait, stop for a moment and let's discuss this. Smile, he might have said, you can't be angry if you're laughing. In my hazy state, it seemed reasonable to do such a thing; more than that, it seemed like the right thing to do. But I couldn't do it because I was still terrified.

This was it, I thought, the way my life will end; as Yevtushenko put it, that moment of frankness at the party, when the enemy crept up. It was too fast. I had seen the aftermath of people who had been in positions just like this. That was so much of what war was about—seeing the aftermath, the wreckage. And I had wanted to get closer, as close as I could. Now I was as close to war and death as I had ever been, and I only wanted time to stop so I could escape.

Ideas of war are necessarily big. They are about good and evil. There is a reason we use the phrase "war zone"—because it marks an area inside of which the world is different. Everything inside that zone is different: the energy of people, their motivations, their fears, their capacity for good and evil. All operate on a different frequency. The closer you get to the center of that zone, as if approaching a bull's-eye, the more clearly you are able to see those motivations and experience them for yourself. The evil that people in wars were capable of, experienced veterans and correspondents would often say, was equaled by extreme goodness. I parroted that view because I wanted some of it to rub off on me. But I also felt I had a real notion of what it meant.

My father, it had always seemed to me, was involved in big ideas, too. The "struggle against communism" was one such idea, and in its purest form it was an absolute. Defeat concerned millions of people, potentially. War wasn't just about fighting. It was about years and years spent cultivating a mindset that you believed would somehow triumph, even over the unseen inventions of future humanities. Those years on Camp Peary, spent teaching generations of young people how to think about their world and their country, and how to defend it, were part of an organized system, perpetuating itself year after year. It was a climate of constant war sheeted with the thinnest patina of civility and bucolic peace. Even as a child, I could sense that. Tyranny, liberty—these were big, attractive ideas, and they stirred something in me. It was rousing to hear speeches about freedom or throwing off the yoke of oppression. I wanted something of those big ideas for myself. But in that moment, on that desolate stretch of biblical road, there were none. It was just a bunch of guys trying to kill me; it was paltry and unexalted. They had their reasons, and they were the same ones in the speeches—resisting occupation and fighting for their country—but they no longer seemed grand because I realized that at the center of it all there was only fear.

Finally I managed to create a hole in the window large enough to escape through. I poked my head out and looked around. Nothing. First my head, then my shoulders—I pushed my way out of the cab and fell onto the ground. For a moment I lay there, unsure of what to do. I was afraid the car might explode. I considered popping my head up above the hood, waving a white shirt, and surrendering to the men who must still be nearby, but they would likely shoot me. Then I heard them shouting gleefully, probably thinking I lay dead inside the car. There was some more shooting, but it was sporadic and it didn't seem directed toward me. I guessed they were about two hundred yards away, even though I could hear their laughter as if they were right on top of me.

My car was up on the median strip. From where I was hiding I could see that the strip stretched off far down the road, an island made of dirt about two yards wide. The attackers might be on their way over to investigate the car, and loot its considerable riches—a computer, two satellite phones, several thousand dollars, multiple tanks of gas, warm clothes, a generator, and the little brass horse my father had given me. If they found me there, well . . .

So I began to crawl away, along the median. I lay on my belly and made myself as flat as possible. I smeared my face as far down into the dirt as I could, filling my mouth with it. I closed my eyes, ostrich-like, and tried to keep my movements as infintesimal as possible as I crawled forward. I was protected by the truck for the first few yards, but was soon exposed. A few more shots rang out randomly. I lay still for a moment, wondering if they had seen me, trying not to breathe too much. A dung beetle appeared next to my face, moving doggedly. I had never seen a more endearing creature, with its perfectly rounded shell; its crooked, spiny legs; and its measured gait. It was going in the same direction. I began to crawl again, too.

I moved and didn't look back. I must have crawled on my belly for at least another hundred yards, like a lizard, pushing my legs up to my hips and back down, swiveling my torso as I did. Please, I kept muttering to myself, please, please, please. And fuck: fuck, fuck, fuck. I did that until I was far enough away that

I could get on my hands and knees, and I moved along in that way for a bit. I was far enough away by then that I felt safer. But I was in the open, on a median strip in the middle of the desert. I had nothing; everything had been destroyed and left behind. The road ahead was filled, I was then sure, with similar people who would kill me if they saw me coming. And there was no question of going back. I couldn't stand up. There was still plenty of daylight left, and not a hill in sight to hide behind. So I just crouched and looked around. I felt like a wild animal—I would have attacked anything that came my way. I was panting furiously and muttering to myself. There were bloodstains on my pants. I must have stayed that way for several minutes.

And then I heard a low rumble in the distance. It was faint, at first, and then it grew louder, and unmistakably stronger. It was the U.S. Army coming my way.

The first vehicles that arrived were tanks. The only people visible in them were a couple of small, goggle-wearing heads, like warts on a turtle. They rolled on by. I thought one would stop, but none seemed to. So I began to wave. As more tanks passed, trucks began to appear, then some Humvees and Bradley fighting vehicles, but those too passed. I got up some courage and stood up. I began to wave more vigorously, and started to run alongside the convoy as it passed. The noise was deafening, but I began to shout anyway. Pretty soon I was running as fast as I could, shouting at the top of my lungs. Still no one stopped. Eventually a few soldiers began waving back at me, like beauty queens on a float. I must have looked so dirty, so ragged and unshorn that they mistook me for a war refugee. "Stop," I kept yelling, "I'm an American." But no one did. And soon the tanks and large trucks were all gone.

Following them were other trucks and smaller vehicles. I ran closer and shouted even louder. Some of the soldiers smiled, or gave me a thumbs-up. More than one made a motion for me to lie down and pointed to the rear of the convoy, as if to illustrate that he understood what had happened, and that more danger was on the way. A couple of times I did actually lie down, but then, seeing the convoy rushing past, jumped up and began chasing it again. I was jogging alongside it, waving my arms when I could, shouting, smiling—anything to get someone to stop. And eventually someone did stop. A Humvee pulled out of the line and rolled off to the side of the road. The man in the passenger seat beckoned me over through the window. I approached with my hands up in the air. "I'm an American," I said. "I got attacked. Please help me."

The soldier had his hand on his pistol. "What are you doing out here?" he asked.

"I'm a reporter," I said. "Reporter. I'm American."

"Who do you work for?"

"*Newsweek. Newsweek* magazine."

His face broke into a broad smile. "Really? Cool. Get in."

We pulled off, and the specialist in the driver's seat spoke up. "We saw you go racing by us back there," he said. "We thought you was one of them CIA guys running around."

"No!" I laughed. "Nope."

He turned around and cast me a quizzical glance.

"I promise," I said. "Not the CIA."

I couldn't reach my father that night. He was in Afghanistan. For a while, though, the world—the parts that were paying attention—thought I was dead. Someone even wrote a story about it. My editors called Janet and told her they feared I had been killed. Faced with my possible death, Janet suddenly seemed to melt, overcome with reserves of love she had, but had never been able to show. Yet on the other side of the country, my mother hadn't heard a thing. I wanted to spare her the pain of worrying, so when I called I chose not to tell her very much about what had happened.

I finally reached my father by email. He was spending more and more time in Kabul. The psychological war was growing, and he was deep inside it.

About a week after the attack in Iraq, the military kicked me out of the unit that had saved my life and sent me back to Kuwait

City. I began to dissociate. It started one day when I began to have death fugues. I was stopped at a traffic light when I suddenly became acutely aware that I wasn't certain any longer whether I was dead or alive. I realized I was confused about it.

The light changed. Cars began to honk. I wasn't sure what to do. Eventually, I determined that I was alive, and drove on. But the fugues continued for weeks, even as I returned to Baghdad for several months that spring and summer to report on the incipient American occupation.

Over time, they morphed into a deep and unshakable depression. When I finally left Iraq, in August 2003, I spent a few days in New York, seeing some friends. Eventually I made my way to my father's house in Washington State, but I don't remember much about that trip. Years later, my father told me that we had taken a hike, and at one point I had stopped in the middle of the trail and started sobbing. He had put his arms around me and asked what was wrong. I was afraid of his death, I told him. I was terrified.

What I do remember is arriving in Seattle the day afterward. I had a hotel downtown, overlooking the wharf, and I called him from there.

"Is everything okay?" he asked. "I'm worried about you."

I mumbled something noncommittal just to reassure him and hung up. I went into the bathroom, turning on the shower. Steam began to fill up the room. I stood for a while watching the shower spew. Then, fully clothed, I climbed in and sank down onto the floor, under the heat, and dissolved into tears. I stayed that way for hours.

Back in Mexico, where I returned after spending six months reporting from Iraq, I rented a hotel room high above the rest of the city, and sat in front of the mirror, staring at myself. I believed my soul was infected. I wanted to kill it, and in the process kill a part of me. But I didn't know how, so I sat in my room and prayed for it to end. Panic swarmed across me in waves that seemed unending. When I wasn't at the mirror, I couldn't get off the floor, or stop crying. The thought came to me: was that why I went to Iraq, to kill myself? I tried to purge myself of it, to cry myself clean. Sometimes the old self-punishing voices came to the surface, and I could hear myself saying things over and over. I choked on my breath. The face staring back at me from the mirror was full of hate. I tried to scream, but couldn't. I sweated and drooled. I vomited and dry-heaved and spat, and still it didn't go away.

I began to see a psychiatrist. He told me that I was having borderline dissociation. I looked it up in a medical dictionary. The fugues were a "state or period of loss of awareness of one's identity, often coupled with flight from one's usual environment, associated with certain forms of hysteria or epilepsy." That made sense; I had had several epileptic episodes in college. The psychiatrist told me I was bordering on psychosis, recommending I begin a treatment of antipsychotic medication. I refused.

The depression got worse. And as it did, I realized that very often my thoughts were coming back to my father. Again and again, whenever I sat down to write, or to look at myself in the mirror, I talked to my father as if he were there. Sometimes these conversations were filled with love and tenderness; at other times they were hate-filled screeds. I thought of the fugue, the loss of one's identity, which was exactly how I felt whenever I thought about him. I began to fear that I was losing my mind. I was so paralyzed by fear and anxiety that I almost gave up work altogether. My mind was ragged and violent, as if one part of me was pursuing another. The more I tried to stifle my fear, the more it raged, until I could no longer control it at all, and invariably I would sink to the floor, or the bathtub, or the bed, unable to move or speak, or sometimes even to cry.

"You don't have a fucking clue about who I am," I wrote one day to my father. "I would bring you down here and treat you like a king, to show you that I can do it, that I can be stronger than you. Those are elements you'll have to deal with. That's how much hate I have inside of me."

Then, on another day, I wrote to him, "I know you're never going to stop loving me. Deep, deep down, someplace that I've never been, somewhere truer than I've ever been with myself, or anyone else, I believe those words."

But the more I thought about him, the more I realized that there was something missing. There was a barrier to our experience of each other, but I couldn't see it. I could only feel it.

I called my father one night. I was so depressed by then that I don't remember much about the conversation at all, except that at some point I tried to confess my fears to him again.

He said, "Don't worry, son, you're not going to lose me. I'm not going to stop calling you, or loving you, or writing you."

But then one day, amid the updates about what was happening in Kabul, he wrote to me that he had run across another American journalist with much experience in Afghanistan. During the course of their discussion, he had told her that his son was a journalist who had been in Afghanistan. Paranoia, which was growing more acute by the day, swept over me. I wrote back a feverish reply:

> I wish you hadn't chosen to tell her about me. I can't emphasize to
> you how small our world is. It may do no harm to you, or to your
> work, to tell people you meet about me. But it could do enormous
> harm to me, or to people I work with. It's very important to me
> that you make no reference to me. It comes down to security, and to
> credibility. I don't want to put mine, or anybody else's, in jeopardy.

I told him I hoped that he understood, and that I knew I was being paranoid. "It's quite possible," I went on, "that at some later time, with people I know I can trust, the situation would be different. In any event, it has nothing to do with you as a person."

My father wrote back right away. "I understand completely your not wanting to have us linked by anybody other than somebody you might trust and so designate. I do want to emphasize that the journalist didn't ever learn my name or with whom I was affiliated, other than a general reference to aid projects. However, I appreciate you reminding me of the walls that must be maintained."

The walls that must be maintained.

This correspondence between us was the first time since my childhood that either of us had explicitly acknowledged the existence of the big secret between us, and the need to treat it with care. Its sudden emergence shook me. Those walls were inside both of us, and they were becoming harder for me to manage. Sometimes I wanted to tear them down, rip them apart, destroy them in a mighty cataclysm. But more often than not I found myself erecting more of them, building others, constructing new and ingenious labyrinths for us to creep through. Maybe both of us were rats, trapped in a maze of our own design.

Sometimes—often, in fact—it was easier just to escape. So I returned to Iraq in the late spring of 2004. As soon as I was there I cadged some Ritalin off a friend, and began a monthlong speed-induced binge of manic work. I wrote for hours on end. I listened to one song, David Gray's "Babylon," for nine hours straight one afternoon. I took needless risks, being driven at all hours through dodgy parts of Baghdad in the back seat of a sedan with the window rolled down. I visited warlords in terribly overrun slums, went to every car-bombing site I could, and partied with great abandon with anyone who was willing.

I carried on with a hazy desire for self-obliteration until, one day, I collapsed on my bed with pounding chest pains. I felt my pulse. It was racing at more than 150 beats a minute.

This period of frenzied activity went on for several weeks, until my allotted time in Baghdad once again came to an end. Then, a week later, I left Iraq and flew to Europe to find my father again, this time in the former Yugoslavia.

CHAPTER 14

Sarajevo, 2004

He spread his arms out, rushed through the airport crowd, and swept me up. My stepmother was nearby, smiling, and the sight of the two of them together, once again in Yugoslavia, was jarring in the extreme. But there we were, standing in the gray morning light outside the terminal of the Sarajevo airport. As in Afghanistan, my father was here on a contract.

The road into the city was walled on one side by rows of low-rise apartments. They went on for mile after mile, grim Soviet-era blocks containing hundreds of small apartments. To the south stretched long fields that once indicated the demarcation line during the Balkan civil wars. From the apartment balconies hung potted plants and vines, colored bed sheets, and ribbons of drying clothes; stuffed onto their decks were bicycles and refrigerators and doghouses and cartons overflowing with junk. And everywhere along the surfaces of the walls, like a two-toned mosaic, were the distinctive pockmarks of bullet holes. The siege had destroyed the city, divided the population, and sent each side to the barricades.

Sarajevo had been one of the most gruesome chapters in the civil war that had torn the country apart. Murderous Serb nationalists, working to carry out Slobodan Milosevic's aims of ethnically cleansing his homeland of Muslims, had targeted Sarajevo in 1997. Serb fighters took up positions on the hills surrounding the city and shelled it continuously for months, and then years, lobbing mortars and rockets down into the center with greater and greater abandon, and sniping at civilians, often women and children. Bosnian Muslim fighters fought back, and the streets of Sarajevo were turned into the site of one of the most intense urban war zones since World War II.

By the time I arrived, direct from Iraq, the war had ended—sort of. Milosevic had been captured. City life had resumed a normal pace, and shops and businesses were booming once again. Many of the Serbs had retreated to an internationally mandated Serb Republic in the hills just above the city. United Nations peacekeeping vehicles patrolled the whole area in armored personnel carriers. We passed some of them on our way down the road formerly known as Sniper Alley, heading to lunch at a nearby Muslim restaurant. My father enjoyed it because of the beef sausage and bread.

I asked him what he was doing here.

Almost a decade earlier, Serb militias under General Ratko Mladic had entered the Bosnian Muslim enclave of Srebrenica and laid siege to its residents. Serbian soldiers slaughtered over seven thousand Muslim men and boys, and buried them in mass graves. The two most notorious leaders of the massacre were still at large and believed to be hiding somewhere in the Republika Srpska. If they weren't there, the people who were would know their whereabouts, my father said.

"So you're hunting war criminals?" I said, only half joking.

He grinned and didn't say much. He swilled his beer and ate a slice of the sausage the waiters had brought. The sun came out, and his glasses darkened slightly. If the peacekeepers left Bosnia, he said, the fighting between the Muslims and the Serbs would begin all over again.

It was disheartening to hear all this. War, or the possibility of war, had become pervasive and constant in my life by now.

Outside on the restaurant's patio, there were several young girls wearing tight pants and bright shirts and talking on their phones. Iraq and Bosnia were both Muslim countries. I saw the bullet-ridden apartment buildings and thought that some things looked the same. I remembered my childhood girlfriend in Belgrade, a bucktoothed Serbian girl named Tatyana who had held hands with me in a bathroom at a birthday party when I was seven. I wondered if she was here. As I watched an armored stabilization-forces peacekeeping vehicle roll down the street, headed toward a military base adjacent to the airport, I wondered if she was even alive.

After the war, the Islamists had returned to Bosnia and started to build. Sunni Wahhabists came from Saudi Arabia and Kuwait and elsewhere in the Arab world. Shiite Iran was also sending faith-peddlers to Bosnia, and they set up mosques to compete with their Sunni enemies. All over, in lieu of housing or schools or clinics or shelters, in lieu of literacy programs and food payments, the Islamists were building mosques. Many of them had fought in Afghanistan, in the jihad against the Soviets. In downtown Sarajevo, young Wahhabi men, bearded and dressed in short white pants and skullcaps, walked purposefully down the streets as if they owned them—and in some ways, they did. Outside the capital, in little villages, Wahhabi preachers were still recruiting for a holy war against the west. Most of the Bosnian Muslims I saw wore Western clothes, smoked cigarettes, drank alcohol, and acted, in most respects, like the secular Europeans they had always been. But the fervent religiosity of peacetime made my dad angry, and righteous. He detested the intrusion of so many mosques, brought by missionaries and zealots, into the country-side; they were bound to sow division and hatred.

I had spent hours with angry Islamic zealots in Iraq, and they were rarely comforting encounters. Looking out at the bullet-scarred alleyways, it was okay to confess these prejudices. It was just to my father. But I wondered if we, too, sounded like fanatics, besmirching these houses of God and lamenting their intrusion into the fabric of the land.

After our lunch, we sat in his apartment and looked out. The city was rose-colored and hazy, nestled in a valley whose hillsides bloomed in spring when the winds came and swept the winter smog away. Flocks of pigeons drifted over the rooftops like schools of fish. It was a beautiful, almost a medieval, sort of peace. But it was only when the muezzin began the call to prayer, like a massive injection of breath into a quiet body, that the city suddenly and immediately felt complete.

One day, shortly after Janet had flown home, my father and I went for a drive. Not even ten years had passed since the worst of the fighting, and yet the land seemed so peaceful. Blue and green fields, filled with cows and horses, slanted off in all directions. Peasants baled hay with pitchforks and stacked what they gathered around wooden poles. The sky was light blue, and high up, a few wisps of clouds were scattered about. We began to pass small villages, and from the road we could see the tops of minarets rising up over the hillsides in some places. It was in villages like this that some of the more radical preachers had made their homes.

My dad pulled off onto a side road, and we veered down a muddy track that led to a small village. Here, too, the fields were full of oxen, carts, and wooden plows. There were several small houses, all looking freshly painted, with bright tin roofs and sturdy metal doors, in the final stages of construction. A few stores lined the only road. At its end, under some low hills, was a giant white mosque—also under construction, but further advanced than the houses. It was the tallest building in town, and held a simple minaret that reached as high as the pines surrounding it.

During the war, the Serbs had leveled this little village, my dad told me. Marauding soldiers had burned the houses, killed the men who hadn't fled, and thrown them and their pitchforks into these same fields. They raped the women. Some people had run away into the nearby hills, which were mined. A few escaped that way. Many more were killed in the forests. All across Bosnia, this pattern was repeated over and over again—villages like this one dotted the hills in every direction. All of them were now being rebuilt.

My father was watching the workers. "They were all massacred," he said with a grimace, referring to the town's previous inhabitants—fathers and sons, mothers and daughters.

He studied the men while I studied his face. It went from admiration to an indecipherable anger and back. He seemed proud of their toil, and then vengeful of the crime that had been committed against them, and then just downcast. At times like these, he had a tendency to become overwhelmed with emotion.

He told me a story about a CIA friend of his, Mark, who had been given the task of interrogating a Viet Cong man during the war. The man had refused to talk. For days, he had been completely uncooperative. Mark knew the man came from a farm where he had, as a child, become very fond of milk. Mark was also raised on a farm, so he sympathized. One day, in an attempt to break the man, Mark brought in a tall glass of cold milk and put it on the table. He didn't withhold it—he gave the glass to the man and let him drink it. He did this every day for several days. Finally, he tried again to question him. "You come from a farm and so do I," Mark said. "And you can go back and have all the milk you want if you talk to me." At first the man resisted, but eventually he broke, charmed by the spell of the milk that Mark was providing.

"All he wanted was a glass of cold milk," my father said. He looked like he was about to cry. Was breaking people that simple, I wondered, a mere question of getting them to see past their seemingly superficial differences to the deeper things they shared? Or making them believe that something which long ago held value and had since been discarded or forgotten was now, once again, available? If this were true, all of us could, with the simplest gestures, the most casual of acts, break one another. We did it all the time, in fact.

My father had always tried to be complicit in my journalism somehow. He was constantly suggesting stories, sending me articles, and emailing me thoughts about some piece I had just done, or was about to do, or should plan on doing at some point in the future. His enthusiasm was infectious, and I found myself pursuing his ideas more often than not. There was nothing he wasn't curious about or interested in, especially if it dealt with Iraq and the folly of the supposed war on terror—which struck me as odd, since he was now toiling in its service.

One day he suggested that we travel to a nearby town to interview some Islamist imams together. We could both pose as journalists, he suggested, and I had to remind him that I actually was one. It would have been fun to go on an adventure like that, but it veered dangerously close to a border I didn't want to cross. It wasn't between journalism and spying—by now I knew they were close cousins, with only a smattering of differences to distinguish them. But I wanted to keep the privacy of my own work, my own sources and methods, to myself.

Right across the street from my father's apartment in Sarajevo was a three-story residential building, fairly nondescript. Inside one of the apartments, he told me one day, lived a man the local Bosnian intelligence services suspected of being an Islamist leader with dubious connections to unspecified terrorist organizations. Sometimes in the afternoons, when my dad came home from work, we would peer out the window to see if the man was home. One day, we looked out to see the man running up and down a set of stairs, loading things into his car. My imagination went wild for a moment, and I had the thrilling sensation that I was watching some nefarious plot unfold before my eyes—packages of nitroglycerine being shuttled quickly from a basement warehouse into the trunk of a waiting suicide car, for example. But then I heard shouting, and looked up to see a woman standing on the landing with packages of food and a yellow blanket. He hurried up the stairs and took the load from her arms. I watched as he carefully descended the steps again and put the picnic into the backseat of his car. She yelled something at him again, and he leaned out and yelled back. They were both smiling.

"Looks like they're going for a picnic," my father said, and grinned.

"Terrorist picnic?" I joked.

"No pork there."

"Nope."

I let the curtain fall.

"Want some peanuts?" he asked.

"Sure," I said.

As he left the room he called back, "Wanna pee, nut?"

One night soon after, we were talking in his apartment. The lights of Sarajevo were lit up brightly. Inside, we had let it get dark.

I was feeling better than I had been the previous year, but now and again I descended into a severe depression. I had tried to stave it off on this trip, but was now failing. Once again, my father's presence seemed to have brought it on. Or I had made it so.

We got into an argument. I accused my father of being manipulative with me, of using the skills I believed he had honed in his professional life to subtly shape what I thought, or how I thought it, or what my reaction to something ought to be. I can't remember the details of the argument, but I remember shouting at him, "You think you're the only one who can manipulate, but I can see what you're doing. Remember, I learned it from the best—I learned it from you."

I had felt paranoia about my father before. But now I couldn't shake the conviction that sometimes I wasn't seeing the real man. My belief was based on the smallest things—a question whose ulterior motive seemed a little too transparent, a suggestion by him that I felt some way that I didn't, the self-confident appraisal about a person or an event that hinted at more knowledge than he was letting on. I wondered if I was being too cynical. Was I seeing patterns of speech and behavior that weren't really there? And was the acuteness of my feelings due to the fact that I thought my behavior was toxic, that I had manipulative tendencies? It was upsetting to think of these possibilities.

I knew I had the same reserves of sentimental ardor as my father—I cried easily in movies or in songs. I remembered something my mother had said: exaggerated behavior in a person usually means just the opposite of what it implies. So I wondered about my father and myself—did we have an exaggerated sense of sentimentality that perhaps disguised intolerance for human weakness in other areas? I wondered whether my father and I shared a vein of cruelty sometimes, and whether that was driving my depression.

There was one incident when I was about six. I used to ask my dad permission for everything, including going to the toilet. One day, as I stood at his knee scarcely able to hold it any longer, I asked him if I could go. He smiled down at me and said no, I couldn't.

I begged. "Daddy, I feel the pee pee so badly."

"No," he said.

I felt like I was going to pee in my pants, and almost did. I jumped around. I sweated. He kept saying no.

Finally, just as I was about to wet myself, he relented and told me that I didn't have to ask permission at home the way I did in school.

So, over the next week in Sarajevo I scrutinized everything: every blink of his eyes, every modulation of his voice, every kink of his body that I thought could signify something—treachery, honesty, sincerity, or some guide to the workings of his mind; I didn't quite know what I was looking for.

My anger at perceived slights took on epic proportions. When we were driving along the highway out of Sarajevo, he pulled over onto the side of the road to show me a beautiful view of the city from a rocky outcrop the Serbs had used as a sniper and rocket position. I didn't want to get out of the car, and told him so. I was tired, and the car felt like a sanctuary. And I wanted us to finish the conversation we were having. But he stopped the engine and jumped out. He motioned for me to come over. I refused. Finally I relented, but said I would only look for a moment. I acknowledged the view thuggishly, and retreated to the car. When he got in, I could see that he was hurt: sad, likely, that I hadn't wanted to share an experience he had no doubt been thinking about showing me for days, and probably weeks. But I couldn't control my anger. I shouted that, just for once, I wanted to be able to finish a bloody conversation without having to stop and look at every goddamned view that came along. In my mind, small details like this showcased his manipulative need to control things, to regulate the conversation or sightseeing so that it proceeded at a pace that was comfortable for him. For me, this was maddening.

That night I told him I thought he had used his spy powers, such as they were, to dubious effect. I didn't see how that could *not* be the case. After all, how could you spend your days tracking agents, gathering intelligence, and using all of your powers of persuasion and concentration to maximum effect, and then simply turn it off with your family, or even with yourself? I doubted if I could do the same with my friends and acquaintances, and indeed had trouble doing so when it came to my reporting. It was exhausting to be on the search for so much of the time. Unless the subjects were official spokesmen, journalists generally trusted those they interviewed on the ground; but if you were a spy, I thought, you always had only yourself to rely on for a sense of people's motivations and agendas, and your own judgments about their sincerity. It seemed a kind of logic that necessarily required spies to shut out people and their sometimes-complicated emotions—or at least to compartmentalize them. Otherwise, it would be too risky.

I began to cry. I wanted to extract this admission from him, to know that what I was seeing and hearing wasn't smoke and mirrors but the deliberate obfuscation of dangerous emotions. I told him I loved him, but I wanted him to be real. I don't think he really knew what I was talking about. We were quiet awhile; he was pensive. Then he asked if I didn't think I might be having some post-traumatic stress issues from Iraq.

I exploded again, convinced that he was skirting the issue. I launched into a full-scale rant about post-traumatic stress, telling him I knew damn well what it was, and I didn't have it, and the issue was truth-telling—he wasn't being upfront with me. I got so frustrated that I began to blubber, and then to laugh. Pretty soon he was chuckling too, until it seemed that there wasn't, nor would there ever be, a way to thread my fears into coherence. When we were a journalist and a spy talking about the nature of truth and deception, it seemed to me as if the world hung in the balance. And then, by magic, we were just a father and a son.

My father said, "I trust you more than anyone, and I love you more than the sky because the sky never ends." There was no way to argue.

Soon after this, my father fell ill. He came home from work early with shivers, a fever, and an upset stomach. He sat on the couch for a while, trying to read, but eventually went to lie down.

I went into his room as he was getting undressed. He stripped down to his underwear and climbed quickly into bed. I went to the window and pulled the curtain aside. It was afternoon, and a gentle winter aura was on the city. There was no movement in the apartment of the supposed terrorist. I let the curtain drop and sat on the edge of his bed, pulling the covers up around his chin. I put my hand on his chest. He asked for a glass of water and I got him one. The bridge of his nose bore two red marks from his glasses. I told him to get some rest.

"I will."

"Sweet dreams."

"Okay," he said, through the clenched teeth of his fever. "Thank you, sweetheart."

I tucked him in some more and left. I stood in the silence for a moment, and went to the window. The light was fading quickly across the city. There were streaks of orange and red on the bullet-scarred buildings, pigeons and bigger birds floating up and down the valley, and a cloud of pre-winter smog hovering above the city. In a few months, there would be sleet and freezing cold, and the smog would gather until it covered the city in a grimy, sooty cloud. Everyone said that Sarajevo was a miserable place in winter. The fighting had been hardest then, and the residents had nearly died from starvation. Bosnians had eventually smuggled in pizzas through a tunnel they dug under the fields by the airport. I imagined, suddenly, the city cast in a halo of brutality, the body of a man wracked with bullets and dying, the punishers leveling blows on him. I imagined the screaming that must have accompanied so many nights. How many loves had died, I wondered. Of those who survived, how many just gave up anyway? I lost myself in the reverie, and then pulled back.

Right now, as the afternoon slipped into evening, it looked peaceful.

CHAPTER 15
Baghdad, 2006

I was living in Baghdad full time. *Newsweek* had moved me there in 2005 to run the bureau. The war I had first reported on had now turned into a full-scale American occupation. An insurgency had been born, and was killing about two American soldiers a day. It was a scary place, but there was nowhere else I would have chosen to be.

One day in the middle of summer, the Baghdad bureau's office assistant, Omar, and I were standing in the front yard of our house in the Green Zone, talking over administrative details. Omar had fashioned a mist-making machine out of spare parts and christened it the Mr. Mister. The two of us marveled silently at his invention. The wizardry of the heat was a superior challenge, but he had met it splendidly. He was an engineer. His country was dying, however, and there was no way to fix it.

His daughter may be a genius, he told me.

"How do you know?" I asked.

"She sits in front of the television screen all day and talks to Shrek," he said, squinting at me through the glare of the afternoon sun. She was only two, but spoke increasingly good English. She was small for her age, but her stubbornness was much greater, and he was grateful for this because it would help her in this difficult life. She showed an abiding love for the world.

While he spoke, he twirled his hand in and out of the cooling air. I lowered my face to see if my cheeks would register the moisture more sensitively than the rest of my body. I closed my eyes.

Omar's brother Tareq came out into the yard with a cigarette in his hand. We all stood together for a while, feeling the moisture before it evaporated in the noonday sun. It was still too hot in Baghdad for the contraption to make much of a difference. It would cool when the sun passed, but that would not be for many hours. In the meantime, the skies would fill with the thrumming of helicopter blades. This house, which a group of Western journalists lived in and worked from, was on a bend in the flight path to and from Landing Zone Washington. When the Apaches and Cobras and Chinooks passed, they did so on a bank thirty yards or so above our house before they headed north, to whatever killing fields required their attention that day.

The four brothers, young Sunni men, had been working with *Newsweek* since the beginning of the war. Tareq had been with us since the winter of 2002, even before the bombs began to fall, when he was working as a translator at the Ministry of Information under Saddam Hussein. The previous government had assigned him to us as a fixer, to help with translation and navigating the city and its people. He stayed on afterward, and brought all of his brothers along with him. Now almost the whole family worked with us in some fashion—as drivers, translators, and assistants in the business of newsgathering, which was as foreign to them, in these conditions, as it was difficult for us. It was this process that brought us together and allowed us to begin to trust one another. Four years on and here we still were, journalists and translators alike, imprisoned in our decaying white office in the Green Zone, barricaded by blast walls and sandbags, and protected by a small phalanx of Iraqi guards. We were perpetually toying with ways to quell the heat, and with it, our sense of summer doom.

The brothers and I went inside for some water and to talk. I asked how things were going. This summer was the worst anyone could recall. The invasion had wrought all kinds of havoc on Iraq, but the ensuing national hatreds that had swept into the vacuum created by the invasion were far worse. Death squads roamed the streets of Baghdad at all hours, killing individuals or groups at will and with utter impunity. Sometimes they showed up at a house or business and issued a warning: a handwritten note telling the occupants, some of whom they identified by name, to leave a house or neighborhood—or sometimes the country—within twenty-four hours, or face death. They often left a bullet with the note.

The unlucky got no warning at all, and the killers just went to work. They raided businesses and homes, lining people up against walls, blindfolding them, reading out their trespasses and their death sentences, and offing them one by one with single shots to the head. I heard about a situation in which they entered an electronics store and lined up all eleven employees against the wall, walking down the line and shooting every one until they dropped. It was only because one somehow managed to survive the shooting and flee the scene—which did occasionally happen—that we heard about it at all. Many stories never fully emerged, and their passing was more often than not recorded in brief, single-sentence footnotes at the bottom of Yahoo! news stories: thirteen killed here, headless bodies found there, a bomb explodes and kills dozens. The death toll continued to climb, and by the time one atrocity had been uncovered, two or three more had taken place, until it seemed as though each event was simply another bubble in a boiling cesspool of chaos.

This was the ugly side of the America my father loved. The America he admired was, here in Iraq, falling to pieces. I watched it every day, fascinated and horrified by the descent.

"My neighborhood has assassinations, not car bombs," Tareq said one day, when the three of us were discussing the constant flux of the chaos. We journalists took stock of the situation on a regular basis as part of our reporting. Like most of them, I would be in Iraq for two-month rotations, with a monthlong break between each visit. Although I saw a lot, I'd miss things, too—the situation in Baghdad could change incredibly fast, and often very violently. We also took stock to keep abreast of security developments in the city.

Tareq handed me a glass of sugary tea and crossed his legs politely. He was short and squat, and like a lot of Sunnis, he wore the customary Saddam-style mustache. He had a short, dry laugh, and he leaned back in his chair to talk. On his lips was always the slightest hint of a smile. He had survived this long, it seemed to say, and he would continue to survive—until they came directly for him, at which point he'd throw it all down, because there was no way he would let them take his family.

They had started to kill the bakers this summer, he told me. Death to all bakers was the order of the day. The killers came mainly from the Mahdi army, a Shiite militia that was fragmenting into smaller, uncontrolled gangs. The militia had lost any semblance of order six months earlier, in February, when an Al Qaeda cell had bombed the golden-domed Al-Askari Mosque in Samarra, one of the holiest sites in Shia Islam. Two or three days after the Samarra bombing, the Mahdi army moved into Tareq's neighborhood and began killing.

"My brother's neighbor," Tareq went on, "was going to the market in a minibus. He was sitting there and a young man came in. An old woman was sitting on the folded chair in the front. The man changed places with her. When the minibus was full of people, he picked up his phone and began talking to someone, and said the bus was going to move. He hung up. Then he picked up his pistol and walked to the back of the bus and shot a man sitting there. Three bullets in the head. He got up and left. No panic. He just got up and left. Very simple; he left. It happens every day."

The day after that, Tareq's next-door neighbor had been killed. A Christian friend of theirs, trying to justify the increasing proximity and enormity of the violence, said that the Shiites were only killing Wahhabis, the Sunni extremists whose ideology drove much of the insurgency, and who often joined Al Qaeda groups as a result. But Tareq's apartment complex must have been filled with Wahhabis because the killings continued indiscriminately.

"This street," he said, "the main street between the houses and the complex—two or three people are getting killed on this street every day. It started increasing about a month ago. There was a bakery there, too."

One day Tareq's wife and brothers were walking to a nearby market when a group of armed men appeared and shot a young man in front of them. Again, no panic. Two more butchers were killed soon after that, and then another bakery was destroyed. An Internet café was set on fire. Tareq began to draw a map as the tally mounted. Another café owner was killed. He sketched a detailed hatching of streets and avenues, with bars for checkpoints and Xs for all the dead, and soon the map filled with Xs. Three main supermarkets were repeatedly attacked, and a man who sold plumbing equipment was killed. One day, as part of the minibus attacks, gunmen boarded a bus and killed eleven schoolchildren, all about fifteen years old, because they were Sunnis.

"So," Tareq said, "the Sunnis started their own death squads, too, and they began to target Shiite minibus operators."

Almost every day I heard these sorts of stories, one more gruesome than the next. Life was reduced to this gross human misery. Baghdad was an open-air prison in many respects, a vast and powerfully overheated jail where the distinction between jailer and jailed, warden and inmate, had been lost.

Tareq and the brothers were enduring the situation, but little by little their abilities to withstand the onslaught were dissipating. Omar talked about leaving, taking his family and moving away—preferably to another Arab country where he could raise his children in peace and religion, but if that was not possible, then anywhere he could go to work without the fear that he might be picked off. Just a few days earlier, a car full of men had followed him for about twenty minutes. It was only at the last moment, when he made a quick turn onto a verge to lose them, that he noticed that two of the men in the backseat were carrying machine guns.

Just then our cook, a young man from the Sadr City slums— where the Mahdi army recruited the most thuggish of its goons— walked through the room on his way outside. "Salaam," the three men each said, exchanging polite smiles. But when he left, the two Sunni brothers smirked.

"Mahdi army," Tareq said, with a glance in the cook's direction.

"Shiites," his brother said, shaking his head.

That evening, after Tareq and Omar had left and I was alone at my desk, I spoke to my father. We usually talked every few days on Skype, or sometimes on the phone, though never as much as he would have liked. Tonight I told him I was planning on writing a piece about Iraq's unacknowledged civil war. All the doublespeak and propaganda emanating from the embassy and the military about what was happening in Iraq angered me—all that disinformation that seeped into our stories day after day, week after week. That wasn't supposed to happen, but it did. But what you did with propaganda was never let up. I had learned from him.

I wanted to know what he thought. "How do you define a civil war?" I asked him.

He said he would think about it and get back to me.

We finished our conversation, and I returned to my reporting. A few days earlier, gangs of marauding Shia militiamen had roamed through a neighborhood called Al Jihad, systematically weeding out Shiites and killing Sunnis on sight. I had spoken to a woman who witnessed the killing, who told me:

We found dead bodies in our neighborhood this morning, which means the gangs started killing during the night. In the morning they

put a checkpoint near the entrance to the neighborhood and started
asking for IDs, and any Sunni was killed immediately. They stopped
private cars and buses and the Shiites were asked to go and the Sunnis
were killed. The gangs also raided houses and shouted at the people
there, "You pimps, Sunnis, we will kill you." And yes, they did.

I had also spoken to some men in the Shiite slums of Sadr
City about what was happening in their neighborhood. "People
nowadays are encouraging each other to carry weapons and be
ready to launch war on the Sunnis," one man told me. "Almost
all the young men in the city are talking about the fight with
the Sunnis." At night, he said, cars full of young men, members of the Mahdi army, were gathering in the streets chanting
war songs before heading out into the city on killing missions.
For these Shia men, the grievances, and thus the war, dated back
hundreds of years—to the Middle Ages, when their prophets and
holy men were killed by brutal Sunni caliphs. The holy grounds
of modern-day Iraq were, in effect, holdovers from centuries-old
struggles between the two strains of the faith. Slaughters in Kar-
bala and Najaf over thirteen hundred years earlier were as fresh
in their minds as if they had happened last week, and with each
new massacre or revenge killing, the time elapse seemed to shrink
even further, bringing the past alive in new and horrible ways.
Many of the men felt it was their duty to take up the cause of their
defeated ancestors, to rid their holy lands once and for all of the
infidels, their Sunni overlords—who were descendents, in their
minds, of the ancient Babylonian dictator Yazid Ibn Mu'awiyah,
whose corruption and excess was later thought to prophesize the
arrival of Saddam Hussein.

"We've been waiting for this moment since we were children,"
a young man told me. He was twenty-six, a mechanic in the Shia
Sadr slums. "The Sunnis deserve to be killed; they are killing our
people in tens every day, and bombing our markets and cities. It
was our grandfathers' hope to seek vengeance. It is our hope, too."

Sunni attackers either responded in kind or, in many cases, brought on these kinds of reprisals because of their own attacks. Over the summer, a group of Sunni gunmen had stormed a Shia marketplace in Mahmoudiya, a town south of Baghdad, and mowed down fifty people. The day after that, a suicide bomber had lured Shia day-laborers toward his truck with offers of work and then detonated it, taking sixty souls with him. The two-day death toll exceeded one hundred people. And so it went. "The Sunnis bomb, the Shia send out death squads, every day, every day," said a man I spoke to now and again, a religious scholar whose calls for moderation had been drowned out by the shrieks and howls of his countrymen. The elementary hatred had gotten completely out of control.

My father eventually wrote to me with a response to my question:

A problem, I think, with monotheistic religions is that they believe, and preach, that they possess the truth. Although people such as Eisenhower can say, and honestly believe, that "it doesn't matter what a man believes, so long as he believes in God," religious Iraqis cannot accept that. Unfortunately, our government in its wisdom continues to define issues as the clash of evil with democracy, a clash between those who love freedom and democracy with those who "hate freedom." That the USG now has rejected the results of democratic elections in Palestine, Iran and Venezuela has not strengthened its demands that Iraqis get with the democratic program. The fundamentalist movements—Wahhabism, Salafism, Hizbullah, the Muslim Brotherhood—have gained strength and in many ways have coalesced since 1910. Those values, not Western ideas of the secular enlightenment, are defining the issues, and they are at war with each other. Naturally, much more is thrown into the Iraqi picture: Baathists, opportunists, insane people, thugs, nationalists, patriots and more. But I don't think those people are defining the issues—sectarian and communal hatreds have taken Iraq to civil war.

Thus, I suspect that the most fundamental question for Iraqis is whether they would be able to continue living as they want to live should the other side dominate. And I further suspect that most now would say they could not. The Shi'a I think probably would see themselves forced to return to the prevailing norms of the Saddam era, maybe with a vengeance such that they would be forced to emigrate, to Iran, for example, where they anticipate they certainly would not be welcomed. Sunnis, of course, have demonstrated they cannot live peaceably if dominated by Shi'as. In other words, the hatreds, always there to some degree, now are foremost in peoples' minds, exacerbated by all the atrocities, such as dislocation from homes and neighborhoods that you already have reported.

I guess, in conclusion, I would add that when a people have leaders who advocate violence, and those leaders are not checked from within the community, and when "strife" is rampant enough, and desires for revenge strong enough that compromise can't be effected, then a civil war exists. I think compromise now would be almost impossible, because the terms of compromise would be impossible. Simply letting apostates return to their homes, and thus desecrate the neighborhood, is no longer a possibility. It's not a question of a difference of opinion. It's even more than a clash of fundamental moral values, as was the case in the U.S. of 1860. It's a question of sin, of apostasy, or defilement.

That night, I went to the roof and lay down. The cement was still hot from the scorching day. A few stars were out. From high above came the steady buzzing sound of one of the ubiquitous spy drones that hovered in our skies, constantly on watch over us.

My father's words lingered in my mind: sin, apostasy, defilement. For an atheist like him, a rationalist and a logician, the words were, to a large degree, intellectual abstractions. In his world, sin could be a powerful commodity, an emotion that could be traded upon, manipulated, and utilized to gain the upper hand. Defilement was an unfortunate but necessary consequence. This violence tapped into that current. Killing begat more killing, and obsessive cycles of hatred and vengeance grew stronger. Far as he was from my reality, from the killing fields and the mayhem, my father nevertheless understood the righteousness, and the terror that struck at Tareq and Omar—and at me—because at that point anyone within the circle of hell that was Baghdad had, to some extent, chosen sides.

I tried to tell the truth about these things, or get close to the truth. Some of the stories I heard made me want to seek revenge on the victim's behalf, and in my daydreams I would elaborate on fantastical plans to do so without getting caught. I imagined myself as an artful avenger, dispensing with human life with about as much remorse as the people I reported on every day—which is to say, zero.

My father understood that. He had been opposed to the war in Iraq. From very early on he believed it was a catastrophe in the making, an egregious error that would stare us in the face for years to come.

I think my father was starting to doubt his own beliefs. All his questions and his endless curiosity about Iraq was rounding out a view to which he was becoming increasingly attached—that the country he loved was in grave danger, and that the organization that he had devoted his life to, the one in whose service he still toiled, was poisoned. As his doubts grew, I think his faith in himself began to crumble.

The more I delved into my father's past, the more I began to lose sight of myself. A certain kind of isolation had crept up on me, and I realized now that it had been creeping up on me for years. I had isolated myself completely from the rest of the world. I had chosen to live in a place that was falling apart.

As I lay on the roof, two more helicopters thundered overhead; and as they arced out over the edge of the Green Zone, four bright flares dropped brightly, fading as they fell, signaling their entrance into the hot zone.

CHAPTER 16

Ramadi, 2006

Luc and I tried to relax in a small room on one of the U.S. forward bases in downtown Ramadi. We had gone there to report on how the military was coping with one of the hotbeds of the insurgency. I was on one bunk and Luc on another, facing me. We lay in this room for hours. Sometimes we talked; sometimes we were quiet for long stretches. Occasionally one of us fell asleep, until the other woke him. Time slipped by.

He pulled out his phone and checked the clock. He carried all of his music on it. There were only a few artists: Lou Reed, Bob Dylan, the Rolling Stones, Serge Gainsbourg, and the Clash.

To pass the time, he suggested we play musical trivia. He began. "An easy one," he said. "On which album will you find the song 'Tangled Up in Blue'?"

"Easy," I agreed. "*Blood on the Tracks*."

He increased the difficulty immediately. Playing me a few seconds of a song, I had to guess what it was. I knew the song—it was Dylan—but I didn't know the title. 'Mister Jones'?"

"'Ballad of a Thin Man'," he corrected me. The chorus reverberated: *Because something is happening here / But you don't know what it is / Do you, Mister Jones?*

Luc smoked little brown cigarettes. We all approached death

from different directions. Sometimes we rushed headlong toward it, suddenly and madly curious, dazzled by its allure. Sometimes we watched from a great distance with utter boredom. Twelve dead in a plane crash? Our fascination with the irrelevant detail made our contempt for the dead that much more acute—what sort of plane? A storm? Anyone famous? Other times, most times, we ran away.

And then there was the waiting Luc and I were doing, the subtle orchestration of events that would bring us into close proximity to the beast. We wanted to slow death down, understand it, and describe it; we wanted to be swept up in its swirling currents for a moment. Isn't that what we wanted?

It was so bright in the Iraqi desert in summer. To avoid the glare, I usually closed my left eye completely and squinted with the right. If not, I began to sneeze. It was a photokinetic allergy. When I was a child, the glare from the snow-covered peaks of the Austrian Alps—at a highway chalet where my dad and I stopped briefly in the summer of 1980, on our way across the Iron Curtain and into Yugoslavia—had thrown me into fits of uncontrollable sneezing.

"What's wrong?" my father had asked, and when he realized that I could only bear to open my eyes into tiny slivers, he put his aviator sunglasses on my head. "We'll have to get you a good pair of those."

They never really helped. In the desert sun, I squinted at the world. Soldiers suddenly disappeared from my vision; I felt the 130-Fahrenheit degrees of heat, but I no longer saw it shimmering.

A marine showed me to the lead Humvee of the convoy we would be taking for a foray into Ramadi. He was a tall Latino, and very muscular. He wore sunglasses with dark lenses and shouldered an M60, one of the big guns, just like Rambo. Soldiers weren't like sailors or racers; their vehicles were androgynous. Their weapons, on the other hand, were cradled and caressed.

"We call this one Lucky," he said, pointing to my vehicle. He showed me how to lock and unlock the door, and pointed to the seat behind the driver. "You'll sit here. We get hit all the time, but Lucky has never been hit. That's why we're putting you in here."

There was an awkward moment of silence as he realized he had somehow cracked the wood that one mentally knocks on. So he bowed to fate. "You guys'll probably get hit today," he said. There was no smile. It was a simple statement of fact.

These marines were from Weapons Company, part of a regimental battalion based in Ramadi—which, in that summer of 2006, was the most violent, chaotic city in Iraq. Much of the city had already been destroyed. Instead of buildings, there was the wreckage of a city that once was. Towering walls of various heights were angled oddly against each other, and the skyline was in ruins. Roofs had collapsed into courtyards, windows had been blown out, powerlines were down, and giant hulks of concrete, rebar, broken steel, and glass lay everywhere on the ground. Repeated American bombings had blown tall buildings to shards, and their dirty remains were scattered across the blight. And there was often not a human in view—only birds that floated in and out of the rubble looking for food or a home.

When I look back now—and I think I was even aware of it very dimly at the time—I realize that I went to Ramadi in part because it formed part of the array of goods with which my father and I would eventually barter. I didn't tell him or my mother about these trips. I kept it a secret, my secret, at least until it was over; until I could go to them and say: Here, look! Here is what I have found out on my own. And then the reckoning could begin. Does this square with what you have told me? Have you told me the truth?

In Iraq in those years, there were simply too many truths swirling around for any one of them to be definitive. Taken together, it often seemed like chaos. I liked that. My job, I told myself in those moments of self-absorbed triumph, was to delve into the chaos and wring from it the truth. Truth permitted all sorts of indiscretions and offenses, not only to others but also to myself, just as it had when I was a child. I often reverted to the mind-set that I was somehow different, invincible, and that the rules that governed the world did not apply to me; that I could skate through unharmed. It was that same feeling I had on the day my father told me his secret—there was a sort of impunity that our illicit world bestowed upon our actions. The world didn't know what I knew, and therefore I had an advantage over it.

The soldiers I saw in Ramadi didn't feel that same advantage. They were terrified—and rightly so, because they felt that their invincibility had run out.

One day, as we continued our reporting, Luc and I were sitting in one of the bunkers at the governor's palace downtown. The marines were watching the streets, or what was left of them, from behind the wire. There was an intersection a few hundred yards down the road from us. Now and again people scurried from one side to the other. A man on a bicycle rode up and down again, seemingly oblivious to armed marines who surrounded him on three sides. Perhaps he was mad. An old man sat in a chair on one side of the intersection. The marines believed that any of them could be insurgents, killers, or terrorists.

Then one of the marines noticed, in the middle of the street, a small box that no one had yet seen. There was no explanation for its sudden appearance. The marines tensed immediately. They squinted through their binoculars at this box. A child screamed giddily and ran up the street. The obvious question: how was this giddiness possible in this situation? The irretrievable answer: it was not. It was a ruse, a trick, and the child must have been complicit with those who had left the box.

"Watch that fucking box," one marine ordered. Several pairs of binoculars swiveled away from the child, focusing again on the box. The lenses on these binoculars were green and shiny, much bigger than average binoculars—rounder, more like eyes, reducing the world to digits of infinitesimal movement.

"Is that fucking box moving?"

"Could be on a rope."

"Who's pulling?"

"That old man?"

"Watch that kid—where's the kid?"

"Is it moving?"

"Can't tell."

"I want the road closed."

"Close alpha now."

"Where's that fucking kid?"

"You see rope?"

"No."

"It hasn't moved."

"I don't care. Shut it down now."

Men and women continued to cross the street, yet now, with the appearance of the box and the child, their movements looked more like a delicately choreographed dance. I focused my eyes and ears on the street: the old woman's clothed frame; the crooked nose of the old man, and his bony, sandaled feet; the whirring of the bicycle wheels. There was no air anymore. The fate of the world seemed to be contained inside this box. No one looked away.

And then a tall man came strolling along. He was lanky, an Iraqi jughead. He swung his arms blithely. He came along, and *whack*—kicked the box and sent it flying down the street.

There was an audible gasp behind me, and then murmurs.

"You were one dead sumbitch."

"Stupid fuck."

"Fucking box."

But the world had been released. The sky opened up again; the clouds drifted. It even looked like it might rain.

Now, near Ramadi, it was midmorning, and we waited on the tarmac where the soldiers were gathering. Four armored Humvees were lined up, including Lucky, the lead vehicle. About thirty marines were getting ready for the mission, which had been described to us as an attempt to draw fire from the insurgents to coax them out of hiding, and then kill them. Those who had been spared this morning's run stood around in T-shirts, talking softly and helping their fellow marines don their gear and load their vehicles. They checked weapons, patted each other on the back, and gave encouragement—because you never knew who would be next, or when death would come. They were getting killed here, too: Americans were dying at the rate of about two per day across Iraq that summer, and when you looked at where those deaths were occurring, Ramadi took a disproportionate toll. Between ambushes, improvised explosive devices (IEDs), and snipers, hundreds had gone down in the last several months alone. They took the bodies of the dead back to Baghdad by helicopter, shrouded them in American flags, and sent them home. Each time a U.S. soldier fell, the resolve to retaliate grew stronger.

Many of the soldiers seemed dead inside already. The sergeant preparing the mission was one such man. He had been in Ramadi for about six months, and had already been IED'd twenty-one times. He was a bald, heavy-chested Southerner who chewed tobacco and smoked. His eyes were hooded and, it seemed to me, full of pain all of the time. I didn't know if he wanted me there, or if he wanted to be doing so much killing, but today he had to accept both.

The air was too still, and the heat was blinding. I looked at Luc, and his face betrayed a degree of uncertainty for the first time. Luc was never uncertain—not once since I had started working with him five years earlier in Afghanistan. The helmet they made him wear was far too big, and it sloped to one side of his head, the chinstrap dangling loosely. He looked like an ambivalent adolescent, bundled up by mother for the winter walk to school.

The sergeant came over to me, checking my armored vest

and slapping my helmet. "If we get hit, the first thing you do when you come to is check your body to see if you're all there." He patted his chest, face, legs, and head in a cursory once-over. "If you're all there, you yell out, "I'm okay, I'm okay." If you're wounded, you yell out, "I'm wounded." If you can yell. If you can't, well . . ." He looked to make sure I understood. "You get out of the vehicle but you don't run away. You wait for one of us to tell you what to do. Got it?"

I nodded.

He pulled open the door and I climbed in. It closed with a bang and a click.

The various companies on the Ramadi base had different missions. Some patrolled the quieter areas. Some did civil affairs work, trying to meet locals and befriend them with offers of tea and money in exchange for cooperation. But Weapons was different. Weapons drove all around the city, and there was no neighborhood that was off-limits. Weapons had only one objective—to draw fire. When that happened, their job was simple: kill.

Fuck it, I thought to myself, because it was too late to turn back, because this was what I had come to see.

For the rest of today, you must not step on any cracks, anywhere, of any sort. If you do, you will die. If you lived by that rule for one hour, it might approximate the obscene attention to detail required to drive in Ramadi. We headed out the base's front gates, passing a few tanks that had been positioned to guard the entrance and exits. Soon, we arrived at an empty intersection that was a popular site for IEDs. The sun was beating down on the footpath, turning it white. The engine growled mechanically. I waited for the blast, but nothing came. And we were through, moving into a narrow street where the buildings on each side closed us off. Then we were just moving forward slowly, waiting.

The sergeant began to talk, directing the private in the driver's seat. "Slow down here . . . watch that sand pile . . . move six inches to the right . . . stop . . . okay, go ahead . . . is that wood?

Clear that plank, stay way right . . . slow down . . . move left . . . more . . . okay . . . gunner, where does that wiring go?"

These streets were empty. They were dirty and strewn with rubbish, including long, dry fronds discarded from date palms. The doors of the houses were metal, and brown walls lined the sides of the road. The traffic islands were canals of dried and caked mud.

There was air-conditioning in the Humvee, but it blasted out hot air. I could see the back of the private's neck. He was young and white, and his neck was burned pink. I couldn't stop clenching and unclenching my jaw. I repeated phrases, and counted their syllables with my toes. Take this right here; four. The gunner swiveled on a moving turret by my side. It was similar to the swivel turret used by Chewbacca, Han Solo's copilot on the Millenium Falcon. The muzzle from the M16 jostled up against my blue flak jacket, which identified me as a member of the press corps.

If a bomb exploded, my face would fill with glass and heat. It could possibly melt off my skull. The worst luck would be if the bomb came from my side of the vehicle. A better scenario would be if it exploded in front or behind us, or came at us from the other side. The better scenario would be if other people died. The worst possible case would be if it exploded as I looked out this window, for no distinguishable reason at all. One of the most memorable scenes from *Star Wars* was when Han Solo put the Millenium Falcon into light speed and it vanished into time. I am not driving, but if I were, I would speed us up right now. Instead, we slow down. We stop beside a pile of sand. It turns out this spot, in time, in space, is not within the vortex. It is negative space; it is dead space.

We set off again and turned on to a broad avenue. There were lanes going in both directions, and both lanes were empty. We had seen a few solitary men moments before, but they had darted into doorways or down curving alleys and disappeared. Our column stopped in the middle of the long avenue with the date palms down the middle, quiet houses on each side. Then we started moving again.

"Get over to the right," the sergeant barked. When the private didn't, the sergeant yelled, "Hey!"

That was the last thing I heard before there was an explosion.

Apparently, we flew. We were lifted high, flung about like a tetherball; five tons of metal and steel, and another half-ton of human flesh, lifted up more than a yard—60 inches high—to the height of my throat; lifted as if by God's hand, shot up from underneath, or within, a pop of the weasel, straight into the palm of the Lord.

I only heard the bang afterward, and I might even have imagined it, needing to attach a sound to the explosion. And then I felt the vehicle crash land, windshield down.

I followed instructions to a T. I felt my chest. The flak jacket was hard. I felt my head. The helmet was hard. I felt my face, my eyes, my mouth, my lips. I am in love with my lips, I thought. I looked at my hands. There was no blood. I felt my legs, and they were intact. "I'm okay," I yelled. "I'm okay."

My father had an itch to push things to the edge. If I asked him not to do something, fearing for his safety, he would do it. He was accident prone, too, which complicated matters. He took a jump at a French ski resort once, right after I had asked him not to, then crash landed and dislocated his elbow. He would forget—deliberately, I sometimes thought—to regulate his insulin intake, sinking into incomprehension and anger before eventually succumbing to an insulin recalibration. He was forever testing boundaries, with himself and with others, in an attempt to prove his invincibility. As a young man, he had taken up diving in Hawaii, where he worked as a tour guide, and once almost died when he free-dove twenty-two yards and barely made it back to the surface in time.

During our hiking trip in the Pyrenees in Spain years before, we had been hiking for about five days when we crossed a vast

stone bowl ringed by stone pillars and bottomed out by a meadow
of swampy reeds. We began to make our way up a long ridge,
over which was another valley that sloped down and circled back
to our starting point. The ridge top was crumbling, and studded
with boulders that would be difficult to climb over. So instead,
we started to cross on a snow field over a deep indentation in the
mountainside.

When we got to the edge of the snow bank, I told my father
I wasn't sure if it was a good idea for us to cross there. The bank
was steep and slippery. He wore leather boots, and his pack was
heavy and poorly balanced. But he just turned around and smiled
at me, starting to kick steps into the snow and, with his hands
out in front of him for balance, to move laterally across the bank,
one step at a time. I waited on the rocky edge and watched him,
trying to guide him from a distance with the advantage of perspective. He was about halfway across when I began to relax. He
was kicking well, and his balance seemed good. He smiled at me.
"This is a cinch!" he said.

And then, in an instant, he wasn't there anymore. I had looked
away, and when I turned around my father was on his back, sliding fast down the snow bank. Worse, he was sliding headfirst.
Below him, a couple of hundred yards down the bank, were the
jagged teeth of the boulder field. Across it was a creeping, ten-
tacled field of yellow lichen. The thin, winding lengths of fungi
were everywhere on the boulders, like a single-bodied organism;
and my father was hurtling toward them, a white body attached
to a clanking frame of metal and plastic, with his head, the most
delicate bloom of all, lodged in its midst. Not a cloud was in sight
in the blue sky. I imagined my father's death; I saw the blood.
It would be a day of blue and red. And, with all those finely
wrought lichen, of yellow, too. All I could see were those colors.

I shrieked. "Dad!" I shouted. "Dad!"

He was still sliding toward the boulder field. His body was
twisting as it fell; now he was sideways. I could hear the scraping
sound he made on the ice. I dropped my pack and started run-

ning, then jumping down the boulders. I fell, but got up and continued. I kept shouting his name. There was no sound from him. Mine was the only noise in the universe then, and it was frantic. I answered myself, more calmly. My voice came back to me from across the valleys, muted and tinny. There are three of us now, I thought. Two of me, and one of him. And he will be gone, so that will leave just the two of us.

"Shit, shit," I muttered to myself. My echo didn't answer.

"Dad!" I screamed. And this time it answered back again.

He hit the rocks. He tumbled. He flipped. The rocks made a low grumble, like dice in a leather cup, and then sharper, like ice cracking. He lay still. His white shirt was still white. I raced down the rocks, stumbling and falling on myself. I banged my knee. Then I was on him. He looked up at me and smiled. The fall had knocked the wind out of him, and he was having trouble breathing. I checked for broken bones, but he seemed to be okay. "I think I'll just lie here for a minute," he said, and smiled again.

I sat down beside him and he stared up at the sky. The high rims of the valley walls were all around us now. We were in a stone bowl whose vertical sides rose up like thousands of thick fingers—columns many tens of yards high, stained orange and brown, and glowing in the midday sun as if they were alive, as if they had been awakened by my father's fall and were staring at us. On the bank above, I could see the long trace of his fall through the snow. The line was smooth and slightly hollow, marked randomly by holes where he had tried to grasp at something to hold on to. A few rocks had been unearthed by his chute.

I gave him some water. "I managed to turn myself around," he said. "I was going down headfirst there for a while."

"I know," I managed to say.

He patted me on the knee and smiled.

Now I unlocked the door of the Humvee and crawled out. Right near me was the prospect of death, just as it had been when I saw my father a decade earlier. It was a marine, the driver who had been sitting in front of me. The bomb had detonated under the engine block—the explosion threw the floorboard up, crushed his feet, smashed his head into the roof, and then somehow threw open the door and tossed him five yards away, where he lay writhing. "Oh my God," he screamed. "Oh my God! Help me, help me!"

I maneuvered around to the other side of the Humvee, helping marines to carry the wounded driver to a less exposed place behind one of the Humvees, and we lay him on the ground. The others, meanwhile, provided cover for us. They had begun to kill as soon as we were ambushed. Bodies, sometimes dressed in black, with kaffiyas wrapped around their heads and carrying large guns, darted in and out of doorways, crouching in the street long enough to get a few rounds off at us. If they lingered too long, the marines mowed them down. The Latino with the big gun stood on his vehicle and let loose with such a clatter of mayhem that I had to plug my ears. He was a madman. Two bodies now lay in the sewage-filled gutters. Another fell in a doorway and stayed there, slumped like a drunk or an extra in a movie, until he was quickly dragged out of sight by unseen hands.

By now the marines had taken off the driver's boots. His feet were smashed and broken. They fed him morphine right away, and he began to grin. His teeth were broken, and blood seeped from his mouth. Is he going to die, I wondered? Why have they taken off his boots? Was that really a priority? His socks were white and fresh, and glowed brightly in the noonday sun. The mothers and fathers at home made sure to send their boys fresh bundles of socks. So his socks were clean, but his feet were in a shambles. The marines had taken off his socks and laid them on his unlaced boots. Now they hovered over his face, talking to him amid the chaos.

Around us, the clanging fire rang on. At the end of the north-facing street, an insurgent armed with a shoulder-mounted RPG bent down and leveled his weapon at us. He was just about to let a rocket go when a marine mowed him down.

Now and again, I heard a "whoo hoo!"—the sound of marines hollering as they killed. With each whoop they had hit another. In the adrenaline, I wanted to live inside that sound. The killers, I was with the killers. I wanted to be a warrior, to vanquish, to identify the enemy and conquer. But I could not.

One of them leaned down to me. "You're doing good," he shouted, before popping back up to let off a few more rounds. "You should have been a soldier," he yelled over his shoulder. "You should have been a fucking killer!"

When I became a journalist, I thought I wanted to know, or discover, the truth. That was the myth behind the profession, to seek and destroy all manner of impurities, to wage war on the propagandists and deceivers, to record history as it was being made. There was the impulse to delve into chaos and unravel from it the truth. But those things were so impossible, really. There were only stories, one after another, these overwhelming stories. The moral world—an incipient universe of malleable laws, a jungle in which Mowgli would have felt at home—was still being formed. There was a terrible privilege to being able to witness people's nakedness, their grotesqueness or their nobility, when they were put in truly awful predicaments—and that included me, and my own.

Eventually, after an hour or more of steady streetfighting, the marines managed to kill or scare away the remaining insurgents, and we holed up in a nearby house to wait for help. A Quick Reaction Force evacuated the wounded marine. The rest of us waited for a while, then tied the broken Humvee to a working one and limped back to the base at a crawl, afraid that another bomb would explode beneath us at any moment.

Afterward, when we were safely back on the base, Luc put his arm around my shoulder. "You have to stop that," he said.

"I know."

"That's the second time you've given me a scare. I saw your truck explode and I thought you were dead."

Luc and I had been in scrapes together before—several—and

each time we had made it through, but barely. "Maybe it's you," I said. "This only happens with you."

But the strange alchemy of the day began to work on me. Later, I borrowed Luc's soap to take a shower. It was a special kind he had brought from France, a gift from his wife and child—a totem that he carried with him in a blue plastic case. When I returned to the trailer we shared, Luc asked me where the soap was. Oops, I had forgotten it. When I went back, the soap was gone.

"I've lost the soap," I told Luc. "It's gone."

His face darkened. His lips pursed. He scowled, absolutely furious.

I got dressed quickly. I wanted us to arrange for our helicopter ride back to Baghdad. We trundled off to headquarters. As we walked, Luc said, "You're going to get me some new soap. I need my soap."

When we got there, I asked the sergeant if he had any soap. "Luc needs his soap," I said, with as much scorn as I could muster. Luc was standing off to one side. He shook his head, livid at my tone. The sergeant brought a small bar of military soap. I took it and handed it to Luc.

"No!" he said. "You carry it."

We were suddenly both very small children. We were reduced to this. The sergeant didn't move, just watched.

"No!" I shouted back. "It's your soap, you fucking carry it." I shoved it into his hands. We trailed out the door, and I walked away first, back to our tent.

I heard Luc's ragged voice break out behind me. "*Assume!*" Luc was screaming at my back as I walked away. "*Assume*, Scott!"

There is no simple way to explain the word, the phrase it conjures, in English. What he was saying was "assume responsibility for your actions." Assume responsibility for your life. Rise to the occasion. Rise! Defend!

I continued walking.

In that moment, I thought about my father. I felt, suddenly

and deeply, very ashamed. I sensed all eyes upon me. I had survived something incredibly scary that day, and yet now I felt as if I could crumble from the inside out. It dawned on me how willing I had been to give up the life he had given me. Why did I keep doing this? And each time with more ferocity, more anger than the time before. I didn't think I had anything to prove to him, or to myself, and yet there I was, in Iraq. This was a solitary experience. It was all mine, and no one, not even him, could take it away from me. Maybe this was why young men went to war—to claim their own hold on life, on death; to wean themselves from their fathers; to kill or be killed on their own terms.

When I called him later, I told him "something" had happened. "I'll tell you later," I said, "but everything's okay, everything's fine."

Two days before my thirty-third birthday, I was back from Ramadi. My father had been writing to me, asking how my "adventure" had gone. I called him. "You'll read about something that happened to me in the magazine," I said, "but don't worry, I'm okay."

When my article came out a few days later, detailing the violence I had seen in Ramadi, he wrote to me. "You've certainly earned your paycheck these last two weeks," he wrote. "I love you, and reading the article (Ramadi) made me as uncomfortable as you anticipated when you thoughtfully called. Dad."

I called him later that night and he asked how I was doing.

"I'm okay," I told him, "but it was pretty bad."

There was a silence on the other end.

"I wish . . ." he started, then, "God, I have horrible dreams about it sometimes."

"About what?" I asked.

"About you being over there. Please be careful, Scotty. Promise me."

CHAPTER 17

Baghdad, 2006

The summer of 2006, when things were at their absolute worst, I was burning through several seasons of *24*, the television series about an American special agent named Jack Bauer who worked for a secret government branch called CTU (the Counter Terrorist Unit). Like some kind of supercharged feline, Bauer seemed to have countless lives, and was forever getting out of near-death scrapes with seconds to spare, killing bad guys and saving the world in the process. Bauer was an advocate for torture, too, and when he managed to bring one of the guys in for interrogation, he never hesitated to break an arm or two, affix the electrodes, or beat the perp silly to get the information he needed. In one episode, he simply took out his pistol and shot a man dead in the interrogation room.

The ends always justified the means with Bauer. That was how the world worked, after all, and Bauer was a faithful servant for the good.

Earlier that spring, I had hired a security company in the Green Zone called CTU to provide guards and consultants, usually retired British or American Special Forces types, to look after the *Newsweek* staff. A couple of them had the same telltale CTU mobile phone ringtones heard on the show.

Almost as soon as I had returned to Baghdad, the Mahdi army launched a full-scale rocket attack on the Green Zone. It lasted several days, and I barricaded myself in *Newsweek*'s office-home with my CTU security contractor, Jacko. The rockets landed perilously close to our house because it was in the fire path of projectiles aimed at the nearby convention center, where the parliament met.

One day, early in the morning, a rocket landed on the sidewalk a couple of hundred yards from our house. It killed two Iraqis who worked at a nearby makeshift carwash and happened to be outside at the time. Not long afterward, at about six in the morning, a rocket scored a direct hit on a house two doors down from us, throwing Jacko and his morning cup of tea straight across the room. It blew a hole in the yard big enough to bury a few bodies in. It shattered thirteen windows on our neighbor's house, blew our kitchen door off its hinges, and broke the lock. We found a piece of its shrapnel in our front yard, like a strange meteorite. It had jagged edges, small protrusions of thin, egg-shell curvatures, and it was layered and delicate like filigree. "That's what'll kill you," Jacko said, studying it. "Go right through you and shred your veins."

I thought about the grenade we had found on Camp Peary as kids, and then put the thing in a drawer. I locked the doors and secured the blast blankets—heavy, leaden shock-absorbing curtains that stretched from floor to ceiling—in front of the windows. I told the staff outside, the guards and drivers, to stay inside their own little protected complex and not to come out, barring an emergency. The whole house was dark. Now and again a blast rumbled out. Sometimes they were close enough to shake the house; other times they seemed to be just distant echoes of thunder. We turned on the television.

For the next few hours, Jacko and I lay on the couch in the living room, distracted from the events outside by Jack Bauer. But I had to get up at least twice every hour to pee, my nerves jittery. "Jesus Christ," Jacko said each time. "Get a grip, bathroom boy."

Jacko and I worked our way through sixteen hours of *24* in twenty-four hours. Cars were getting blown up. People kept getting killed. Bauer kept saving the day. He was immune to death. He usually killed three or four bad guys during each episode. He had a daughter, but was never able to spend much time with her because the imminent collapse of Western civilization was placing substantial demands on his time. Then she got kidnapped and he saved her, and all was redeemed. For a while, Bauer's daughter went to work for CTU as well, as an analyst, and together father and daughter fought crime—she from the bowels of CTU's command center, and he from the tough streets outside. Terrorists had killed his first wife, which complicated the family dynamic further. Bauer loved his family, but he loved his country more. Or maybe he didn't love it more, but he was more loyal to it. Maybe Bauer was an emotional cripple, with nothing left to lose. Sometimes it was hard to tell.

Eventually, three days later, a friend flew in and found me on the couch, in the darkness, wearing a T-shirt speckled with potato chips and the same clothes I had been in for three days.

"You looked like death warmed over," he told me later.

Long before the era of Jack Bauer—of 9/11, and terrorists plotting to inject mustard gas or sarin into subway lines, or blow up commercial shopping malls—my father started taking me along on some of his work trips. Out in suburban Michigan, ours was a more prosaic kind of guerrilla theater. But some of the actors were the same: Arabs, Chinese, gumshoes from the FBI (for whom my father reserved a particular kind of scorn because they were mere policemen, he said, focused exclusively on issues of law and order—the lock-up or liberty—and those were such simple formulas, so inadequate for the world's complexities).

I knew he worked for the CIA by then, but I didn't know much more. Our home in Southfield was, I soon realized, a kind of ground zero for the Middle Eastern connection. My father's number two at the fake insurance office was the mysterious Lebanese man I had met, and although I never got to know him very well, I did come to understand that he was well connected—which was saying something, because in Michigan in those years, half of the miserable, exiled Middle East seemed to have decamped to our bleak northern city.

But there were other interests further afield—bigger fish, perhaps—and they were beginning to take my father to distant locales. We often went to Ohio on these trips. There was a man there who I later learned was a volunteer access agent for my father, just as my dad had been for Robert in Mexico twenty years earlier. That meant the CIA used him for introductions, which his position and long years in town facilitated. Ohio, of course, was a big military state. The Air Force had bases and schools there, as well as officer training centers, the Air Force museum, and plenty of small conservative colleges that attracted students, foreign and domestic, interested in strategic and military affairs.

Ohio also had the Cincinnati Reds, one hell of a good baseball team.

One day my father and I drove down from Detroit. We had a rental car, having ditched the old Buick. It was spring, blossomy and humid, allowing us to roll down our windows, breathe, and enjoy being with each other on the road like this. These trips, off on adventures, were the best times with my father.

He told me we were going to see a friend of his who was retired. It was for work, so I should be on my best behavior. We pulled up to a long, low house in a florid suburb—a Miami Beach transplant in the middle of Ohio. Inside, it was all fuchsia and white leather and feathers; there were ceiling fans and teak paneling and small white dogs underfoot. The man was tall and thin, with well-groomed hair, and he wore slip-on shoes. He had been in the air force, too. His wife, she of shell-hard hair and a perfect smile, lingered in the background.

We made small talk for a while, and then my father and his

friend moved into the living room. The wife took my arm to usher me away. She wore lots of makeup and sported a brightly colored blouse. "Would you like to see our porch?" she asked.

The porch was mostly empty except for a giant cage at one end, which housed a parrot. "I'll be right back," she murmured, closing the door on her way out. I sat on a hanging vinyl swing set. My feet just barely touched the floor.

She eventually came back and handed me a drink with a straw and a piece of fruit in it. She led me over to the parrot cage. "He talks," she said. "You can teach him words." She said something, and the bird responded gamely with the appropriate answer.

"Round on the end and high in the middle," I said. "Oh-hi-oh." She giggled.

I peeked through the windows and could see my father and his friend bent over a table, discussing something over spread-out papers. My father laughed, and then quickly turned serious again.

The man's wife stayed with me for a while and we talked to the parrot, but eventually she left and said that if I wanted more juice I should knock on the door and she'd bring me some. "Make yourself comfortable," she said, nodding to the vinyl couch, and I did. But the parrot went quiet, and so did I. I kept looking in through the windows to watch my father. He was serious. He had a pen and was drawing something. I could hear the rumble of his deep voice, like long-distance radiowaves coming at me through a pack of wool sheeting—no annunciation, just a steady hum of electricity, connecting his head to mine through all these solids.

The thing of it was that Jack Bauer was forever doing the wrong thing and pissing off the wrong people, and even if his screw-ups were for the right reasons, the net result never seemed to equal out for him in exactly the way he, or we, would have liked. I thought about that day in Cincinnati as I was lying on my couch in a darkened room in Baghdad, watching Jack Bauer shred his

life to bits. I thought about that day and others like it because
while in most ways my father was nothing like Jack Bauer—no
intelligence officer really is. Bauer was an archetype for a man
who was profoundly, existentially lonely, willing to sabotage his
life in various ways for the praise of those he respects: a few words,
a note, a nod of recognition. Saving the world was the ostensible
goal, but I always got the sense that it was almost a sideshow com-
pared to the succor of kind words and admiration and respect.
As with Bauer, my dad believed in the possibility of doing some
measure of good, and wanted to be seen as a purveyor of accu-
racy to those who adjudicate the moral world. It is astonishing,
the myriad ways we can wreck or remake our lives, the ways in
which our sacrifices are so disproportionate to the reward.

It wasn't until years later that I found out what my dad had
done, and was doing, on those trips to Cincinnati. My father was
interested in a Chinese military officer. This man, Xiang, was in
the United States on a scholarship and studying with the U.S.
Air Force. Xiang was a senior-ranking officer in the Chinese air
force, and because of this his presence had raised flags with various American government agencies, including the FBI and the
CIA. The FBI wanted to surveil Xiang, and arrest him if it could;
the CIA wanted to recruit him. My father, in Michigan, was the
closest field officer around, and so he took a particular interest
in Xiang. The trick was to figure out how to meet him. And this
was why we were in the house of the access agent in Ohio.

During these meetings, the two spies devised a plan whereby
my father could be casually introduced to Xiang. The plan called
for a female FBI agent who would pose as my father's fiancée
and accompany him to a baseball game. My father posed as a
State Department officer working in Washington, D.C., who
traveled to Cincinnati regularly to visit her. The access agents in
Ohio would arrange to take Xiang to the same game. It would
be a cultural experience, they'd say. My dad organized for the
female FBI agent and himself to be sitting a few rows down from

Xiang and the access agents, one of whom was female. During the seventh-inning stretch, the two women would spot each other in the crowd, wave, and agree to meet up later. In this way, my father and Xiang would be thrown together haphazardly. It would be up to my father to take advantage of the situation and make inroads with Xiang.

When the time came, it worked perfectly. My father met Xiang, made friends with him, and the two of them agreed to meet up again later for some other, equally benign activity where they would begin to get to know each other better.

So over the coming months, my father began to cultivate Xiang. In Ohio, and later in Boston, where Xiang moved on the next leg of his American tour, the two of them became increasingly friendly. Over time, my father slowly revealed that he would be interested in knowing more about Xiang's activities with the Chinese air force and, if possible, to know more about what the Chinese military was involved in. As time went on, Xiang came to trust my father, and began to tell him stories.

Xiang was from Beijing and had two children, a boy and a girl. In 1989, when the Tiananmen Square demonstrations began, Xiang's son had participated in the protests. He was a pro-democracy activist and was soon to be a college student. But he got caught up in the security nets as the secret police and army chased waves of students across the square. In the melee, some overly zealous member of the police or army struck Xiang's son on the head with a baton. He fell to the ground. He suffered major head trauma, and had to be hospitalized for months. The beating was too much for Xiang to forget.

By the following year, my father and Xiang were meeting often, usually in a shabby Boston motel room where they would talk for hours. By now they were joking with each other. They exchanged stories about their children. My dad showed Xiang pictures of me as a boy, and Xiang did the same of his son. "I remember telling him that if anything ever happened to you, if anyone hurt you the way the Chinese police had hurt his son, I would be so unthinkably, so murderously angry," he told me once.

One night, Xiang volunteered to provide my father with sensitive information about the Chinese military. They stayed up late into the night, with my father asking as many questions as he could. He took copious notes. I don't know all that Xiang revealed to him, but the information did provide evidence of Israeli perfidy.

The next morning, my father went into the Boston CIA office and filed a cable to Washington. With very little editing, the cable was sent directly to the national security adviser with an "urgent" note attached. That afternoon or the next, the cable was returned to my father with a note from the adviser. "Excellent work," it read. "Congratulations."

That was all Bauer needed—a nod from the president, say, a quiet thank you. Of course, families need more. They need differently. Spies—real spies, not the Jack Bauer simulacrums—need like the rest of us. But I suppose to be a spy also required that one leave unanswered, or unasked, the question of the profession's effects on his or her emotional life. Anything else, I realized, could be a serious liability. After all, that's how foreign agents got to you—by pressing on your weaknesses in exchange for information. That's what the CIA taught its case officers to do. It must have also taught them how to protect themselves against the same tactics.

On a visit home around this time, I remember going out to dinner with Janet alone one night in Spokane, Washington. She started drinking white wine, several glasses, until she was quite tipsy. She flitted her hair, an old habit, but now the curls were no longer as lustrous—they were straighter and drier. She glanced around the restaurant, trying to piece her thoughts together.

"You know," she said with a sad smile—she wanted me to understand that she didn't want what she said to be taken badly, because I was his son, after all, and she knew where my loyalties were—"he always told me that his work was his work and that it doesn't affect us, our marriage, or our family. But I don't think he sees it." She looked at me to see if I understood what she was saying. I nodded. So she went on. "It's like he can't actually see that there's a carryover. I mean, hello! He's a spy, for God's sake!" She took another swig from her wineglass and fiddled with her food.

"How do you think it affected you?" I asked.

She shrugged, because some things don't need to be said. She laughed. "He's, you know, good at getting people to do what he wants. He's charming."

"He is that."

"And he's so smart."

"Do you think it makes us all weird?" I asked her. "I mean, none of us really trust each other."

She looked at me. "Oh, Scott, I hope not," she said. "No, I don't think so. It's just different."

But I also knew, or felt, anyway, that in Baghdad I was somehow trying to match my father. I sit here all cooped up like this, I thought, watching it all on television one day, trying to awaken it in real life the next.

When I was in high school—not in Michigan but in Virginia, right around the corner from Langley, the CIA headquarters— my father had an alias. Alan something-or-other. He had a driver's license that showed him in a mustache and glasses and bore Alan's name, and I used to spot it now and again on the telephone stand or in the kitchen next to his wallet and keys. I picked it up once and looked closely at the picture. I fingered the card's plastic edges, examining the watermarks and reading the details.

Height: 6 feet
Weight: 185 pounds
Hair: black
Eyes: brown

But everything else was wrong: the date of birth, the address, a funny kind of dead look in his eyes behind the thick, square bifocals. I remember feeling like an intruder had come into the house and was sitting by the phone, as if waiting for the owner to get home because there was something urgent the two of them needed to discuss.

In 1989, shortly after we had moved to McLean, Virginia, my father pulled me aside and handed me a small card. It was red, white, and blue, and listed the names of several countries, including Saudi Arabia, Iran, Iraq, Pakistan, and Afghanistan. Beside each name was a series of letters and numbers. The markings showed the origins of the anonymous diplomatic vehicles that were on constant patrol around the suburbs of northern Virginia. Most diplomats were allowed to drive wherever they wanted; but when they did, they aroused suspicion. If I saw any of those countries' vehicles nearby, my father said, I should let him know immediately. I carried the card around in my almost bare wallet, next to my social security card and driver's license. But I never looked at it or pulled it out, and eventually it grew weathered and torn, until finally it disintegrated and I had to throw it away.

Then, when my father moved to Spain in 1992, we had to pass a battery of psychological tests. I was called in to see a CIA psychiatrist. He sat behind a small desk, a white-shirted, bespectacled little man with a sheaf of papers and a checklist. I had been smoking a lot of dope the week before the test, and my blood was filled with THC. I knew I was going to have to take a blood test, so I just came out with it: I told him I had smoked pot, but he couldn't tell my dad.

"Anything else?" he asked.

"Is this going to change whether we go to Spain?"

"Anything else?"

"No. Pot. That's it."

He took notes. He didn't look like a psychiatrist. And he likely wasn't; he was probably a government interrogator. Maybe he was the same one who issued the polygraph tests my father hated so much. But I was scared he wouldn't let my parents leave the country because of my indiscretions.

I had to fill out a long questionnaire at home and return it. I answered all the questions and checked all the boxes. What would you do if . . . ? How do you feel about . . . ? What is your best . . . ? What is your favorite . . . ? And how many . . . ? And what kind . . . ? There was a score, but I never knew what it said, or if I passed or failed—or which of those would be worse.

A few days later, I went to pick up my father at Langley. I waited outside, in the parking lot. The building was a giant silver box. It was my first time there. A couple of guards stood behind some bulletproof glass in a hut, but otherwise I saw no people. There were American flags everywhere. Not a piece of litter on the ground. The grass was ultra-green. I turned off the engine and let the radio run. Finally I saw him coming out, walking briskly. I loved the way my father walked; he was as at home in his stride as a gunslinger. But he looked stern. He saw me, but he was sucking on his cheeks in concentration. He slid into the passenger seat and instructed me to drive us to a nearby park. He wanted to talk.

We parked near an open stretch of grass and got out. I knew what was coming. I never should have trusted that interrogator. My dad asked me why I was smoking pot, and I told him it wasn't as bad as all that.

"Look," he told me, "you can smoke it if you want, but if you get into trouble with it, I'm not going to help you out."

Lying on my dirty couch in Baghdad, watching Jack Bauer beat the world into submission and compliance, I thought about all of those moments with my father and his company. And all of it—the FBI man and his parrot, talking with Janet in Spokane, the CIA psychologist—felt like theater, an imagined world. And yet it wasn't. I knew that the work he did was necessary and important. Every country had people like my father—people who protected the rest, sheltered them, and made tremendous sacrifices for some notion of the greater good. But this work took a toll on these people. And as much as they might try to shelter their families from the lives they secretly lived, it was nearly impossible to keep those worlds apart, to keep one safe from the other.

My father was able to contain a huge amount of conflict within himself—more, I think, than most people. It was a tremendous feat. Within the CIA, people like him, who worked as case officers in the clandestine branch, were often referred to as "the chosen ones." This was no accident. They had to be particularly skilled at juggling those razor-thin boundaries where identity shifted into mask and back again. They had to understand people more than they understood themselves, anticipate them, think for them, and feel their way into the dark places no one else could. Psychologically, it was a colossal challenge. They were chosen, cultivated, and groomed by masters of manipulation for lives and careers that would require all of their emotional energy. It was no wonder if their resources could only stretch so far.

CHAPTER 18

Washington State, 2006

During one of my breaks from Baghdad, I went to visit my father. It was summer, and we decided to take a trip.

As we drove, I looked over at him beside me in the truck. We were traveling alongside the wheat fields and low, blue ridges of the Huckleberry Range, toward our land. The land, what we called "the property," was a hundred acres of pristine timber on a ridgeline of forest west of Addy, Washington, which was nearly a ghost town. The nearest big town was Colville, almost twelve miles away. It was mountainous terrain, full of bears and deer, and flush with the small, pungent berries that gave the range its name. To the west and down a hill, the Columbia River lumbered by in massive silver glory. And east, down a steep incline, were several meandering farming valleys that produced hay and wheat, and that welcomed Mennonites from back east, and solitary types who wore their John Deere caps like uniforms.

Our spread was near the summit. My father had bought the land in 1974, a year after I was born. A great deal had changed since then, but the road to the property had not—and nor had the Columbia, which scrolled along like a nickel vein through granite.

The towns out there, the ones that still had heartbeats, lived around main roads, with their one or two stoplights, diners, and one-stop shoe stores that sold tailored leather business attire alongside steel-toed loggers' boots. On days the stores were closed, we'd see families in the park. The kids were barefoot, the mothers pregnant. The fathers wore caps with bald eagles spread out on wide bills.

Warm air blew through the windows of our Nissan truck, and with it the smell of hay and the tang of wildflowers and smoke. The sound of cicadas bounced around the walls of the cab like violin notes. Before going to the property, my father wanted to see his friend Ernie. As we rounded the summit, the view south and east converged to a narrow valley with two walls of trees. From there began the six-mile descent into Rice. My father amused himself by coasting the whole way down; with spare use of the brakes, we drifted past the old llama farm and all the way to the river. The llama had disappeared since I had last visited. It was too difficult to get water, and the owners had put the house up for sale. As the descent steepened, he pointed out a road named Scott. And a little while later, another named Johnson.

We pulled into the gravel lot next to the Rice store. On the far side of the road, a ribbon of grass had grown high and was swishing back and forth in the wind. At one end of the lot stood an open hangar, and just outside it Ernie was bent over, working under the hood of my dad's camper. Ernie used to own the Rice store, but he had been forced to close it, too. These days, people did most of their shopping upriver in Kettle Falls, ever since the Wal-Mart opened there. No point in making an extra stop just to get coffee, Ernie said. While Ernie and my father talked, I walked down the road and stared toward the river. I could just make out its edge, a thin blue strip of currents moving in two directions at once. Over the years, the river levels rose and fell. The summer I was eight, it was the lowest I had ever seen it. A fellow could swim across it if he really tried. He would drift in the currents—first one way, then the other—but he would reach the opposite shore.

My father had his foot up on the camper's tire when I walked over. Ernie turned back to the rotor cap he had fixed and adjusted his own cap, with a wolf on it, downward. "The more you leave this thing, the worse it gets," he said. "You leave anything too long it's going to choke on you. Come on, I'll drive you up there." He dropped the hood and dusted off his hands, nodding at the camper. "I know how she's running now, anyway."

I followed them back up the hill in the Nissan. Ernie and my dad made an odd pair. Ernie was the kind of guy whose respect my father coveted: a character with firm knowledge of specific elements, like machinery or wood; someone whose intentions were as transparent as they were tractable. Ernie had his own trailer down the hill, with pictures of wolves on his walls and porcelain wolf sculptures in his makeshift living room. I was sure he was Indian somewhere back there. He hesitated taking money from my father for the work he did on our camper.

We reached the top of the hill and pulled in. My father opened the gate we had erected to keep hunters out, and we coasted on to the little meadow at the end of the road where we always talked about building a house someday. It was immediately cooler underneath the ponderosas and cedars that surrounded the clearing, creaking and groaning, shedding their needles and bits of tar. Wisps of cloud sped by above, propelled by the currents and the lure of the floodplains that stretched out below.

We unloaded the camper off the Dodge, mounted it, and then stood around the trucks for a while as Ernie and my father talked about the price of land and the cost and cut of cedar wood. Ernie, with a reed of grass in his mouth, nodded approvingly at several cords of wood, and my father said he could come up anytime and cut down as much as he might need. We were silent for a while, and then, looking at my father, Ernie inclined his head toward me and said, "Must be nice to have him back, huh?"

My father nodded, and put his hand on my shoulder. "It sure is."

"You being careful over there?" Ernie asked me, glancing at my father. "Your dad told me about it."

I said I was.

He drew a blade of grass across his mouth. "You think it's gonna get any better? You think those Iraqis are gonna make it?"

I shook my head. "No, I don't." I shucked my feet along the needles. Ernie adjusted his cap. My father started to say something analytical, something about the Middle East, but I shot him a look. He stopped short.

Ernie said roughly, like a command, "Well, you be careful, all right."

"I will. Thanks."

My father tried to smile, but his normally strong mouth loosened. I figured he was hurt that I had tried to tell him to keep quiet. I just didn't want to hear about Baghdad—not right then, when I would be back so soon.

We shook hands, and Ernie tipped his cap down low, climbed into the Dodge's cab, and rumbled off.

After breakfast the next morning, my father cleaned the camper's Formica counters with boiled water. A dead wasp lay on the windowsill and another buzzed around the curtains, looking for a way out. He couldn't remember when he had cleaned the windows, or anything inside. It might have been the last time I'd been there with him, he said.

He wandered outside and began digging at something in the ground. I watched from the back window.

"Come take a look at this," he called out.

I climbed down onto a stump. My father was poking the end of his stick through the soft needles of an eight-inch-tall white pine. "See how small it is," he said. "I planted this eight years ago and it hasn't grown at all, not even an inch."

"It doesn't get any sun," I said.

But the sun would come, spear through all this, and penetrate somewhere.

He licked his lips and looked around as if to verify. "Is that what it is? I planted them all over. This is the only one that hasn't grown."

"I don't know," I said.

He looked up at the sky. The ponderosas heaved in the wind.

That night I laid my sleeping bag out on top of the bed in the camper and crawled in. The light from the campfire glowed through the plastic door. My father came over and laid his hand on my chest and smiled at me.

"Good night, Scotty," he said. "Sweet dreams, my sweet boy."

"Good night," I said, and smiled. He had never lost his habit of tucking me in, and I had never lost the habit of expecting it now and again if he was around. I was in the safest place I could be right then, but I knew in just a few days it would all be stripped away again. I felt the pressure of his hand on my sternum, enjoying the way he rubbed the blanket and patted it down. Then he smiled and turned away, disappearing.

When his flashlight passed underneath my window, I crawled to the far side of the bed to watch him. He would sleep in the back of the pickup that night. He sat on the tailgate and pulled one leg up to take his boots off, then thought better of it and moved off to the edge of the road to pee. He turned off his flashlight and darkness flooded in. To see him I placed him in the corner of my eye, like he had taught me. He wasn't seven yards away, but his form was already dissolving into the thickets of branches. Then he moved, slightly, and I caught him. He looked tall. His face was a white blur. He was watching the stars.

I woke up in the middle of the night. I opened the door to a sky full of brightness. I'd never seen so many stars, not even here. There were too many. They were framed by black treetops. The forest was singing in creaks and whinnies, clicks and groans. It could wipe you away if you let it, if you let yourself float to the upper branches where needles flew off into the void, where the whole world was visible. When my father was living abroad, he used to come here between assignments. He spent weeks alone with the trees. When he and my mother were divorcing, he had sought refuge here. He cooked on the fire. He washed in the river. He'd slept alone under the sky. I never had; I was always too scared. I still was. I stood in the doorway for a while and let the cold wind blow. Out there, it looked like the moon had set the world alight with wind, and now it was racing to flow away, to come together in some new form before time simply ran out. I stayed that way until it got too cold, and closed the door again. The wind blew on.

When I woke the next morning, the sun was already high. It was too hot to do much work, so we decided to take a picnic to the river. The road passed by peach orchards and tree farms, and followed the bends of the river winding slowly to the north.

We pulled into an empty space at the riverfront. Off a newly built dock, two jet-skiers were revving their engines. Years before, we had stockpiled several gallons of cherries from a tree on the banks here. We had clambered up the branches, told jokes, and bragged about who had the biggest cherry; but since then, the park service had laid asphalt over what used to be the sand-and-gravel parking lot. The cherry tree was gone.

I took our lunch and headed for the far end of the beach.

We walked toward a couple of old aspens that had been there since I was a child, and sat on warm logs. The river was still low and flat. Across it, the hills of the Colville Indian Reservation were reflected as a jagged strip, separating blue from yellow. On the opposite hillside the sun was getting brighter, and the contours of swales and ridges had begun to glow. A slab of light crept across the water like a moving shelf of lava.

When I was a child and we returned to America in the summer, the one unchanging constant was the land of the Columbia. In and of itself, there was nothing particularly stable about it. We had no house there, nothing built that we could turn to for shelter. There were hardly any people—only the strange man on an adjoining property who kept wolves, or the solitary neighbor who fed the deer from his back steps. Over time, I would come to notice the community shrinking. The wind peeled the houses of their paint; the walls sagged and crumbled. But when I was a child, it never seemed to change much at all. You could stand in the middle of the road and hear the trucks long before any were visible, and the certainty of that distance was a form of safety in itself. The banks of the Indian reservation were untouched by roads or houses. From our side of the river, the hills there stretched on in a naked, sunlit glory.

My father and I had often gone to the banks to swim, stripping to nothing, slipping into the cold water and drifting on our backs. The river was always green, and clear to the bottom. My father brought little white bars of soap, and we stood in the shallows and scrubbed off pinesap and pitch and seedling. I swam out as far as I could into the currents and began to drift downstream, and then pulled myself back in. We lay on stones and watched clouds as the wind dried us. And we sat in the shade of the quaking aspen and listened to the clucking the hard leaves made, like castanets, and the whistle of the wind through them. There *was* no God, my father said, but for the god that lived in those waters and trees and hills. There was the land itself, and nothing else. When you died, you passed into nothingness. After you were gone, what you left behind was ephemeral, with the life of a single man's memory; the legacy you left was incarnate in who you had created. Life was a great and unyielding mystery, but it was the questioning that gave it shape and form. We were just passing through, like driftwood.

After our lunch, we decided to drive further along upriver. We followed the road north, past Kettle Falls, which the Indians called *Swah-net'-qhu*, and over to the other side of the river, where the land flattened out and tracts of farmed watershed began to appear. I wanted to go on this drive with my father precisely because it would be long and meandering. It offered up a chance for discovery. But because there were so many distractions, it also made it easier for me to ask him things he didn't want to discuss. I had been trying for years with varying success. Now I returned to our longest-running conversation. I did so artlessly, with the bluntness I knew he hated. As a young man in Mexico, he had acted as an extra in movies and done a few cigarette commercials. And he had contemplated being an actor full time. I thought the two careers mirrored each other well, and I wondered if he did too. "Do you think being an actor helped you to be a spy?"

He stiffened. "Acting is make-believe," he said. Case officers—he never called himself a spy, only I did—weren't making anything up when they worked; they weren't pretending to be people they weren't. Nothing, in fact, could be further from the realities of being an intelligence officer or engaging in the art of espionage.

It was my turn to stiffen. I was determined to extract an admission that my suspicions—about the natural links between the performance of one's own life and the manipulation of another's—were real. His actor's charisma and ability to make life seem large must have come in handy, sometime, at least once? "But there has to be an element of fantasy, no? What about when you have to convince someone that you're not actually a spy— that you're not what you really are, and what they believe you to be? Doesn't that involve some acting?" I thought back to Camp Peary, and the café along the banks of the York River, where Jeff and Reid and I used to go for malted milkshakes.

But my father was quiet. He had decided it wasn't so, and no amount of wheedling for another answer on my part was going to convince him. "I only pretended to be someone else once, in Hong Kong, in the seventies," he said.

"Oh?" I had never heard this story.

He had flown from India to Hong Kong to intercept an Indian businessman who had been posted to North Korea. My father wore a fake mustache, adopted an appropriately British name like Attenborough or Marks, and acted "prim and proper." The Indian was only too happy to oblige a representative of the Crown, but it turned out that he had nothing of value for my father or his colleagues.

"I can do a decent British accent if I try," he said. But when I asked to hear it, he balked and said he'd do it later. He was too angry to indulge me any further.

We fell silent. My curiosity on this point—the moral tone of his work—had become a sore spot between us. I asked him why this was the case. We pulled into a service station and I let the engine idle while I waited for an answer. When his father died, he had told me that he wished he had "assessed" his father better. That was the language of his work; it was the CIA case officer's job to "assess" potential agents for recruitment. Officers must determine the individual's psychological makeup, weaknesses, hidden desires, and strengths. They must form a well-rounded picture. Then they must act on it. They must exploit it. They do it again and again in their attempts to keep the upper hand on their enemies, to extract information and loyalty. They do it with the necessary people at first. And then, I imagined, it became second nature. The natural inclination grew stronger, and thus the circle of those who would be tested expanded. Eventually, I imagined, you did it with everyone, until finally it was done back to you.

"I don't mind you asking me questions," he said at last, and let the pause linger. "What I don't like is being interrogated." He had often urged me to "develop my elicitation skills" when I was talking to him—or, for that matter, anyone. He didn't like my directness. And I, in turn, balked at being told I was too blunt, although I knew I was. Perhaps my methods offended his sense of how subtly and cleverly information could be obtained, if done right.

"I'm not interrogating you," I shot back.

My father stared out the window and chewed on an apple. Ahead of us was the truss bridge, and underneath, the snake of the Columbia. I wondered if he was having a diabetic low; he seemed slightly slower than usual. But then I realized that he wasn't looking at anything outside. He was concentrating on something else, something invisible in the cab—the seedling of doubt that had again sprouted up on the seat between us.

"I'm not," I persisted. "I'm not interrogating you."

He looked over at me with an expression as overflowing as the waters we were near. But his voice was even and controlled, just a notch below its usual timbre. "Are you sure about that?"

Part III

The Stranger within my gates,
He may be evil or good,
But I cannot tell what powers control —
What reasons sway his mood;
Nor when the Gods of his far-off land
Shall repossess his blood.

—"The Stranger," Rudyard Kipling

CHAPTER 19

New Hampshire, 2006

I often asked my mother about my father. She was reluctant, at first, to discuss my dad too much because she felt a certain amount of loyalty to him. The failure of their marriage was theirs to share. And my mother took responsibility for her part.

I suspected that the long years spent living in a world of secrets had taken a toll on my father. I didn't know exactly how, though. But my mother had wondered about it too. And I wondered how it had affected her.

"Well," she said, "he *was* a commercial officer." We were sitting in her family cottage. My aunt, Linda, was there too.

"He wasn't. He was a spy," I protested.

She nodded and looked down, picking at her cuticles. Somehow it seemed necessary to her, even in hindsight, that he be both.

Like all of us, my mother sometimes lied; hers were especially about my father. These were not harmful lies, or malicious ones, or even intentional in any meaningful way. They were simply the result of the way things were. To change just one word in a sentence of your past can change everything. Between us, there was—and still is—an endless reckoning of how to do it.

My mother came from a family of diplomats. She had been

well drilled in the art of adaptation. It was a family virtue; rigidity was a cardinal sin. She had accepted the news of my father's recruitment into the CIA as a government bureaucrat's daughter might, with great joy and excitement. Her father had been a real State Department officer. And my mother and her sister had grown up all around the world, like me.

After she and my father were married in Mexico, over the long summer of 1969, when her friends were wearing flowers in their hair and smoking pot, my father went to Washington, D.C., for interviews and then, after he was accepted, instruction and indoctrination. My mother took to the change willingly. As his wife, she would come to help my father in his principal task: identifying and recruiting Soviets overseas. In the summer of 1971, they left the United States for India on his first foreign assignment. They flew to San Francisco, then to Hawaii and Hong Kong, and finally landed in Calcutta at 3:00 one morning.

At the social events she attended, while graciously playing the role of the pretty young wife, my mother carried out other, less obvious duties. She assessed Soviets for their potential to become defectors. My mother had very little in the way of training—she brought no specific knowledge about what a good defector would or should look like—and yet my father trusted her intuition and observational abilities.

That was how my parents came to know Sergei and Natasha. Natasha was Ukrainian, thin and dark. Sergei was Russian, blond and handsome. The four met at a party hosted by a Mexican diplomat. In those days in India, the art of espionage was a social affair. Lawn parties, croquet matches, cocktail soirees—these were the halls and mirrors where spies dwelt.

My parents invited the couple over for drinks one night. The men tried to impress each other with theories of capitalist excess or Keynesian dynamism. My father trotted out some glossy American catalogs from Sears Roebuck and put them on the coffee table to whet his guests' appetite for Western material pleasures, but they went unremarked upon. Both of these men lacked a certain ruthlessness, or experience. They were both new at the game.

Soon, the two couples began to spend time together regularly. Their playgrounds were wide and yellow sandy beaches, with the pale brown sun sitting low over an easy green ocean. There were usually slow-moving figures in the distance, thin fishermen with their long wooden prows pitching silver filament along the horizon. The squawking of the gulls was like an ever-present multitude of voices trying to tell them something in a language they could not understand. The great wash of the Indian Ocean surrounded them. At nights, Sergei and Natasha drank from the bottle of Jack Daniel's my father had given them, and my parents sipped their gifted Stoli's.

"What did you think about Natasha?" my father asked, after evenings spent with the Russians. "Or Sergei? What did your intuition tell you? Did you have a feeling they're for real, or do they want to defect?"

She thought, considering all the time they'd all spent together, that maybe they did, yes.

My father hoped that was the case. He put away the Sears Roebuck catalogs soon after. He didn't make a point of highlighting his eight-track stereo or his record collection or his newly bought Italian leather shoes to show Sergei that he was living the high life. He was genuinely glad for the friendship.

The fact that Sergei was KGB didn't change much for my mother, either. She wasn't interested in politics, and ultimately she didn't give a damn if they wanted to defect or not. Natasha was her friend. She was there when my mother was pregnant with me, watched her grow big, cheered her on, and promised to be there for her after the birth.

But after I was born, my mother *did* begin to have a problem with the double life she was leading. "For the most part I was struck by what a wonderful husband and father he was," she told me, "and how he doted on you, and you were the center of his life.

I saw him as almost perfect, and felt that I couldn't measure up to him and his expectations. I saw him as even-keeled, unflappable, solid, very intelligent, and articulate. I also thought of him as positive and optimistic. At the same time, I felt he had unrealistic expectations. He was judgmental, and critical of my shortcomings and negative feelings. I felt guilty for not measuring up to his expectations."

In 1975, two years after I was born, she wrote in a journal that my father "seemed to be uncomfortable with the expression of any emotions other than positive ones and to want to suppress them." She wrote:

> In a discussion, if I get very excited or get angry, Keith's response
> is to tell me to calm down and control my emotions. If I get angry,
> he would get angry with my anger, then clam up and carry a long
> grudge. He seemed to want to shut out all conflict. I have become
> afraid to show anger, as if having that emotion makes me a bad
> person. I try to repress it, control it. I've felt that unless I was
> positive and even-keeled all the time, he'd come down on me. I
> cannot express emotions of fear, sadness, frustration, impatience,
> nervous anxiety, etc. When I do, I feel guilty . . . guilty for having
> these emotions.

My mother worried that her critique of him was unjust, that he didn't deserve this kind of unruly psychological grilling. She worried that much of her angst was of her own making, and that he was doing his best under difficult circumstances. But she ended up feeling bad all the same.

Over the years, she also began to notice one of my father's more marked traits—his exaggerated sentimentality. It reminded her, she told me, of the way actors are in musicals. It was hard for her to pinpoint and describe the quality, but it was as if he was too effusive, and it seemed to her sometimes that his emotions lacked depth. She started researching personality types.

"Isn't it true that even if you're retired, you're still not allowed to talk about it?" Linda asked, sliding the lid off a pot into which she plunked squash. The windows of the cottage had steamed, and beads of water dribbled down, leaving inky pools behind.

"We became quite good friends with some of the agents," my mother said, looking up from the table where she had been doodling on a notepad, her brow furrowed as she struggled to draw these memories into clarity.

"But didn't they know you were in the CIA?" Linda asked.

"They probably did, but we were playing this sort of game," my mother said. "We were pretending that we didn't know."

"What did they do?" Linda put down the knife and stood with her hands under her chin like a squirrel, as if ferreting away the information for some future time.

"There were all these unknowns," my mother said. "That's what the whole thing was all about, to find out. Keith would say, 'Lee, what does your intuition tell you? Do you have a feeling that they really are for real?'" Her eyebrows raised with the memory.

"You were hoping they were going to defect to the U.S.?" Linda asked.

"They were KGB, but in the end it turned out they weren't candidates for defection."

"So then what?"

My mother grappled with the memory of her friends, and the possibility that never came to anything. "For me, at that young age, it felt like a betrayal of trust."

There was a silence. "But didn't Keith tell you that's how it was?" Linda asked after a while, chewing thoughtfully on a piece of celery.

After so many years, all that seemed to be left of the strangeness of that time was this confusion about what it meant then and what it means now. There was not much to cling to, nor to be bitter about. Nevertheless, seduction only ever works when everyone enjoys the idea of it, and by the end of their marriage my mother did not.

"The problem for me was that we got involved with these people as friends," she said. "There was a fine line between the professional relationship and the friendship."

In 1977 I was four, much too young to know anything, but for months my father had been working on a Soviet named Gregori.

He had had some small success with Gregori at first. Gregori had warmed to my father's advances, and accepted several invitations to dine at our house. Gregori had downplayed his importance. He was just a bureaucrat, he often told my father with a laugh and a shrug, a low-ranking official with little access to sensitive files or valuable classified information.

And yet my father was still thrilled at the sight of the man casually flipping through the pages of the Sears Roebuck catalog with his wife, picking out this or that luxury item. He was even more thrilled when, a few weeks later, he dropped the couple off on a dark, residential street near the Soviet compound, and watched them disappear carrying a new stereo and two pairs of highly prized blue jeans purchased from the catalog.

It wasn't long afterward that Gregori began telling my father how disgusted he was with the Soviet system. He could pinpoint the exact time of his disillusionment, he said; it had been while he was still in high school and one of his favorite teachers had disappeared. He was told not to ask any questions. This was an exciting development, my father knew, but it was also dangerous. The Soviets could possibly be "dangling" Gregori and setting a trap for my father. He told his superiors at the station about his concerns. "Don't worry," they told him. "Get him."

Gregori had no real knowledge of the operational matters of his office at the Soviet embassy, nor access to any sensitive documents, so my father began by asking for very basic information that would verify Gregori's bona fides and establish his willingness to cooperate. What was the internal structure of his office? Who were the undercover KGB officers? What was the physical layout? And could he draw a sketch of the offices and write the names of the people working in each one? Gregori did this without compunction. Again my father dropped him off in a side street after a circuitous tour through a darkening New Delhi.

Around the same time my father was cultivating Gregori, he was introduced to another Soviet—a man named Oleg, an economics professor who worked at the Soviet embassy. Oleg seemed harmless enough, and so did their meeting—a chance encounter at a neighbor's dinner party—but it gave my father the inroad to invite the professor home to dinner a few weeks later.

Oleg was gregarious and cheery, full of lighthearted anecdotes about the dismal state of affairs at home. To read a Soviet newspaper, he joked, one must begin with the obituaries, to learn of those who have finally escaped. Oleg had a kind of preposterous hilarity, like a Cold War Roberto Benigni, and my father wondered if here, too, was another potential recruitment.

As they sat down to dine, Oleg excused himself. He was an obsessive, he said. He was constantly washing his hands, and he must do so now.

My father laughed and waved him off to the washrooms.

After dinner, Oleg told my father that he wanted to reciprocate the invitation. But it would be impossible to meet at his house, he said, without giving a reason. Instead, the Soviet suggested they meet in a week's time in the main dining hall of the Ashok Hotel.

And so it was that, a week later, my father arrived at the Ashok hall, an old-style dining room that harked back to the height of the British Empire. Oleg was already seated. He was as jovial as usual, and they ordered cocktails and chatted. After ordering, Oleg said that he must excuse himself to wash his hands. My father waved him off once again.

No sooner had Oleg disappeared, however, than another Soviet appeared, slipped into Oleg's seat, and introduced himself.

"We need to talk," he told my father.

Thoughts of Gregori immediately sprang to his mind. He was suddenly worried. Gregori had been opening up more and more of late. He hated his own system, he had told my father.

"Okay," my father said. "Let's talk."

The man took out a small tape recorder and placed it on the table between them. "We've been watching you for many years now, Mr. Johnson," he said. "Ever since you were in Mexico."

"Why?" my father replied, in the expected tone of befuddlement. After all, he was just a lowly bureaucrat.

"We've been watching your contact with Gregori from the very beginning, and now you're going to be in big trouble with the admiral," said the KGB officer.

"Wait a minute, you dumb shit," my father said, "you've got the wrong guy. I'm not in the navy, and I don't care what any admiral says about me."

The Soviet turned the tape recorder on. The sound was indistinct, but my father could clearly hear his and Gregori's voices. He tried to grab the recorder, but the Soviet snatched it back.

Gregori *had* been dangled. My father tried not to appear rattled.

"You may continue working Gregori," the Soviet told him, "but under our direction." He then offered $50,000 for cooperation.

"Fifty thousand?" my father laughed. "I'll earn that much next year clipping coupons from my stock options." And anyway, he persisted, why would the Soviets be so interested in the cooperation of a lowly economics officer?

He stood up to leave, and the Soviet followed. As he passed the maître d', my father gestured back at the Soviet. "He'll take care of the bill," he said, and walked out.

In the spring of 1973, several years earlier, my parents had gone on a trip to rest and relax. Friends of my father's, another CIA couple, were living in Katmandu, and my father wanted my mother to see the mountain kingdom before I was born. After a week at a nearly deserted beach in Malaysia, they flew up one day in April, when my mother was six months pregnant. They sat side by side in the bulkhead seats, just behind the cockpit. A man next to my father warned him that if they didn't touch down at the very beginning of the runway, they risked crashing. The runway was under construction, and the final extensions at the end hadn't yet been completed.

When the plane came rolling in, the runway began to unfurl beneath them without the plane touching down, and the man gave my father a look. And my dad turned to his new wife. "This is it, Lee," he said, and clutched her hand.

The plane crashed on the unfinished runway and caught on fire. It went catapulting down over the runway extension, a drop of several yards, and as it did the cockpit came unhinged and spiraled off to the side, leaving them exposed to the air but still moving forward. Just before reaching the second step, the plane came to a shuddering halt. My father jumped down off the smoking wing and held out his arms to my mother. And she, pregnant with me, leaped into my father's arms from the burning wreckage through a gaping hole. Several people in the rear died later from injuries sustained in the crash.

My mother, who had been in car races with her college boyfriends, run reckless through her teens, and loved life in so many forms, was suddenly quiet. In shock, and terrified of miscarrying—and of the greater fears that lay suddenly visible on the horizon—she put her head in the arms of the other CIA wife and prayed. Those Nepalese mountains were so glorious; the winds rolled over their peaks and curled like waves. The mountains rose into a sky tinted with the black of space. But there she lay in their midst, one of God's trinkets.

My mother went into labor in July of 1973, in Madras. I was big and she was very small. She lay in the bed at the hospital all night. My father paced the rooms outside. The rains had come again, and outside the streets were flooded; but the inside of the hospital was dank, white, and antiseptic. She pushed until she couldn't anymore, and by that stage it was too late or too dangerous for a cesarean. The doctor had to act quickly. She was experienced, but overconfident. She rushed in with a pair of metal forceps and clasped my head, pulling me headfirst into the world and crushing my malleable skull along the way. I emerged misshapen and bruised. The pressure of the forceps had bashed my head, and it began to swell. It turned blue, then black.

There was a neurosurgeon on call that morning, and he was summoned immediately. On my first day of life, he performed emergency surgery on me: he pushed my skull back out, pressuring it back to a form much like a Ping-Pong ball pinched by fingers, and then released it with a pop. But my head continued to swell and bruise, and I was a mess of contusions for a while. For a year they thought I might be irreparably brain damaged.

My mother recalled waking up in bed to see Sergei and Natasha in the hospital delivery room, before she had even been allowed to hold me. The Russians were the first nonrelatives to see her, all sore and bloodied, and desperate to go home.

But my father remembers it differently. The Russians did come, but only when my mother had been cleansed and bandaged, and had held me in her arms for the first time. Sergei and Natasha brought me Matryoshka dolls, and for my father a Cuban stogie; for my mother they came bearing sympathy and considerable Russian love.

Now, years later, my mother struggled to find a word for how she'd treated them. She fiddled with her pen. She uncrossed her legs and looked at me. "You have to woo them," she finally said, as if the word were the final piece of a mental jigsaw puzzle she had been struggling with for years.

Linda took the squash out and laid four pieces on the board. "How do you choose what people to be friends with?" she asked.

"We invited them over to our house for drinks," my mother explained.

"But how did he pick which person to begin with, to even bother with?" my aunt persisted.

We lined up at the counter and ladled squash and steak and peas on to our plates. The windows had started to clear up.

"You probably have a lot of CIA guys around here and there," Linda mused, more to herself than to us.

"They have all kinds of covers—regular covers and deep covers," said my mom. "Keith was a regular cover, most of the time."

Linda took a bite of the squash and chewed with her eyes closed as she thought about this.

"He was almost a deep cover," my mother said. "He did function as a commercial officer; that was his job. He had to know how to do that job, but then underneath . . ."

"What's a deep cover?" asked Linda, her eyes still closed, the celery poised at her mouth like a paintbrush.

My father had told me about "illegals," sleeper spies sent to different countries to wait for instructions from their headquarters. They lived as locals for years—sometimes decades. Their children grew up as natives, knowing nothing of their father's or mother's job. They remained dormant until the day a handler called them from their slumber. "The time has come," they would say. There were also spies who worked outside the confines of the embassies, in regular jobs—as energy consultants or investment bankers— who had to take that extra measure of precaution to keep safe.

But deep cover was something else as well. To me, cover involved the family protecting the secret together: the way my father spoke to me sometimes, with the timbre of his voice lowered just a little; the way my mother whispered about the difficulties of her past; the way the first answer to a simple question for all of us (where are you from? Or, what does your father do?) was always a lie—distorted, shortened, or abbreviated.

When I was young, the Russians came to our house and played with me in my crib. My father and Sergei used the living room to discuss the world. My mother and Natasha cared about each other, sharing in motherhood.

Sergei and Natasha were my parents' friends for a time, until they simply weren't anymore. There was nothing dramatic about the ending; it began when my parents left India. They met as friends a few more times in America and elsewhere, but it wasn't the same. The reexamination afterward niggled at my mother. What was the point, after all? It began to feel like a betrayal—not that the game existed; she knew better than that. But that what had seemed like real friendship was also, in fact, an elaborate ruse. Beyond the immediate goal of recruitment was a void, a space cleared of figures or light or anything at all. It seemed a relationship destined for failure. Simple pleasures became, in hindsight, opportunities for endless examinations of motive and interest and calculated response. When she and Natasha had laughed so gleefully at the sloping figure of the fisherman caught in the surf, was there some ulterior motive? They had become involved with each other as friends, or so it had seemed, but the line between the professional and the personal got blurred and was eventually erased altogether.

Even as she tried to cope with the difficulties of living in India and of being sick, my mother also became increasingly unable to sympathize with or understand life with my father. He tried to lift her spirits, to buoy her, but he failed. She tried to live up to her own expectations, and failed too.

And to herself, she explored some of the reasons why. She wondered about my father, who was alone in bearing her burdens. "He has an intolerance of human weakness," she wrote. "Also, his exaggerated sentimentality with me undermines the depth of his emotions, makes them seem superficial. It seems he always wants me, everything, to be happy all the time, with no conflicts or emotionally jarring experiences (like in a musical)." She continued:

> *What is my response to these qualities? Anger. A sense of things being fixed, inflexible. A sense that these characteristics have created a barrier between us. I find myself suspecting him. No trust . . . I read in that book that this kind of behavior masked deeper harsh*

tendencies. I noted: "Keith once said himself that he was afraid that
subconsciouly he might have harsh, cruel tendencies." I paid little
heed at the time.

Not long afterward, my mother left India and returned to the
United States. The end of my parents' relationship was complicated, but the years of living in the shadows of the CIA hadn't
helped.

I was six when my parents divorced. I remember my mother
standing in the driveway at our house on Thatcher Road in McLean,
Virginia, before she drove off in her little blue car. Wind and rain
enameled the spring cherry blossoms into a street of dark tar.

My grandparents came to help my father with the separation.
My grandfather walked me home from school in the afternoons.
The sidewalks were filled with cracks. I scrupulously avoided
every one, not wanting any more bad luck.

My mother had gone to live in an efficiency apartment not far
away. When I went to stay with her, I slept on a pull-out couch in
the small living room. When I got up early, I watched cartoons on
her little black-and-white television and waited for her to wake
up. We made breakfast together—English muffins with butter
and jam, and bowls of cereal—and sat at a round table in the sunlight. We swam in the neighborhood pool. Sometimes we visited
the zoo, or the Smithsonian Institution, or even the Museum of
Natural History, because she knew how much I loved dinosaurs
and trilobites and fossils. At night we listened to *Peter and the
Wolf*, and I let her hold me when the sinister-sounding violins
played, indicating the black forest where the wolf was lurking.
She tucked me in and pulled the covers up high, kissed me on the
forehead, and told me how much she loved me. I don't remember
my father during that time at all; in my memory, my life with him
began just after. It was as if he simply disappeared for a while, the
period when I was saying goodbye to my mother.

CHAPTER 20
Mexico, 2006

In the spring of 2006, on another break from Baghdad, I asked my father to go on holiday with me in Mexico. He had just returned home from another tour in Bosnia as an independent contractor.

I picked him up at the airport in Puerto Vallarta, and we headed to the little town on the Pacific coast where I was staying. We turned a corner and drove down a muddy road, where women in brightly colored robes were selling Huichol beads, straw dolls, and clay statuettes of the Virgen de Guadalupe. A dirt road paralleled the beach. A few young guys wandered by, carrying surfboards. We passed women in sundresses, dogs resting in the shade of cars and tin porches, and hibiscus and bougainvillea springing out from the underbrush and the sides of houses. The road wound up and around the north end of the village, and the ocean spilled out below, underneath a sloping terrace of wild grass and neem trees and acacias that held black frigatebirds, iguanas, and geckos. He wore sunglasses. I felt like we were a couple of gringo thugs.

The war in Baghdad was as bad as it had ever been. There were revelations about Iraqis being killed in CIA detention facilities. It seemed like the world was coming apart. I asked him where he was going next. He stared out the windows at the shirtless brown men pouring cement and laying tile, but if he noticed them he didn't give any indication. "I have . . ." he began, and smiled to himself. "I've been having some moral qualms."

I turned sharply and looked at him. "Oh?"

"I might not go back again," he said. It wasn't clear if that meant anywhere, or just to the places that provoked the moral qualms.

I asked him if it was the first time he had felt that way, and he nodded.

"It must have been something pretty serious," I said, trying to draw him out, but he shook his head, uncomfortable with specificity. We kept driving. I reminded him about the CIA contractors who had been accused of murder, those who had been implicated in torturing Iraqis in CIA detention facilities, and those in the Abu Ghraib prison scandal. He knew about all of this, of course. He nodded in disgust.

"I don't know," he said. "We'll see."

The last time my father was anywhere near here was almost forty years earlier, when he had brought my mother to Puerto Vallarta for their honeymoon. This stretch of coast was nothing more than a string of fishing villages then. You could stand at one end of Puerto Vallarta and see the other end. There were two taxis in town, and a couple of thousand people. They rented a little bungalow right on the beach for eight dollars a night.

During the honeymoon, my father spoke to his cousin, Graydon, and invited him down to join them. This was made much fun of in years to come. How could you bring your cousin on your honeymoon? Graydon brought his fiancée. They were a young quartet, full of romance and possibility. The beaches they lay on have disappeared since, buried under cement and rebar.

We settled into our house, just above the beach, where the sound of the breakers rolled from day into evening and night. I put him in the room where I normally stayed and moved my blanket out onto the couch in the living room. I asked if he was comfortable and he said he couldn't be more so. He plugged in his computer to show me pictures later. He arranged his insulin kit on the bedside table. He carefully spread his clothes out on the dresser. He admired the art on the walls. Meanwhile, I went outside and got stoned on a whim, for I didn't smoke regularly, and came back.

"It's beautiful," he said. "Just gorgeous."

We went to sleep to the sound of the ocean. The waves crashed and retreated and crashed again as darkness fell and the whirring ceiling fans came to life and began to thump.

The next day I took him up to the hills in the next town over, where I had bought a small, fixer-upper house. The hills were lush and verdant, filled with palms and Higueras and Parrotta trees, where birdnests filled with eggs hung down like burlap sacks. In the hills there was a pond where iguanas and parrots lived, and horses roamed among the palms freely. From the top of one hill was a view that stretched all the way down to the little town below, and beyond that shone the blue panel of the sea. Burls of clouds rose up from behind the hills and crept along horizontally. My father talked about building a house. He took pictures and gazed out through the trees, enraptured.

On the way back home, he brought up an article I had written a couple of years before, about an Afghan warlord named Pacha Khan Zadran who had been a particularly nettlesome figure for the Americans. Zadran had probably been responsible for an ambush and nighttime attack on me and my friends near Gardez a few years earlier; his thugs controlled the area we were working in, and had the sources to know where we were at any given time. Later, when my father had gone to work at the CIA's base in Khost in 2004, Zadran had continued to be a problem; the warlord was still operating in and around Gardez and Khost. Sometimes he fought alongside the Americans, sometimes against them. As we were driving along through the canopy of trees back to our rented house, my father lamented Zadran's fate. "They should have killed him," he said. "I told them they should."

And then he added, "But they never listen to me—that's why I can say things like that. I'm not important enough."

I didn't say anything. After a long silence, he asked me if something was wrong. I shook my head. We drove along under the valley trees, which were dry, still, and unbloomed; dusty-looking.

"I'll be excited when they come up with a real, viable desalination machine," he eventually said, as if to no one in particular. "That'll change a lot of things."

I kept on driving. He said nothing more. We turned into the town and made our way to the house, where I collapsed on the sofa.

I wondered if his outburst had been a sudden expression of a desire for revenge—if it made sense to him that the perpetrator of the attack against me years before should just have been killed. A warlord couldn't, of course, simply be killed. Or rather, he *could*, but not for an offense like that. It was simply a fantasy of sorts. I had never heard my father express the idea that someone should be killed. If most people's dads said those kinds of things, I thought, it would seem innocuous.

That night I brought up again the CIA contractors in Iraq accused of murder. They had tortured Iraqis in dank prison cells and gotten away with it. My job, as a journalist in Iraq, had been to find the full story behind it. But I didn't know anything more than anyone else. "They were contractors," I said, vaguely. Were they really like you, I wondered to myself. I couldn't square the idea I had of my father with this much larger reality.

He changed the subject. It made him uncomfortable, but I didn't really care. I wanted him to be uncomfortable just then, to see how it felt to get grilled, to be uneasy. He asked a question, and moved the conversation on to something else. He began taking pictures of me. It seemed that he could hardly keep his attention on one thing for more than a few seconds. I couldn't stand it. I told him I didn't want to be photographed, but he went on taking pictures anyway.

That night, we went to dinner at a restaurant that overlooked the town square. I asked for a table on the edge of the floor, near a broken palapa roof. The light in the corner was dim. To the side of the roof a full moon had risen. Around it, a thin halo amplified the moonlight and cast it in an out-of-focus haze. I ordered wine. I looked at him across the table. He sat with his arms crossed and looked at me. His sun-kissed face seemed angry; his brows were furrowed. I waited for the wine to come, and when it did, I finished it quickly and ordered another.

"Good wine," he said.

"Mmm."

My heart was beating hard. We started talking in general terms about his work—I had taken his advice to work on my "elicitation skills." I asked him suddenly if his career had made it more difficult to establish personal relationships or intimacy.

He scrutinized me. I was sweating. Over the years, his privacy had come to seem to me like a precious commodity. Sometimes I wanted his confessions; sometimes I wanted nothing. He told me he couldn't think of anything about his job that made it especially difficult to have personal relationships. He said he didn't understand what about my childhood was strange or weird. "What was stranger about your growing up than . . ." and he mentioned another family whose parents worked for the State Department, and whose moves and constant instability mirrored my own in virtually every other way.

So I told him. It was strange to come home and find one of his drivers' licenses with an alias I had never heard before sitting on the microwave. Or have a CIA psychiatrist examine my mental fitness for another of his foreign postings.

"Where?" my father asked, incredulous. "Where did that happen?"

"In Virginia," I said.

"A psychiatrist?" he asked again, unbelieving.

"Yeah." I nodded, sipped more wine, and leaned back in my chair.

"What did he want to know?"

He had a list of questions and he was checking off my answers on a piece of paper, I told him. "Oh, and there was also something I had to fill out at home."

"There was?" He was struck.

"*That* was weird."

"What kind of questions?"

"If I had taken drugs."

"I don't remember that at all."

"Really," I muttered, marveling at how he could have forgotten something, which, at the time at least, had seemed so monumental. But he shook his head. "No," he said, "I don't remember that at all."

I sat staring at nothing in particular for a long time. A few tables away, an elderly couple was finishing off a pair of drinks and it struck me suddenly that the woman might be trying to listen to us. The couple was quiet, perhaps only contemplative, basking in the evening air and the unencumbered view of the hills, where a thousand small lights were spread like floaters in a fishing net. But for a moment all I heard were dangerous words, like "CIA" and "operations," words that had no place on this soft night. His eyebrows were arched, and I was glad that he was facing away from the rest of the diners. Did I engineer this on purpose—this subtle removal, far enough away from the crowd so that the others would have difficulty in hearing us, or working out what remained unspoken between us? Did I, as he had so often accused me, direct him here to interrogate him, to get the answers I wanted to hear? Instinctively, I brought my hand up to my lips and made a sign for quiet with my fingers while looking past him at the other table, and without skipping a beat his voice descended a pitch and his head bent down a few degrees. This was part of the game, too. These subtle shifts are part of any human exchange but, with us, it took on something of the cloak-and-dagger. I wanted to be able to relate to him on this level, to speak his language of secrecy.

He asked me what else.

"There were a lot of weird things," I said.

We were silent a while.

"What about Tlatelolco?" I asked.

"What about it?" he said. "I wasn't there on the night of the big massacre. I was there another night. I think you're confusing two nights." Then he laughed. "Scotty, I wasn't involved in any massacre. I never saw anything like that. I promise you."

I actually knew this by then, for as I dug I had realized that I had conflated the dates of two separate incidents. I had, on my own, absolved him of any crimes. But I wanted to hear it from him, again. Ultimately, I wanted an acknowledgment that my memories, real or imagined, were at least something—that I hadn't dreamed it all, that his faulty and selective memory was not mine, and that I was not crazy if I remembered my life with a twinge of fear, sometimes, or paranoia. I may never know how much of that fear could be chalked up to my own genetic makeup, the quirks of my brain chemistry, how much my own sensitivity to life trumped, in the end, whatever my father did or did not do. As wonderful a father as he was, and is, however, a part of me still needed to hear him recognize that both of us—me just as much as him—were children of the CIA.

CHAPTER 21

Washington State, 2007

The following year, in January, when the weather had turned cold again, I left Iraq. My assignment over, I flew out of that dingy Baghdad airport and vowed never to return.

I went to visit my father, of course.

The two of us left Spokane early one morning and drove north, toward the Canadian border. It had been snowing on and off for a few days, and hay spiked up through fresh drift. We passed Fairchild Air Force Base, which had supplied the B-52s that had napalmed Vietnam in the 1960s and, a generation later, daisy-cut the bare hills of Afghanistan. The sun emerged, and the water on the road glowed. Long pastures rose and fell unevenly in graceful swells, one side cresting as another dipped into milky troughs. Through them, like an oil slick, wavered the road.

As we drove, he told me about a day almost forty years earlier, when he flew from Mexico City to Langley, Virginia, for his first interview with the CIA. I asked him what the interviews were like.

"Ordinary," he said. "For the most part."

I chuckled. By then, I had come to have a tempered understanding of the word.

"What you'd expect if you were interviewing to be a spy," he added.

"And what was that?" I asked.

His interrogators wanted to know if he had ever done any drugs. He had not. Had he any homosexual desires? He did not. Had he ever had any dealings with communists? No, he assured them. My father was a patriot through and through.

This land we were driving across had made him that way, he reckoned. This land and others like it spoke to something deep inside him. He remembered the flight up from Mexico because he saw America, the physical landscape, in a different way than he had before. Some synesthetic impulse kicked in that day.

It was an American Airlines flight, a propeller plane. "It started coming down real early as it was coming into Washington, D.C.," he said, "and it was flying real slow, and we were flying over the Appalachian Mountains."

He paused at the memory, smiling faintly.

"They had music on," he said. "I was listening to the music and it was coming in kind of late in the afternoon—the sun was setting, the shadows were long—coming in over those green mountains and little farms and meadows and streams down there. It was just unbelievably beautiful, America, and the song 'America the Beautiful' came on and I was listening to that. To land in the capital where I was almost certainly going to be hired by the government to help protect America—it was a thrilling experience for me, it really was. I've often thought of that part of it, fields of grain unfolding off to the side and me looking at the setting sun. It was very romantic."

This was my father's country. He had grown up here, in the Northwest. Both of his parents had eked out pioneer existences in this area around the turn of the century. My father's mother, Marjorie, came from what people around here still called Okanogan country, far from most of the other settlers, on the remote western edge of the Columbia Plateau—a corner of the world that lay under the sheen of the Cascade Mountains and a wide expanse of sky. It was lonely, vast country, singed with the last vestiges of a continent that would never exist again. My great-grandfather Jesse James Coulson was a photographer, farmer, Quaker, and friend to the local Indian tribes. Jesse James had a mane of black hair, and a large, straight nose. He worked the fields in front of his house and took Marjorie along for the company. Sometimes in the summer, a Colville Indian would show up unannounced and work alongside them in the fields. At night, the Indian would tell Marjorie grisly, gruesome stories about a world she could never know. The Indian came and went. The years passed. And Marjorie soon grew into a young woman.

A few years earlier, my paternal great-grandfather, Jens Petter Johansson, had left his home on the southern tip of Sweden. He had boarded a steamship and sailed to New York. After landing, he headed west. In Michigan, he met my great-grandmother. They trekked across a still incomplete America to Idaho, where they married. He slimmed his name to Pete Johnson and insisted everyone in the family speak English. He worked at anything he could: he sold bottles of fresh milk and cut cedar for the lumberyards. In 1906, Sally gave birth to my grandfather George, the last of their ten children. When George was a child, Pete took him on milk runs into town, and when the delivery was finished, Pete retired to the local bar to slog whiskey with the rest of the Swedes. George sat outside in the winter cold, drumming his mitten-clad fingers on the newly laid curbsides. One summer George met Marjorie, while she was visiting her sister, who was married to George's brother Clarence. By then, Marjorie was a shy, pretty, redheaded Quaker girl who could recite by heart pages of mournful Longfellow poems. They were married in 1934.

Four years later Marjorie delivered twin girls, but both died within days from lung complications. My father was born on a cold, winter day in Spokane, Washington, in 1940, the same year Joseph Stalin sent a mercenary to Mexico City to find Leon

Trotsky. As the only child, my father was doted upon. There would never be any other children.

The Johnsons never lived anywhere for very long. Just months after my father was born, George got a job as a county agent—a sort of traveling agricultural savant whose job it was to make sure the farmers, cattle-raisers, and herdsmen in the area were getting what they needed. George moved his little family to St. Mary's, in Idaho. One of my father's earliest memories is standing in his dad's office in St. Mary's and peeing into a brass spittoon where cowboys and ranchers still spat their tobacco juice. But George was restless and soon moved east, to Ronan, a cow town on the Flathead Indian reservation in Montana.

George wanted to join the army. He liked the idea of saluting people and being saluted. He could have found a place for himself in World War II, he reckoned, but only within certain parameters. He would not have enjoyed being in Bhutan or Corregidor, lying in the mud shooting at people, slogging through trenches, or performing triage on a severed companion. He would have preferred being a well-dressed officer inspecting meat, say, or performing some other bureaucratic function. George sent off an application. The army rejected him, extolling the critical importance of his work as a county agent, and so George stayed home as the war swung into full tilt. Marjorie cultivated her victory garden, as President Roosevelt had instructed. They sat around a little wooden radio and listened to news from the Battle of the Bulge and Verdun, from North Africa and Italy and beyond.

And then, one day, Marjorie walked out on them.

"Your mom's leaving," George nonchalantly told my father. "You'd better go and get her."

Terrified, he chased her down and found her tottering along in a dark cloth coat, her figure slightly plump and her red hair frizzy. She was crying quietly. My father tugged on her coat, pleaded, and brought her back. That night, like so many nights, George crooned his son to sleep with these words that my father still sings:

Sing your way home at the end of the day
Sing your way home, drive your troubles away
Smile every mile, for wherever you roam
You will lighten your load
You will brighten your road
If you sing your way home.

My father and I kept on driving through the snowfields that day, looking east and west as the rollers went by, and out to their edges, where farms stood in solitary glory. Every few miles there were long, straight roads that led off the highway—roads that led only to lone farms. Giant stands of leafless poplars surrounded the barns. The sky was an enormous spinning wheel above us.

My father found it difficult to be in the outdoors without commenting continuously on the marvels it offered. His sensory requirements were paramount. He interrupted himself and me to point out the beauties he saw: a rose-colored limestone cliff, woven braids of hay, a dark-red orchid, an old wagon wheel. He watched diligently, taking it all in, reporting back to me. He read road signs at a distance and announced what they said. He framed photographs in his mind's eye. "What I see is what we liked to call the real America," he said, watching the countryside unfurl around us. "Rural America, small-town America; I was always, always part of that."

We had reached the top of the steep grade and he slowed the car. Spread out below was a maze of rough-hewn canyons and rust-colored buttes with striations. This part of the Columbia Plateau was dry, frosted in parts with a thin covering of snow. It dipped and rose in jagged, horizontal planes, steepled with thin, rounded towers of sandstone and basalt. Overhanging it all were terraces of rock, whose lips dangled precipitously over the lower ledges in even panels all the way to the dry river bottom below. Somewhere in that maze was the Grand Coulee Dam. Beyond that, the river pooled in dark-gray blooms, and then there was the

Colville Indian Reservation, and the town of Nespelem, which is where my father wanted to take me. We sat there at the top of the grade and looked at his beautiful country.

"I remember . . ." he said, letting his thoughts wander. "You know, I always wanted to do something in my career that was meaningful, and I once came close to leaving the Agency because I wasn't sure that most of what I had done . . ."

He stopped. I waited for him to go on.

"I did some fun things in India," he said. "You were born there, and I'd been cultivating a Soviet, which was what I set out to do. Still, a lot of what I had done was a waste of time, I knew—meeting an agent clandestinely at night to hear reports of the activities of the Communist Party of India . . ."

He paused again before continuing. "And I learned during the course of that that there was one person in one office who read my reports. One person read them, but the finished things didn't matter to anybody, except in the most general way. It was a piece of the puzzle, but it wasn't a critical piece."

He looked over, arched his eyebrow, and grinned. I smiled back. "Of course," he said, "today Kerala is controlled by the Communist Party and it is the best-run state in India—they have a high degree of literacy, high participation of women, less corruption, and on and on it goes."

He looked out the window and ran his hands over the wheel. "And there we were, skulking around trying to figure out whether the Communist Party was in danger of taking over Kerala State." He shook his head. "There were other areas where the Communist Party activity was more developed and nefarious. The Marxist Leninists—they were true murderers and thugs, and that was something to be concerned about, but the Indian government had that well under control and was surveilling them far more effectively than we were."

We kept driving, and eventually pulled into an American Indian–themed restaurant on the side of the road. Inside, the walls were lined with vinyl records and pictures of John Wayne and Clint Eastwood, and in the corner a jukebox played Elvis. The other diners looked up at us as we came in. We ordered, and the waitress returned with salads with blue-cheese dressing, a hamburger for my dad, and a Reuben sandwich for me. We ate, listening to Elvis and country music, and examining the old movie posters on the walls. There was *Fistful of Dollars* and *The Good, the Bad and the Ugly*, and one with a close-up of John Wayne sitting in the desert looking tired and hot. People used to say my dad looked like Clint Eastwood.

At the table behind us two men were talking about the Iraq war.

"What in hell is he gonna do with more troops?" one said.

"Mm-mmm," said the other. "It's a damn shame is what it is."

My father looked at me, and we both listened quietly to the conversation, which continued on in a similar vein. "God, I'm glad you're out of there," he told me.

After lunch, we continued on. The road curved around and led into the town of Grand Coulee, where there were a series of small government-issue blockhouses painted in primary colors. They reminded me of Play-Doh. The dam wall above rose many tens of yards high, casting a shadow.

"God, I can't imagine living here," I said.

"It'd be like living under the Berlin Wall," he mused.

But we crossed the river on top of the dam and turned left, and soon we were driving along the riverbank again—only now we were right above it, and the ground looked to be stone. The canyons opened up. Flat clefts of rock were tabled evenly, stretching away like giant paving stones on a godly walkway. Some of the land looked like a baby's chubby fingers, and some of it like a father's backhand slap. The road wound along, rising and falling beside the river.

I was driving slowly, winding alongside the bank of the river below. In the distance, a new range of snowy mountains had emerged, and their peaks stretched as far as I could see. "That life," he said, waving a hand. "It was a life of gifts of dubious quality and cocktail parties and that kind of thing, but was it really as honorable a profession as my dad's? My dad's work was designed to help farmers, not to counter anybody—not to deliberately go against anybody."

"Did you feel like you were straying?" I asked, wondering whether he felt like he had abandoned some set of core values. But he shook his head and looked out the window. "No," he said, and pursed his lips.

In 1945, my father's family left Ronan, dragging a trailer. A day after their departure, a spring storm raged through town and hurled a lightning bolt into their house, splitting it in two. Halfway to their destination, Spokane, the trailer caught fire and began to burn. My father remembers it: the road, the late afternoon, the flaming wreck in the middle of the tar. After that, they never stopped moving. They lived in Idaho and Washington, Oregon and Montana, and never for very long in any one place—a year, maybe two.

In Spokane, George got a job as a traveling salesman, selling bottling equipment to the creameries in small towns and cities. On V-E Day, and again on V-J Day, after the atomic bomb was dropped twice on Japan, Spokane erupted in celebration. Whistles blew. The sky was filled with confetti. Car horns honked.

He and Marjorie began to receive brothers and cousins returning from the war. There was Virgil, who had been belowdecks cooking potatoes on a battleship in Pearl Harbor when a commotion had shaken the hull. He ran up top and threw his cooking spoon at the planes swooping low overhead, their gray sides painted with bright rising suns. Another cousin, Stanley, had been in the Pacific when his ship collided with another cruiser and sank. He had saved another sailor's life. Raymond had been fighting the Germans in North Italy with the 10th Mountain Division. There were more, and all of them, at one time or another, came to visit George, Marjorie, and Keith. They generally wore their uniforms, complete with caps and medals, and my father stared up at them in awe. The feats that these returned men had accomplished, were, for my father, utterly heroic. These were lives lived on an improbably high plateau.

The parades for returned soldiers imprinted themselves on my father's imagination indelibly. The shining medals on the men's lapels, their height and heft, and the obvious ecstasy their presence inspired was evident all around in the screaming of the crowd and the trumpeting of horns. For those moments, it was as if a door into the possible had been opened. What was on the other side was bright, responsive, and heroic.

In 1948, George moved the family to Colville, Washington. They stayed there for six years, which, until my father retired from the Central Intelligence Agency more than fifty years later, was the longest he would live anywhere. I pictured my father as a young boy, ten or twelve, with a bright smile and sad, downturned eyes, sitting with George in a raggedy straw hat with a feather in the side, driving through the golden fields. I wonder whether it made my dad want to run, as far and as fast as he could.

George and my father went to grange meetings and farmers' houses. He brought along his .22 and they hunted squirrels. In the summers, they trolled backcountry roads. They picnicked on the Spokane Indian Reservation and ate under shade trees by rivers, which were largely undammed in those days. They fished in Lake Pend Oreille, and George taught my father the names of horses and their marking colors: red roans, buckskins with chocolate-brown tails, red-and-white appaloosas, and the little two-tone pintos the Indians rode.

My father's best friend in Colville was a gap-toothed energetic boy named Roderick, whose vitality immediately attracted my father. "Come on out," Roderick said on the day they met. "If I'm not there, I'll be coming around the barn with a couple of dogs." This self-confidence impressed my father. Roderick was all-boy, as if he had been pulled straight from the pages of *Adventures of Huckleberry Finn*.

My father and Roderick were pals for three or four years. But when my father was twelve, Roderick died from spinal meningitis. My father was a pallbearer at the funeral.

There was a time, right after Roderick's death, when my father didn't have any close friends. He lay on his front lawn and watched the shapes in clouds, and played in the street alone. It is tempting for me to think of him as lonely and isolated, set off from friends by circumstance, such as Roderick's death and his transient lifestyle. But that would be selling him short. He was lonely sometimes, but probably no more than most kids, and he was remarkably resilient for someone with few stable patterns in his early life. He made friends easily, and kept them. He wanted to be liked, and he was.

Still, partly to fill the void left by Roderick's absence, and partly because it was what boys his age did, my father joined the Boy Scouts. Vic, the scoutmaster, was one of George's friends and became a mentor. My father used to go to Vic's house just to listen to him talk. He was vivid and learned, and he taught modesty and resourcefulness.

Vic wasn't religious, but his wife was a Christian Scientist. When Vic got sick with a cold, and then pneumonia, which quickly turned into a full-blown septic infection, she wouldn't allow him to go to the hospital. She prayed nonstop for his recovery instead. One of Vic's friends stopped by one day to check up on him, saw that he was close to death and, against the protestations of his wife, whisked him off to the hospital. But it was too late, and Vic died. My father thought Vic's death was an injustice bordering on the criminal. Like murder, he said. It was a needless adherence to faith in the face of all reason. He was enraged. He was overcome with frustration, as if a series of fantastic opportunities had been snatched away from him.

We had been driving for half an hour through the forest. The hill had peaked and begun its descent when we rounded a corner, and a populated valley opened out below.

"Stop here," my father said, and I pulled over.

Below was the town of Omak. We looked at it for a while, a low, brown settlement at the base of another mountain rise. Beyond that, the Cascade shelf began. A few clops of snow dropped out of the trees and onto the banks. A light wind blew through the upper branches. I opened the window and let the cold air waft in. It was eerily silent, except for the wind. It felt like a dead place, or else something so alive that any sound would burst it right open.

"You asked me once if I ever wanted more appreciation for my work in the Agency," he said after a while, "and I didn't. That was enough for me."

"It was?"

He thought about it for a while, then looked at me and nodded.

The America that my father fell in love with that day on the plane from Mexico to Washington seemed everywhere here. As we resumed driving, a black hawk dove suddenly over the fields and stalled three yards over the snow, flapping and turning. He rose again, with several powerful kicks of his wings. I didn't think any living thing would be in those powder rollers; the whiteness was massive and foreboding.

I looked over at my father. I suddenly felt proud. I told him so.

"You are?" he asked, surprised.

I nodded.

When my father was ten, he was reading voluminously: Zane Grey's adventures of the Old West, Mary O'Hara's *My Friend Flicka* (the tale of a young boy who disappoints his parents with his constant struggles in school, but is later redeemed out on the ranch when he saves a horse's life), and Johnston McCulley's *Zorro* adventures. "Zorro" is Spanish for "fox," and was the secret identity of Don Diego de la Vega, a fictional nobleman and master swordsman living in Spanish-colonial California. He defended the landless peasants against tyrannical governors and shiftless villains. One of Zorro's signature traits was his penchant for publicly humiliating his foes from atop his sturdy horse, Toronado.

Another of my father's boyhood heroes was Roy Rogers, the "singing cowboy." Rogers was the embodiment of the all-American hero. And when my father wasn't devouring the exploits of cowboys and Indians and the seekers of justice of the Great Plains, he listened while Marjorie read to him from her thick volumes of Longfellow and Whitman.

My father was the best reader in his fourth-grade class. But he also talked too much, passed notes, got caught sticking his dip pen into the floor, and flirted with girls. Each time he misbehaved, Miss Rhodes kept him back from the lunchtime recess and made him memorize eight lines of poetry. Pretty soon, he had worked his way through all of the poems Miss Rhodes had in stock. After a while, she appointed him the chief reader for the daily twenty-minute reading session.

Marjorie wasn't affectionate with my father. Maybe it was her Quaker past, or a particular version of New England austerity, that held her in check. On a visit to a friend's house, my father watched jealously when his friend approached his mother, and she put her arms around him lovingly. Marjorie was also sinking into a depression. She and George argued all the time. A doctor recommended that Marjorie try smoking to calm her nerves, and she did. But then she and my father began to fight. He often felt that he was the object of her anger. During one argument between them, George intervened. My father was about to leave the room when he overheard George whisper to his wife. "Well," he said, clutching his wife's arm, "if you didn't want him, why did you have him?"

The summer of 1954, when my father was fourteen, George got another job. This one was different. His employer was the United States Agency for International Development. George would be an agricultural adviser to the University of the Punjab, in Pakistan, thousands of miles and two oceans away from Colville, Washington. The family would be leaving for Lahore in a matter of weeks. My father was ecstatic. George threw away those items he deemed unsuitable for the voyage—such as an antique pinball machine and my father's vast comic book collection—and bought new things instead—such as a shortwave radio and a baseball mitt. My father sold his horse, and gave his dog Taffy to a friend to keep until he might return. He wasn't sure when that would be.

Late that August the family boarded a converted B-29, now called a Stratocruiser—the first time on a plane for any of them. A few days later, they were met in the southern Pakistani port city of Karachi in the middle of the night. When the first light appeared and they were able to make their way into the city, my father saw street people for the first time. Such a thing was unknown in Colville.

His first impression was of an atmosphere of intense white and heat, and a lethargy in which untethered caravans of camels and donkeys meandered down decrepit colonial avenues, and vultures scavenged for carcasses. Even in those first days he was in awe of the mournful call of the muezzins, so many times a day, and the sari-clad women who swept the streets, all of whom were either Christian, or Hindu untouchables. Tongas—elegant, two-wheeled carts pulled by fine horses—veered down the streets as taxis.

They took up residence in a rapidly expanding part of the city, Gulbarg Colony, in which most of the foreigners lived. My father fell in love with Lahore, which was to say India—for even then, seven years after the war of partition that split Muslim Pakistan off from the motherland, Pakistan was as Indian as it had been for thousands of years. The city was home to the largest mosque in the world, left over from the Mughal Empire fifteen hundred years earlier. People had been trading on the streets of Lahore since long before the city was a stopover on the Silk Road. Pakistan was a freshly minted military dictatorship, but to my father it was full of promise. People earnestly believed things would improve: that their lives would inevitably pick up as a result of the huge amounts of American foreign aid that had begun pouring in.

My father began to read Kipling, the great documenter of the British Empire that even then still lay over Pakistan like a slowly receding fog. He roamed the streets, absorbing everything. And he adapted, more than his parents ever could or would, to his new home with the easy sensibility of a teenager, and the hunger of a young man in search of a new identity. Marjorie, who much later came to regret that she either didn't know how to, or simply chose not to, socialize with Pakistanis, relied on her son. When the two of them traveled north to Peshawar, capital of the outlying tribal areas, to visit a gun market and the Khyber Pass with friends, Marjorie was struck by the way Keith casually sauntered into the crowd with some locals. She was sitting at some streetside vendor's stall, beside the hunched frame of a friend who was recovering from typhus, and surrounded by piles of rotting meat. Suddenly there he was, on the hill above her, in the middle of a throng of gun sellers—four or five of them on each side, and her son towering in the center like some young icon of the empire, the weight of the world so visibly absent from his smiling face. The vision of it stayed with her.

My father was enrolled at a missionary school called Woodstock in a Himalayan hill station, a former British resort town. Scripture classes were mandatory every Monday, Wednesday, and Friday. Church was held on Sunday, and chapel on Thursday. And for the true believers, Saturday was reserved for something called Christian Endeavor. Christian Endeavor, or CE, as it was known, was held at the girls' hostel, on top of the hill, and so my father and his new band of friends very often went.

Academically, my father did fine at Woodstock, but he very quickly earned a reputation as a troublemaker. He argued points of scripture with the teacher, claiming personal umbrage at her constant reference to the Hindus and Muslims in class as heathens. At lunch one day, when the student monitor asked my father to lead the table in prayer, he stood up and solemnly bowed his head. "For what we are about to receive, Oh Lord," he intoned to the silent room, "make us truly thankful, for Chrissakes. Amen." He earned demerits—the currency of punishment at Woodstock—faster than anyone else. His teachers kept him back on Saturdays, the only day students were free to wander into town on their own. One teacher told him he was, very simply, the naughtiest boy who had ever been to Woodstock.

But George wasn't happy in Pakistan. He detested his work. He found the Pakistanis lazy, unmotivated, and quarrelsome. So he decided to move once again, back to the familiar shores of America. My father wanted to stay on, but George wouldn't hear of it. And so they flew to Europe in the summer of 1956, and from there headed back across the Atlantic aboard the RMS *Queen Mary*.

During the voyage home, another boy on board told my father about rock and roll, and how Elvis had changed the world. Resigning himself to having left Pakistan, my father then and there decided to become American again. But not just any American—he decided that he would be an all-American boy, maybe a bit like his dead friend Roderick. My father was going to embrace everything about the United States that he had missed by being away. When the ship docked in New York, he immediately set out in search of a jukebox. He listened to Elvis Presley trilling "Don't Be Cruel." He fell in love again.

The family drove across the country back to the Northwest, the land of their births. During that drive, my grandmother sank further and further into depression. She had not wanted to leave Lahore, and now was suffering from severe culture shock and disappointment. They wound up in Oak Harbor, a small fishing town on the far western edge of Washington State. It was quiet and lonely, the starkest contrast to roiling Lahore. They had no friends or family there, and little to appreciate except a tremendous view of the imposing peaks of the Olympic Mountains across Puget Sound and, day after day, a gray Pacific Ocean that lapped at the pebbled shores, and the detritus of miles of unbroken forest.

My grandmother's depression hardened, until she refused to talk to either my grandfather or my father. My dad cornered Marjorie one day and delivered an ultimatum: unless she got out of her depression, he would leave home and join the marines. He could pass for eighteen. He refused to live under her gloom any longer. And so, whether because of his pronouncement or for some other reason, she began to return to the world of the living, and my father was spared the prospect of having to follow through on his bluff. But it had taught him a valuable lesson. The bluff had worked, hadn't it? The means were ugly, but the end was achieved.

I sped along the road as he recounted these memories to me. The fields were cast in afternoon sunlight that came from behind us and lay on the snow rollers like honey. Huge rainclouds levered toward the east, pending over Mount Spokane and rising hundreds of yards into the sky.

"My father never tried to influence what I would do with my life," he said, looking out, "though he did not want me to be a farmer. It was too uncertain a future. He didn't think I was straying—in fact, he was proud when he could tell people, 'My son is on assignment for the State Department,' which was always how he framed it."

We drove along in silence for a while. I could imagine what he was thinking. Fifty years later, nothing much had changed around here, from almost any perspective. It was a timeless sort of country. That's what he liked about it.

Then my father remembered something else. In the early months of his training—after he had passed his interviews and lie-detector tests, and was well on his way to his first foreign assignment—he took a trip with some fellow students. There were four of them in the car one day, sharing stories about their lives. My father was telling them about his home back in the Northwest. "I was saying something about where we lived or what my dad did," he remembered. He looked out the window as he told me, lassoed into great tranquility, as if it stood in counterpoint to something inside him. "And I kind of shared the thought with them that I had some misgivings about this career, this life, because I admired my dad, whose work was really dedicated to helping people, and who did things that were directly beneficial for the people involved; I was thinking of the county agent years. I wondered whether my work was going to be as meaningful as my dad's had been, or was . . ." He trailed off, pondering the possibility of it all over again. Then he said, "It wasn't something I clung to or ago- nized over, but on that ride something came up in conversation that triggered that response, so it was in me . . . I said that I tried my best to be true to myself, and in terms of what I was doing.

"And I remember this girl quickly jumped in and said, 'Of course it's meaningful,' and went on to talk about getting the key piece of intel that informs the president. And I knew all those stock answers, but I also knew that it wasn't something that hap- pened on a day-to-day basis, or even week to week, and there was something more wholesome about my dad's work."

I wondered what that must have felt like—to know that you are about to embark on a path, as my father had said, of dubious distinction, and do it nonetheless. How long would it take you to learn the path? Would you ever be able to? My father had had misgivings on that day. But he didn't let them linger for long. It was a simple calculation, followed by a lifetime of trying to make it right, to make it work, to have a double life and live each with love and devotion. I had followed my father, but somewhere along the way I had gotten lost.

CHAPTER 22

Baghdad and Amman, 2008

For several months after I left Baghdad, my thoughts kept returning to Iraq. When I finally did return, a year later, the civil war was ending. My editors had asked me for one more tour. I was given the assignment of investigating the origins of the insurgency. Why had it happened? Who had propelled it forward? We knew the generic answers to these questions, but they wanted me to dig deeper.

Car bombs and death-squad killings had all but disappeared. Tareq and his brothers, save one who had fled to Europe, were still in Baghdad, but they seemed more relaxed. They were once again going out to restaurants along the banks of the Tigris; their children had returned to school. City parks had reopened and there, on lazy afternoons, families gathered cautiously. Worry had melted away, replaced by sanguine acceptance.

I knew what I was looking for this time. I had been trying to work my way into the assignment, getting close to people who knew about the insurgency, who had fought against it or participated in it. I knew I was getting close when I met Pete.

Pete worked for an American intelligence agency as a kind of jack-of-all-trades. He spoke Aramaic, the language of Christ. He was an Iraqi by birth, but his parents had fled to Michigan in the 1970s and raised him there. Detroit and its suburbs were filled with Iraqis, most of them Christian, who had fled Saddam Hussein's regime. He graduated from an American college, married an Iraqi woman, and had two children. He had come back to Iraq around the same time I did—during the invasion in 2003, or shortly thereafter—and, also like me, he had been there on and off (more on than off) ever since.

We spoke regularly, often late into the night, going through packs of Marlboro Lights and glasses of whiskey, or juice and tea. I queried him about his work, his life. I tried to get close to him, to make myself accessible and trustworthy. I followed my father's advice and tried to be someone whom Pete would eventually trust. Sometimes during our conversations he grew quiet, answering my questions with nothing more than a yes or a no, or stopped talking altogether. He was twitchy and nervous, but his gaze was intense, and when fixed, it transmitted a measure of the anguish he endured.

One day a couple of weeks into my trip, Pete and I were having lunch at a chicken restaurant. Pete took off his sunglasses and reached for his cigarettes. He lit one and blew a stream of smoke between us. "Those guys, you know, our friends?" he said, and paused as a skinny waiter set down two glass cups of black tea, half-full, with sugar. Then, "They're a legal criminal organization, man."

American contractors and Iraqi security guards sat at nearby tables mowing through huge plates of rice and chicken, kebab, pillau, raw onions, and warm, diamond-shaped Iraqi bread. Pete looked at me sideways and carefully fashioned another horn of smoke as he cradled a pair of mobile phones. He leaned in close. "They can do whatever they want," he said. "I could never work for them." He paused and spun his wedding ring.

Our friends. Sometimes he said it with a nod of his head in this direction or that, as if they might be just around the corner, or sitting at the next table. Sometimes he called them the ORA, the Office of Regional Affairs, or the OGA, Other Government Agency—formless euphemisms for the CIA, words I thought only called attention to it more. Sometimes he just said "them."

"Why not?" I asked.

"Because I can't lie, I can't lie. Man, I've got so much stuff in my head I can't sleep anymore. I've been here too long."

He took a long drag on his cigarette and rubbed his temples. Then he glanced at me quizzically. "You journalists, you always want to know more, and more. There's this curiosity." He paused, as if this fact was somehow antithetical to the very idea of survival—which it might have been, in his case. Or maybe it just felt grotesque, since so often journalistic curiosity could appear to have no real purpose. Either way, it was incongruent with the necessity of having to lie about what you did know to those you loved. Withholding became, at some point, a fabrication all its own.

"I used to have that curiosity," he said, "but I'm not curious anymore, you know? Not at all. I just want to forget now. I want to erase what I already know. I want to fucking erase it all, man. I haven't talked to anyone in years. I don't tell my wife, my family. They don't even know what I'm doing over here. She doesn't know, and I'm not going to tell her."

The most that Pete could do, it seemed, was to withhold information. And this was a problem because Pete had fantastical plans for saving Iraq, plans in which he played a leading role—as a broker, say, between two warring communities, or the middleman to a gathering of tribes who couldn't agree on the rights of passage through disputed territory, or a savior to his own beleaguered Christian people in the north, persecuted and threatened every day. Hanging over all of the daily chaos of Iraq were the plans to make Iraq an oasis for businessmen, to put a McDonald's in every province, to kick the Kurds out of the federation once and for all. The vision of a peaceful Iraq was out there on the horizon; he knew it, and could see it. But now we were talking about how you got there.

"So that's all you do?" he asked me, because my role must have seemed so inadequate to him. "Write stories? About what?"

I hesitated. Then, "So, your family," I said, deflecting. "Not even when you're old?"

He shook his head. "Not ever."

He didn't know what to do with the cone of silence he had created, or brought into existence, and what effect it had had or was having on the people who lived in its shadow. Should he extend the protective coat he wore to everyone, he wondered, or maybe just warn them away from himself? He felt compelled to help, but he didn't want his mission to include any more lost lives.

Pete told me about a time when an Iraqi soldier he thought he had befriended later tried to kill him by giving out his GPS coordinates to a group of insurgents. Pete found the man and called him in, putting the question to him directly. The guy denied it—swore on his life that he wasn't a traitor. Several Iraqi colleagues held him down in front of Pete and said, "Do you want us to cut his head off? Just say the word and we'll do it." Pete declined, but he told his men to take him away and "set him straight," and after that nothing was heard from him again. Pete didn't know if he had lost his head or not, and he couldn't stop thinking about it.

"These guys are going to be loyal to us until it doesn't work for them anymore, and then they're not, and we won't be, either," he said. I asked what the idea was in the meantime, when all of those allegiances were being sorted out, when people were figuring out what they really believed and who they could really trust, and who they'd go to in their moment of panic. "The idea?" he asked. "The idea is that in the meantime, things will get better, the situation will improve, people's lives will improve." He shook out his cigarette with a dismissive motion, and the ash fluttered onto the floor. Looking around at the assortment of men in the bar, and then at me, his eyes went soft. His mouth curled into a question because he wouldn't let a smile bloom, and he twitched his head. "That's got to happen, because if it doesn't, then think of all the collateral damage we'll have then. You see where I'm going with this, huh? Do you?"

I said I thought I did.

We sat there in silence for a while. One of his phones rang and he answered it, speaking fast Arabic for a few minutes before hanging up. I picked up his sunglasses and tried them on for fun, and he grinned and generously offered them to me. I handed them back, excusing myself. I remembered everything he said. I went to the bathroom and scratched it out quickly on a notepad, stared at myself in the scarred mirror, and then slunk back into the room, water on my face, relieved.

"What about our friends, anyway?" I asked, nodding vaguely toward the door. "You work with them much?"

He shook his head. "I don't want to." He looked around. Then he leaned in again with the half-smile. "They do whatever they want here and they get away with it." He was talking quickly, his hands crossed in front of him. "They run around this place like they own it—and they do, in a way. It's all about deception. You never know who they are. Some contractor. Some guy who says he's with KBR or CRG or whatever. You just never know."

"I'll never talk to them, will I?" I asked, and added as an afterthought, "Or I guess they'll never talk to me."

But even as I said it, as I looked at Pete, I thought about my father. Maybe I'll tell Pete, I thought; I've been withholding long enough now, too. He could know. What should I say? My father was—well, he was one of them, I'd say, he was one of our friends, you know, the Office of Regional Affairs. I might even tell Pete a thing or two. Hey, I'd say, you know what the guys and girls inside call it sometimes? Christians In Action. I know them well. I grew up with them and played with them; I loved them. Pete would get a kick out of that, I thought.

But, damn, he looked scared.

Then Pete interrupted my thoughts. "No," he said. "No, and you don't want to. Because if you say the wrong thing, you're gonna attract the attention of people whose attention you don't want, and they'll have ways of getting back at you. Suddenly you'll have troubles with your finances. Or they'll destroy your reputation. Or something else will happen. You see where I'm going? You don't want to screw around with these guys. You can't talk to them, but you don't want to talk to them, okay? You see? You see where I'm going with this?"

And I said I thought I did.

Iraq was such a lost place, he said. It just wasn't simple, and it never had been. People had switched roles. The killers wanted to come in from the cold. They were tired, besieged, and betrayed. In some cases, they wanted to work out deals for themselves. Others had seen the errors of their ways, renounced the fascist ideologies of the death squads, and come to terms with the occupation that had stripped them of their families. Many had simply drifted toward ambivalence as the chaos grew and dwarfed them.

Pete had already been in Iraq for several years by the time I met him. He had only been home to Michigan a few times to see his wife and child. He kept most of what he knew and had seen to himself and the people with whom he worked. He knew he was damaged, he told me—he could feel it. He wasn't the same man. He hadn't seen it coming, but had felt the change once it was upon him. He wanted to go home, but couldn't draw himself away. And he was constantly being called upon—by his American colleagues, by Iraqi friends and acquaintances, by almost anyone who felt some measure of his alienation—to help out in some way, and in every case where he could, he did.

I sometimes asked him questions I knew he couldn't answer, such as the real name of an informant or the details of an interrogation, just to hear him say no. I felt satisfied that he was telling me the truth because he was so obviously struggling with it. He began sentences and ended them abruptly halfway, realizing he couldn't say more.

I thought about my father when I spoke to Pete. I sometimes

replaced the image of one with the other. I realized I wanted my father to tell me that he felt the same way as Pete: that it was difficult to be so isolated, that life down inside the rabbit hole was a kaleidoscope, and that if I had trouble, sometimes, believing him, he understood.

"I wish sometimes I could just erase it all," Pete said to me one day while we were having tea. "But I know I can't."

"I'm sorry," I said.

Pete wanted to help me and himself. He told me that I needed to meet a man he knew, a prominent tribal sheikh from Al Anbar province in western Iraq, where the Sunni insurgency had been born and flourished. Pete told me this sheikh would be able to tell me what I wanted to know about the insurgency. He lived in Amman, Jordan, now. "He's your man," Pete said.

We were quiet for a time. Pete twirled a cigarette around his fingers, playing with it. He looked outside, and back at me. "He works with our friends," he said quietly.

That was in winter, when Amman can be cold—snow falls occasionally and children run into the streets to have snowball fights. Next door in Baghdad it will never snow, and sandstorms turn the skies red and black at high noon. But it was arid and pleasant in Amman when I arrived. The plane banked in low over the desert wadis, and a weak winter sun scratched in through the windows.

The sheikh sent one of his drivers to meet me the next morning. He took me to a spacious downtown office space where I waited in a smoky lobby. An assistant eventually led me into a large, well-lit room where I saw a robust man in his mid-forties sitting behind a desk cluttered with papers, and an ashtray where a cigarette burned.

We exchanged pleasantries for a while, and then I told him what I was after. He smiled and dismissively waved his cigarette, which he smoked through a telescopic holder. Then he spoke for almost an hour: about his home in Anbar, his frustrations with the Americans, and his efforts to work with victims and men who had been wrongly imprisoned. He denied having anything to do with the insurgency. He told me he was a businessman. And then we both sat back.

Pete had told me that the sheikh worked with the Americans, but now the sheikh was denying it. I decided to press him. I asked him what his relationship with the Americans was like.

He shook his head. "No . . ." he said. He was quiet for a while, and then went on talking about the same things as before.

Eventually, I interrupted him. "I don't understand," I said. "I thought that you . . ."

The sheikh shifted in his seat to quiet me. He looked at me for a long time while he smoked his cigarette. "This is a very difficult time," he said. "Very dangerous."

I nodded.

"Many of my people are getting killed, you know. Very many."

I kept quiet. But he didn't say anything else, so I said, "I know. I'm very sorry."

We sat there in silence for a while longer. An assistant brought in a glass of orange juice for me, as well as some candied dates and an ashtray.

Eventually he smiled. "How can we trust you?" he finally asked.

"You know Pete," I said. He nodded. "Pete is watching me."

But for the sheikh the situation was not lighthearted. "It's very difficult," he said. "Very difficult, very complicated."

"I understand that."

"Now is not the right time."

I told him there might never be a right time. He just shook his head.

I sipped my orange juice and ate a date, waiting. I didn't intend to leave without getting what I had come for. And I felt the sheikh was softening. I heard my father's voice again: *Be the kind of person who, when he defects, comes to you.*

Eventually he pushed a button and said a few words in Arabic, and then sat back, sipping on his cigarette holder the way an asthmatic might—with quick gasps, holding his breath on the uptake as if he was reluctant to let too much of anything go. A few minutes later, a young man walked into the room and sat down quietly in a chair directly across from me. He was wearing jeans, a blue shirt and red sweater, and loafers; he was clean-shaven. I stood up and we shook hands. The sheikh pointed to him. "This man," he said. "He might talk to you."

I still don't know his real name. But the one he used that day, and every day that followed, was Abu Ahmed.

Abu Ahmed and the sheikh spoke quickly in Arabic, and then the sheikh turned to me. "Go ahead," he said, nodding toward the young man.

I turned to Abu Ahmed and told him I wanted to know how it all began, how we wound up here, and why he was now sitting across from me. Abu Ahmed looked at the sheikh and said something. They both smiled. "He says he'll tell you if I say it's okay," the sheikh translated, and smiled at me. "What should I tell him? That he should put his life in your hands?"

I nodded. "Yes, tell him it's okay."

The sheikh sucked at his cigarette for a few moments and watched me. Then he said a few words and nodded to Abu Ahmed.

That morning, Abu Ahmed began to tell me his story. It continued over the next several days. Sometimes we met in luxury hotels—always at corner tables that I deliberately chose to be as far away from prying eyes as possible. Jordanian intelligence was always watching him, he said, and he had to check in with them all the time. He didn't like to stay in any one place for too long. Once he took me to a smoky teahouse and led me to a back room, far from the other patrons, until he got uncomfortable thinking we had been there too long and we had to leave. We also had a few conversations at the sheikh's office. Another time, we just sat in a darkened SUV parked on the side of a busy road, and talked as the traffic roared by. Later on, I met up with him in Iraq, with Pete, and the three of us sat for several hours at a candlelit table and drank tea and Coke. Pete and I smoked as we listened to the story of Abu Ahmed's life.

Abu Ahmed was a terrorist. That is, he was a radicalized Islamist with ties to Al Qaeda in Mesopotamia—the name that Al Qaeda had given to its organizational structure in Iraq. Abu Ahmed had once belonged to that vast and amorphous violence. Broken down, the past was much more nuanced. The fighters he had known and helped comprised nationalists, Baathists, criminals, Islamists, Wahhabis, Al Qaeda *Takfiris*, foreigners, mercenaries, and—most miserable of all—those men and women who, because of American aggression, accidents, or circumstance, were simply out for revenge, hellbent on making the sadness that the war had brought into their lives go away by returning it in kind. All of them were fighting. Many were dying. Many more were rotting in jail. Only a few of them were the planners, the organizers, and the thinkers. Abu Ahmed was one of these. That's why he was so dangerous.

Abu Ahmed had grown up in central Iraq in the 1970s. Those were tough years in the country, and he had turned to religion at a young age. Saddam Hussein frowned on too much religiosity among his people, justifiably concerned that it would lead to the undoing of his power. But Abu Ahmed was undeterred, and at thirteen he became a Salafist—a member of a fundamentalist Sunni sect with origins in Saudi Arabia that preached close adherence to a strict interpretation of the Koran, much like fundamentalist Protestants cleave to the strictest interpretations of the Bible. In due course, he became a teacher. Sometimes he went on road trips with the most promising of his young students, into the backcountry of southern Iraq, visiting with desert Bedouins and living as itinerant travelers. But trips like these aroused the suspicion of Saddam's brutal secret police, and when he was seventeen Saddam imprisoned him for seditious and undesirable teachings.

Abu Ahmed told me about his father. He was kind, and he supported his son through the long months spent in captivity. The father came to visit the son in jail every week. He brought him fresh clothes from home. He smuggled in money so that his son could bribe the guards occasionally to save himself from the prison's weekly mass punishments. In Saddam's Iraq, they both knew, no one was spared. "His injustice filled us," he told me. Three times the young man went to jail for his beliefs, and three times he emerged righteous in his anger.

The American invasion of Iraq was both the end and the beginning for Abu Ahmed. No longer would he ever have to endure the dictator's punishments and humiliations. But the invasion presented new challenges. Like other Salafists, he believed it was sacrilegious for foreign forces to occupy Muslim lands. Another Salafist, Osama bin Laden, had opposed American troops being based in Saudi Arabia during the first Gulf War. In May 2003, around the same time I was settling into Baghdad as a reporter, Abu Ahmed attended a meeting of about fifty Salafist imams and religious scholars at a safe house a few miles south of Baghdad. The men agreed on a plan for war against the Americans. They would gather arms from storage depots, collect money left behind by the regime, and steal intelligence files from government offices.

Later that month, on May 20, the fledgling insurgency struck its first blow against the Americans, ambushing a U.S. military unit in Baghdad.

Over the next several years, Abu Ahmed rose through the ranks of the insurgency. At first he focused on logistics: supplying and transporting weapons and supplies, organizing safe houses, and coordinating operations between different cells. His wife drove when he had weapons to deliver because American troops were less likely to search a car with women or children inside. By 2005, he had become one of the senior strategists for the fifteen-hundred-strong Army of the Faithful, a Saudi-funded group that was responsible for some of the most spectacular attacks against American forces. He lived like a hermit for the most part, he told me. The only people who knew where he lived were his two brothers and his father.

But his world began to unravel in the beginning of 2006, when a gang of men blew up one of the holiest shrines in Shia Islam, the Al-Askari Mosque in Samarra. The bloodbath that followed was what I had spent most of my time in Iraq documenting. Those years were far and away the worst the country had endured, perhaps ever. Abu Ahmed's world was turned upside down, like practically everybody else's. "We lost control of our people," he told me late one night in Amman, as we were sitting in a dark corner of a hotel. When the group's bankrollers realized what was happening, they cut off funding and supplies. "They wanted to prevent a sectarian fight," he told me. They had experience in Afghanistan—they remembered the factionalism that had torn apart the Afghan mujahideen after the Soviet withdrawal, and they wanted to avoid a repeat in Iraq. But it was too late. The civil war unfurled with a mightiness and savagery that no one could control.

Abu Ahmed was a steady, quiet man. He had a slight stoop and delicate hands. He looked like a graduate student. He wore thick glasses. When we spoke, he usually placed both elbows on the table and leaned in close, with his hands under his chin. He looked either directly at me or down at the table. Now and again he peered around, but for the most part his attention was directed solely, unflinchingly, at me. He spoke quietly, urgently, but every now and again he laughed and his eyes crinkled up at the sides, and the mirth spread broadly across his face. He seemed a man full of emotions: compassion, rage, love. And sadness, because soon after the Al-Askari Mosque attack, Al Qaeda approached him, he said, and asked him to carry out a special recruiting and fundraising mission outside Iraq. For whatever reason, Abu

Ahmed refused. A few days later, Al Qaeda responded by kid-napping his father, taking him to a secret location, and decapi-tating him.

Abu Ahmed told me this the night we sat in the dark corner of the hotel. "My dad always stood up for me," he said. He was lean-ing on the glass and looking down at the table. He met my gaze and then lowered his head. His eyes were full. "He stood up for me during Saddam's time, when I was imprisoned three times. It was difficult for a father to stand up for a son during those times, when the son is a political prisoner." He looked around at this sinister luxury. "It was tough for him to say, you know, he's my son, this is my son."

He looked away. He coughed, twisted a ring on his finger, and adjusted his glasses. "Families are . . ." he started, and then just said, "We are very close with our fathers."

I nodded. Then we were silent for a long time. I was think-ing hard. After a while, I noticed that I was holding my pen in a vice-grip and staring at Abu Ahmed. I realized that I wanted to tell this man—a virtual stranger—more than I have ever wanted to tell anyone else, that my father was a spy. There was a sudden urgency to the conversation—urgency about who my father was, and who I was, and what this man sitting before me could tell me. It seemed to me that my world and my father's world had con-verged in him. It felt to me like Yevtushenko's "frank moment at the party, when the enemy crept up." Only the enemy wasn't an enemy at all; he was a friend.

And suddenly all the years of my father's lessons flowed into a kind of coherence. As a journalist, I wanted to tell Abu Ahmed's story. But I realized that I also felt, for the first time, the thrill of what my father's work had been. I wanted to recruit Abu Ahmed to my side; I wanted us to be allies. I wanted to be the one, as my father had told me so many years before, to whom he would come when the time was right. Further, I wanted to wrestle from him the kind of information that only a spy should be able to summon.

Who did he work with? And how did they work? What were his motivations? I wanted Abu Ahmed because I desired, however briefly, to slip into my father's skin. I wanted to touch that wall, put my hands on it, feel its contours and smell its construction. I wanted to lean against it, feel what heart beat on the other side.

Before I had a chance to speak, Abu Ahmed continued with his story. It didn't take long for him to respond to his father's killers. Within days he had tracked them down. He killed them, or had them killed. He did it summarily, without the slightest doubt. Beheaded, unflinchingly. An eye for an eye. "Everything was out the window after that," he told me.

Some senior Al Qaeda figures contacted him personally to apologize. But Abu Ahmed didn't believe they were sincere, and refused their offers of compensation. "They told me, 'If you hadn't killed your father's killers, we would have,'" he said, "but I was convinced they had planned this."

His revenge was complete, but now he was on his own. Fatherless, being pursued by the Americans, and no longer able to trust the insurgency's strongest supporters, Abu Ahmed was a hunted man. He was all alone.

This was when people like my father stepped in, I thought.

I went back to the sheikh repeatedly in those days in Amman, in between meetings with Abu Ahmed. As usual, he sat behind his desk, and the desk was as much an illusion as anything else. He was who he said he was, partly, the same way Abu Ahmed was, or my father was, or I was. All of our identities become muddied to some extent: you are what you need to be, or what other people need you to be, at any given time. You pull from yourself the thread of some other man's life and weave it into your own. That's how you protect yourself.

The first time I went back, the sheikh greeted me amiably. "So," he said, "now you know."

"Hardly," I said, and we both laughed.

The sheikh told me how he had come to know Abu Ahmed.

As a tribal leader, the sheikh had been working with the war's orphans and victims for a long time. But he also knew and, to a certain extent, sympathized with the insurgents. He recalled the first time he saw American and British troops enter the town of Al Qa'im, a dry and desolate smugglers' outpost far to the west, on the border with Syria, where many of his tribesmen were from. "A lot of resistance came from my tribe," he said. "They were living between us. We didn't even know their names, but we knew.

"I remember there was a meeting in my uncle's house, and we learned that the British were coming to Al-Qa'im. My tribe asked them not to enter the village, but to stay outside. We are conservative; we didn't want to see outsiders. Then on the second or third day, they did the opposite—they entered the town. I remember when the fighting started. I was going to my house and it just started, a really big fight. All the women started to clap their hands and make the *helahel* sound [a high-pitched screech], supporting the resistance because they had warned the British: we don't want you inside. The image is still in my head—you just saw people running, all the young people running, taking their Kalashnikovs to fight. No one organized them—no one said to them 'you should do this or that'—they were just fighting the way they thought they should. Honestly, I was proud. That image will never leave my mind."

But as time went on and he watched the insurgency rage out of all control, he began to have doubts. Iraqis were killing other Iraqis. The Americans weren't leaving—and the violence was only making them angrier, which meant they would stay longer, and kill more of his people. Very shortly after the invasion, Al Qaeda fighters entered the sheikh's town. "It happened immediately," he told me. "This really started the distortion. When you saw these people—they don't have shoes; they were stupid, ignorant. They started coming in all over."

The cycle of violence had begun, and he realized that he

needed to do something. An Iraqi friend told him that maybe he should start working with the Americans. Long before the tide of cooperation between Sunni tribal sheikhs and American forces began, this sheikh started seeking out his own partnership. It wasn't easy going. Because he was a Sunni from a troubled province, the Shiite-led government harassed him regularly, and even jailed him twice for alleged ties to terrorists. The Americans helped to bail him out of jail on both occasions. The sheikh, in turn, began working with the Americans to build up a network of people who could successfully penetrate the hardcore elements of the insurgency and weaken it from the inside. "Yes, the Americans help me," he told me, "and it's not because I have blue eyes, it's because I'm fighting terrorists. We're fighting these fucking stupid people—we're trying!"

For a long time, the sheikh had been eyeing Abu Ahmed from a distance. He knew the young man by reputation, and knew that he was dangerous. So he set about on a slow course to persuade the fighter to switch sides. They met for the first time in 2005, when Abu Ahmed was "still stuck in the fighting." But the sheikh worked on him. "It took a few months," he said. "I started making him meet people affected by the violence. I gave him money to help widows and poor people. He started to do humanitarian work, and he could see the effects immediately. He could see how they got better. I told him the wheel was running—time was running out.

"It took about a year. Then his father was killed, and his face started to change. I asked him, 'Why did the parents of these orphans die?' I said, 'We don't want the Americans to stay forever as the occupying force, but who will lead us when the Americans go?' This was not a jihad. Iran was going to run Iraq. The enemy of my enemy is my friend, I told him, for the time being."

One day in mid-2007, the sheikh sat down in Baghdad with a group of Americans in civilian clothes—CIA case officers—to talk about getting rid of Al Qaeda in Iraq. "We started to discuss the future and our talk came around to names," the sheikh said. "The Americans knew who Abu Ahmed was, and they were interested in him, but they were more interested in capturing him than working with him. They asked what I thought. I said, 'We can't kill all the terrorists.' They knew I knew Abu Ahmed. I said I would convince him. They said, 'He's a terrorist.' And I said, 'No, don't judge him. You can use him as a spy.'"

A few weeks later, the terrorist met the American spies. A few weeks after that, they began to work together in hunting Al Qaeda.

Abu Ahmed wore a leather jacket on most days that winter. Whenever I saw him he was unfailingly polite and courteous. He was gentle, but also brutal. One night when we were talking at a hotel, the lobby was suddenly filled with music: drums and the wailing of women. We walked to the lobby just as a wedding procession was making its way into the restaurant. Beside the bride was an older man, thin and bearded, and he was holding a small video camera, filming the scene with a benevolent smile on his face. Abu Ahmed's eyes locked on the man. I was sure he was the bride's father. When I looked over at Abu Ahmed, he had a smile on his face and his eyes were wet with tears.

I thought about him hunting down his father's killers. He was a father himself, and he had a son. Was he in the room when his father's killers were killed? Did he cut their heads off himself, and just not tell me? I looked at his hands. They were thick and strong. It seemed possible. I wondered why he was talking to me.

I spoke to my father one night after meeting with Abu Ahmed. "I'm speaking to someone from your world," I told him, without going into too much detail, as was our wont.

He laughed. "Be careful," he said.

So this, too, was part of my father's America—this gray, in-between world, where the killers come when they come in from the cold, and where the men who wait there to greet them bide their time. And where people like me can visit, for a time, if we're lucky, or good, or patient, or because it's where we feel the most comfortable, too. Things sometimes fall apart, and this is where we might start to put them back together again.

It was after ten o'clock one night, when we were sitting having tea, that Abu Ahmed explained his motivations to me. "It's the thoughts, the ideas, that are dangerous," he said. "It's the thoughts that will bring the men to jihad, not the other way around. The people we are trying to kill are the ones who make the thoughts."

I wondered if his CIA handlers saw things the same way.

"I'm still in the resistance," he told me, "but it's a new tactic, a new strategy. Al Qaeda is the harm in our way now, so we have to remove it. But the road ahead is still jihad—there are just more enemies now." He smiled.

"What are they like?" I suddenly asked.

He looked askance at me.

"The Americans," I said. "The CIA? What are they like?"

I felt like he knew what I wanted to know, maybe more than I did. I had come with questions about the insurgency, but I had been led to men like Abu Ahmed, and to the men who controlled Abu Ahmed, men like my father. Is there a spy behind every insurgent? Within every insurgency, are there legions of men like my dad, trying to keep the scales tipped to the right balance? Too mean, and it all goes belly-up; too light, and the war goes on forever.

I thought I might get something spectacular from Abu Ahmed, some secret admission, some shard of knowledge that I didn't know. But when he spoke of the men he worked with, "our friends," it was as if he was talking about his own children, or mine, or the parents we could have shared in some other life. "They're very respectful and understanding," he said, "very smart. They know about our heritage, our culture, and our behavior. They have talents and curiosity."

I thought about Abu Ahmed sitting around a table with my father, just like this, and the questions each would ask. There would be mutual fascination. They both shared the same aim because men like them didn't get together like this, the way that we were now, just to tell stories. They got together to act. They were men of action.

"The ones who need to be killed," Abu Ahmed said, "are the ones who create the thoughts, and the ones who need to be killed are the ones who give justification for these thoughts, and the ones who need to be killed are the ones who write for publishing the thoughts, because then he has reached a point of no return." He looked at me. These two worlds, then, his and mine, were not mutually exclusive.

"If there are still thoughts, there is still Al Qaeda," he said. "The insect is still there. She can always rebuild and create another. If you kill the group and leave the queen bee, you've done nothing. They will keep regenerating. The brain of the insect lives."

He told me about the operations that he and his new American friends had mounted. Sometimes he gave them information for targeted strikes, air assaults, and other covert operations. Sometimes they worked together to intimidate the thinkers and organizers into believing that they were about to be killed, which provided enough incentive for them to leave the country, where they might be arrested or make some other fatal error. Sometimes he wrote screeds lambasting their ideology that he posted on the Internet. He and the Americans had a list, he said, of people that needed to be quieted. There were sixty-three names on it. Five of those had to die.

"Sometimes, I used to get jealous of the Americans," he said. "Every little thing, whether it is important or not—they analyze it, they find out what it means. They never throw anything away because they know they might need it at another time. They even work on holidays."

I nodded. I thought about my father's scanning eyes, aware. "Is it strange," I asked, "to go from wanting to kill them to working with them?"

He nodded. "It is. Yes, it really is."

One night, after talking for a long while at a teahouse, Abu Ahmed said he wanted to go to my hotel. It was good to change locations now and again, he said. He wasn't worried about safety; he just didn't want to linger too long in one place. That was fine with me. We got to my hotel and went to a corner table in a dark part of the lobby restaurant, and ordered more tea and water.

I asked him about Al Qaeda. He said that from a purely religious standpoint, there wasn't all that much that separated him from them. They both believed many of the same things. Then he talked about the divisions in the movement. The wing that supported the Egyptian cleric Ayman al-Zawahiri was in a feud with Osama bin Laden. Abu Ahmed subscribed more to bin Laden's view, which he said was the more moderate of the two.

The new reality was one kind of Al Qaeda versus another, less tolerable, version. There were always going to be bad men, and then men like this, living in the in-between space. They couldn't really feel comfortable anywhere else. Someone had to talk to them, engage with them, bring them in from the cold. Someone had to be there waiting for them when they were ready. That was what men like my father did—what few others wanted to do.

And what if it changed, I asked. What if the long-term interests started to diverge? What if the Americans eventually found they no longer had any use for him, or for what he was in a position to provide? It had happened before, and probably would again.

But Abu Ahmed understood this perfectly. "I am still in the resistance," he told me again. "I am on your side, but just for now."

For now, but never forever. Forever was only for the initiated, like me, because I had taken the oath my father gave me and never broken it with strangers, not with Omar or Tareq or Abu Ahmed. They only needed to know what I decided was right to tell them, and nothing more.

Pete thought he knew what was coming. What was it he had told me? I thought back: "These guys are going to be loyal to us until it doesn't work for them anymore, and then they're not. And we won't, either. In the meantime, things will get better. They have to. Because if they don't, then think of all the collateral damage we'll have." And Abu Ahmed was, Pete had said, the CIA's "ace in the hole."

The last time I saw Abu Ahmed was in Baghdad. We met at a hotel near the Green Zone. Uniformed Americans and Iraqi sheikhs in dishdashas meandered through the long hallways together. He had told me he was going to organize some more meetings for me. But I didn't have time, I told him. I was going to leave. I *wanted* to leave; I had to.

"Did you get what you wanted?" he asked me.

I nodded. "I think so."

He shook my hand. He looked at ease, like a man who believed in what he was doing, whose heart was still.

I never told Abu Ahmed about my father. I almost did, once, and then I stopped myself. Instead I just said, "You're a very interesting man," and he smiled.

But I told my father about Abu Ahmed.

"What have you done to protect him?" my father asked, and I wondered, what are you telling me here?

"Have you been careful? It's important that you protect him," he said again. "It's the one problem I have with journalists . . ." and trailed off, because he knew that I knew what he meant. What can seem like betrayal can have honor, while the supposed virtue of truth-telling can become a vulgar and exploitative tool.

I suddenly understood what Chris had been talking about in Paris so many years before. The betrayal in journalism came the moment when you sat down, alone, to put forth to the rest of the world what you had learned. The people you had spoken to— those who had trusted you with their most intimate secrets— could very well feel betrayed by what you would do then, no matter how noble your intentions or pure your instincts. At that moment, your aims and theirs took divergent paths.

And it went further. Your subjects weren't the only victims; this was the moment when you left behind that *other* you—the questioner, the seducer. The feelings you had: the sympathy, the urge to empathize and understand, the need to bond; so much of that got left behind, too. The abandoning of a part of one's own self to the page, the self that had connected with the world, was perhaps the ultimate betrayal.

So had I been careful with Abu Ahmed? Had I been careful with my father?

I said I thought I had.

I had tried my best with the assignment. I tried to see Abu Ahmed for what he was, as I had been taught, and I also tried to see through him to the reality that lurked beneath. I tried to see him as a journalist would, and as a spy would, too. I didn't know if I had succeeded. I didn't know if there was anything there. I thought there was, but I wasn't sure.

"Good," my father praised me, when I sent him the story. "Good job. It's a wonderful story."

I wasn't sure if it was or not. But I knew that a story was all it was, or would ever be. This was as close as I was going to get to being a spy, to recruiting someone, to seeing his life from the inside; I knew that. And it was okay. My father and I saw things so similarly, but we acted so differently. He was a spy. And I was a journalist. He was a father, and I his son.

I would have liked for the two men to meet. They would have understood each other. Although, who knew? Maybe they did.

I knew my father was struggling with the discrepancies between the oaths he had taken to the Agency and his own moral imperatives. For so long, I realized, I had been trying, and failing, to find that moment with my father when the curtain would collapse and his authentic self would peer back at me. For so long, I didn't believe I was seeing it, and I wanted to. I had wanted to see him as the spy or the journalist sees its prey. But my father, the man, wasn't in hiding at all; he wasn't cached in some dark corner of the world waiting for me to find him. He was staring back at me, waiting for me to see that he had always been there for me, and had always loved me.

The blindness of others is so readily apparent, but rarely do we recognize the blindness within. Until, suddenly, we do. I wanted to run away from myself, and I did, but I ran away from my father as well. I couldn't always find, or adequately fuel, the love he wanted me to have for myself. I started running, and I never really stopped, because I was too afraid of what I might see if I turned around and looked at myself. The enemy that Yevtushenko talked about, the enemy that crept up—that enemy had sometimes been me. Because as much as my father ushered me into a darker world, he also never left my side.

The idea of seeking out the truth in other people's lives, in this country or that, or in this war or that, was one way to avoid looking for it where I knew it would be hardest to find—or once found, hardest to bear—and that was inside myself. I had tried to get into my father's head, searched for the telling detail and the moment of frankness. But it doesn't always work that easily, for I couldn't shine a light on him and remain in darkness myself. Yes, there was betrayal in journalism, broken promises, untold or unkempt truths and half-truths, lies small and large, and I trafficked in them with as much flair as any spy did—even more, some might say. But I didn't want to hide from myself anymore, or betray my own life.

But now, on this rocky shore, there was silence.

For many years, my father nurtured a fantasy about the end of the world. It was a dream he cultivated as a means of escape when he was driving across the country alone, or on long walks with his dog. In this fantasy, a new dreaded disease or famine or some other ungodly horror had befallen humanity, but somehow my father had survived. Perhaps there were other survivors, somewhere, but only small bands of them, and they were as yet unconnected to him. For now, my father was alone in a pristine wilderness. He imagined himself piloting a sturdy plane and fly-ing from one large city to another, unlocking the gates of zoos and freeing captive herds of wild animals to roam the avenues. From there he would travel across the country by road, attaching the ends of fences to tractors, tearing them out of the ground post by post—a lengthening latticework of ruined walls. He would free herds of bison and cattle, and horses, opening up the barricaded spaces of the world.

He had also worked out the details of this apocalyptic scenario into a neat and orderly series of staged devolutions. The mystery of the human vanishing was left aside. But there would be bill-boards to rip down, buildings to topple, and dams to burst. These were acts of great and anarchic liberation, in which he would set free entire populations of imprisoned animals to roam and plants to grow in peace, in a world of boundless possibility. Natural decay and erosion would also play their part. What seemed to con-tain a semblance of stability, such as the nearly finished roof on a house, would quickly fall apart. Great sheets of rain would enter the smallest holes and make them large. Wood and iron would be turned to moss and rust, and his kitchen would become a patch-work of colorful hives and mold. In this new forest, televisions might flutter for a time, like butterflies twitching on the ends of tree stalks, and then shutter themselves in darkness. Lights all over would stand down. Institutionalized luminescence would cease to exist.

For a period, ants, cockroaches, and insects of all sorts would flourish. Then larger animals would eat them. In time, he would feel changes in the air; temperatures would cool. The sun would come to have an additional identity; so would the moon, the trees, and the stars. By night, alone, he would marvel at the beauty of the world.

It would be a place free of sin, and even the possibility of sin. It would be beautiful and breathtaking, my father's song against the world. The whole idea was inhumanly eerie.

"Wouldn't you be lonely?" I had asked my father after he had told me this during a visit home.

He just smiled.

"Do you wish you could have that world?" I asked.

"Sometimes," he said.

There had been times I was afraid to think at all, afraid to allow myself the freedom to peruse the valleys of my mind. I feared that if I did, I would fall into an abyss out of which I would never be able to climb. But here was my father's imagination so openly on display. His world was a tapestry of devotion, nurtured in his mind; and like a child, he could conjure it forth whenever he was lonely. In a way it was a picture of the life he had actually lived, only it was cast in a vivid and dreamy solitude. His life and this dream shared one key element—the profound uncertainty that there is anyone out there who is truly on your side. My father's imagined world was masterful, and though I could imagine the dream, I could not fathom enduring the existential loneliness of the dream's twin reality the way my father had, and for that I was awed, and kind of tired, and ultimately simply glad to be awake.

"You know," he had said, and put his arm around my shoulder as we walked, "We don't always have to believe the same things."

Epilogue

My father and I are walking along a rocky, boulder-strewn beach in South Africa. It's a cloudy day, but warm, and the ocean is flat and steely, with the occasional lip of swell breaking up closer toward us, then receding back out into the deep.

He's been stopping to take pictures of the rocks, the yellow and red lichen, and the odd branches of driftwood scattered about. I have gone on ahead, skipping from boulder to boulder, moving toward a rickety wooden staircase that leads up to a promontory from which the vast expanse of southern ocean glows. Seabirds are ducking over the rocks, and from high on the escarpment above us comes the sound of the wind rushing through these last barriers of the trees before it reaches us and the open world. There's no one here. I am only aware of my father behind me, following the tracks I've made.

I stop. I begin to turn my head. And as I do, everything slows. I have seen this before—this slowing down of the world, this almost audible protraction of time into its infinitesimal digits. The ocean is suddenly frozen. A seabird collapses in a gust and stays there. The rocks are white globes—worlds of stone, I think, perfected this way over millennia. And to think I have never, ever seen them before.

They are everywhere, these stones, and their rounded imbalance separates me so hazardously, so oddly, from the figure of my father, which, I can see, has begun to fall. He is like a tree, I think, as I feel my body begin to lurch in his direction. So tall, so elegant, so straight, and he is falling to the ground. From this distance his eyes look closed to me, almost peaceful, but I can see the paleness in his face, the paleness I should have seen before, the same color I now see reflected in this stony shore.

As he falls, I can see the angles, the percentages that change in his descent. What at first seemed like such a long way to go is now cut in half, and then again, until that straight ramrod body of his is almost to the ground. I never take my eyes off him even as I run and leap and jump to reach him. But I am not in time—the angle is no more. There is just a sliver of light between him and the stones below, and then there is not even that. Just a slight bounce as he lands, and I see his head rise up a few inches, then go down again, with the world as still as it ever has been.

I scream.

Then, finally, I am on him. He is nestled in those stones like a plant unloosed, ripped from its roots and cast about in the shallows. For a moment there is no sound, no movement at all.

And then the silence breaks. He breathes. With great difficulty, but he does. He opens his eyes, and his big brown irises stare at me. His two front teeth are shattered. But he smiles and puts his hand on mine. "Thank you," he breathes.

"I'm sorry," I say. "I'm sorry."

But he shakes his head and lies in my arms, and the world begins to move again. The ocean washes up onto the rocks in a sudden burst, and the seabird is off. I lean down and cradle his head.

Acknowledgments

I would like to thank several people, without whose wise counsel, support, and wisdom this book never would have seen the light of day. I am tremendously grateful to Georges Borchardt, who believed in me and helped me to understand what I was writing, and why.

Barbara Galletly showed an early and intense interest in the book, and helped me to navigate the initial hurdles. The indefatigable Kate Johnson has stayed with me throughout, steering me through challenges, rejections, and successes, and for that I am very grateful.

Henry Rosenbloom and the team at Scribe believed in this book when few others did; I will never forget that. Julia Carlomagno was a terrific reader and a wonderfully precise editor. The design team deserves special thanks for including me in its decision-making process.

I'd like to thank everyone at W. W. Norton, particularly Jeff Shreve, a tireless advocate and wonderful supporter.

Thanks to Annie Cobb, who read early drafts and counseled me through the writing and the emotional hazards of the project. She is a fine writer, and her belief in me over many years was a real gift. Thanks also to Joe for the house and fine company.

I am grateful to the Iraqi staff of translators, drivers, and security guards who worked for *Newsweek* during the years I was there. They enriched my experience of Iraq immeasurably, and their dedication, loyalty, and bravery through years of hardship was remarkable.

Thank you to Luc Delahaye for the friendship and the honesty. I'm grateful to Rod Nordland for teaching me how to work in places like Afghanistan and Iraq; and to Peter Baker, for months of adventure in Afghanistan. I thank Babak Dehghanpisheh, Joshua Hammer, Michael Hastings, and Joe Contreras for their friendship, and for the many conversations that helped to shape the ideas in this book. And a special thanks to Christopher Dickey, a fine mentor and friend, who taught me so much about family and friendship, and the value of the written word.

None of this would have been possible without the loving support of my family. My mother, Lee, consented to multiple interviews and endless questioning, and through it all showed a great deal of patience. Janet Johnson gave me valuable insights and support, and I'm grateful for the loving relationship I have with her today. Her daughter, Amy, has been a wonderful sister for many years. Linda Ainsworth provided love, humor and a place to write. I thank Ben Riggs for his honesty and for the continued love and support he gives my mother.

Several people who shall remain nameless helped me in ways small and large to understand the CIA and the world of secrets. Thanks to C., A., S., G., P., and M. Thanks also to all the children of The Farm—those with whom I spent my childhood and those who came before and after.

I benefited from the documents discovered by the National Security Archive, and from the poetry of Yevgeny Yevtushenko. My gratitude also goes to several people in Mexico, who shall remain nameless, for their friendship and love. Their lives were affected by the difficult years of the Dirty War in the 1960s and 1970s, and I'm thankful that they shared their stories with me. Abu Ahmed and several unnamed people in Amman helped me to understand the insurgency. I'm grateful to the crews in Cape Town and Seattle for years of adventure and hilarity. And thanks to Ernie for taking care of the property, and of my dad.

Most of all, I owe a tremendous debt of gratitude to my father. Over many years he showed an unbelievable degree of patience and love with me as I waded through this material, which was often very difficult for him. I am lucky to have him as a father.

And through everything, my wife, Alison, has sheltered me with love, care, and devotion. She is a fine editor, a wonderful and patient listener, and the love of my life.